IN THE EMPIRE OF
GENGHIS KHAN

By the same author

OLD SERPENT NILE – A JOURNEY TO THE SOURCE
FRONTIERS OF HEAVEN – A JOURNEY BEYOND THE GREAT WALL

STANLEY STEWART

IN THE EMPIRE OF
GENGHIS KHAN

A Journey Among Nomads

HarperCollins*Publishers*

HarperCollins*Publishers*
77–85 Fulham Palace Road,
Hammersmith, London W6 8JB

www.**fire**and**water**.com

Published by HarperCollins*Publishers* 2000
1 3 5 7 9 8 6 4 2

Copyright: Text © Stanley Stewart 2000
Photographs © Stanley Stewart 2000

The Author asserts the moral right to
be identified as the author of this work

A catalogue record for this book
is available from the British Library

ISBN 0 00 255904 8

Set in Postscript Linotype Galliard by
Rowland Phototypesetting Ltd,
Bury St Edmunds, Suffolk

Printed and bound in Great Britain by
Clays Ltd, St Ives plc

A Cinzia,
con amore.

Contents

Acknowledgements

Travel writers bear a special debt of gratitude. This journey would have been impossible but for the countless unrecorded acts of generosity by people along the way. In Mongolia itself the remarkable traditions of nomadic hospitality are as strong as ever, and from one end of the country to the other I was welcomed, warmed, fed and supported by people who saw nothing remarkable about their own generosity and to whom I must have appeared as a curious and possibly demented figure. I remember them all, and want to record my gratitude to them.

Here in the UK, Julian Matthews of Discovery Initiatives, Nick Laing of Steppes East and Stephen Penney of Intourist, all offered considerable help, while Sue Byrne of Buddhism in Mongolia and Jambaldorj of the Mongolian Embassy were generous with their knowledge and advice. Patsy Ishiyama offered much direction and reassurance on matters equine while Lyn Waters in Istanbul helped to point me in the right direction. In Mongolia Helge Reizt and Kate Glastonbury of Nomads Tours & Expeditions gave invaluable assistance and advice. Thanks are also due to Ganchimeg, Oyungerel, Inkhtoyah, Louisa Waugh, Una Murphy, and Livia Monami.

Crucial to the success of the journey were my two interpreters, L. Bold and G. Mandah, who shared the joys and the privations of riding across Mongolia, with an uncomplaining enthusiasm. Both were wonderful colleagues and remain dear friends, whose contribution to this book is immense. I owe a special debt to U. Munkhzul who shared insights about her own country, as well as wonderful companionship, over two years. She missed the journey, only to embark on one of her own. I am grateful once again for the wise and sensitive editorial comments of Rebecca Waters. As always I am greatly indebted to Christine Walker of the *Sunday Times*, who not only commissioned my first article on Mongolia, but has provided considerable support with a stream of commissions ever since. In somewhat different guise, a part of chapter seven first appeared in her pages.

Mongolian names and words are transliterated into Latin script with a bewildering variety of spellings. I have opted in most cases for a form that is acceptable to modern historians, but in places consistency has been sacrificed to ease. Purists may be appalled by Genghis and Kubilai but general readers will avoid the irritation of familiar names rendered in unfamiliar guises. I have been guided throughout by the excellent annotated translation of *The Mission of Friar William of Rubruck* by Peter Jackson and David Morgan published by the Hakluyt Society in 1990. Most of the quotes from Friar William however derive from the earlier translation by William Rockhill.

Finally I would like to acknowledge the tremendous contribution of Cinzia Fratucello. Her support has been unstinting, and it has been a joy to share the labours of this book with her. It has benefited enormously from her encouragement, advice and scrutiny. The result is dedicated, with love, to her.

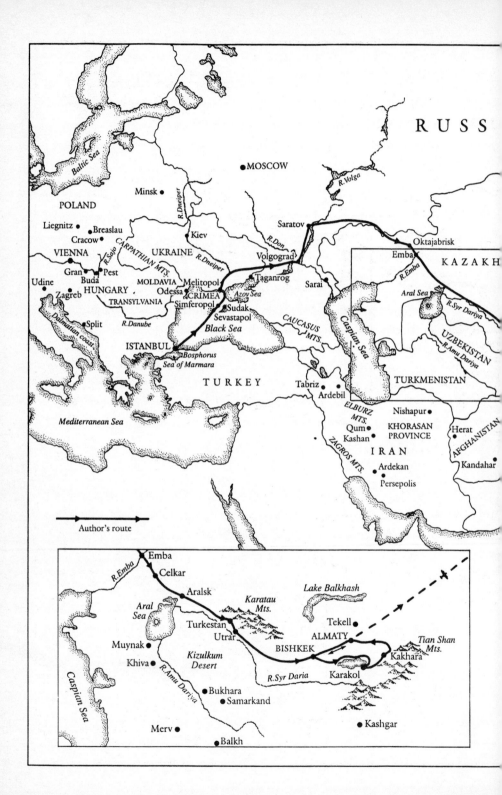

0 250 500 1000 1500 KM
0 250 500 750 1000 MILES

I A

● Barnaul

Irkutsk ● *Lake Baikal*

TAN

Ölgii

ULAN BATUR ● Dadal
Qaraqorum

Lake Balkash

MONGOLIA

MANCHURIA

ALMATY

Issyk-kul Lake MTS.
KIRGHIZSTAN
TIAN SHAN

Shang-tu ●
BEIJING ●

AJIKSTAN

[See detail below]

CHINA

Yellow Sea

BURMA

South China Sea

INDIA

Greatest Extent of
the Mongol Empire
1280 AD

Moscow ●

Qaraqorum

Baghdad ●

Beijing ●

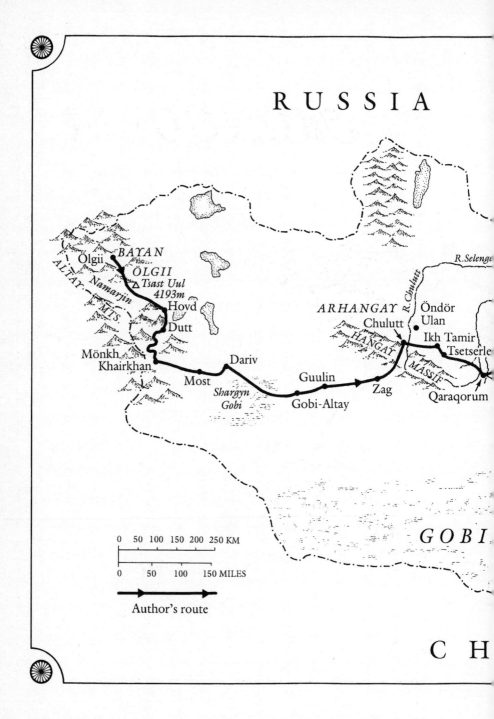

RUSSIA

BAYAN
Ölgii
ÖLGII
△ *Tsast Uul*
4193m
Hovd
Dutt
Mönkh
Khairkhan
Most
Shargyn
Gobi
Dariv
Guulin
Gobi-Altay
Zag

ALTAY Namarjin MTS.

R. Selenge

ARHANGAY
Chulutt
HANGAY
MASSIF
Qaraqorum

Öndör
Ulan
Ikh Tamir
Tsetserle

R. Chulutt

GOBI

C H

0 50 100 150 200 250 KM

0   50   100   150 MILES

Author's route

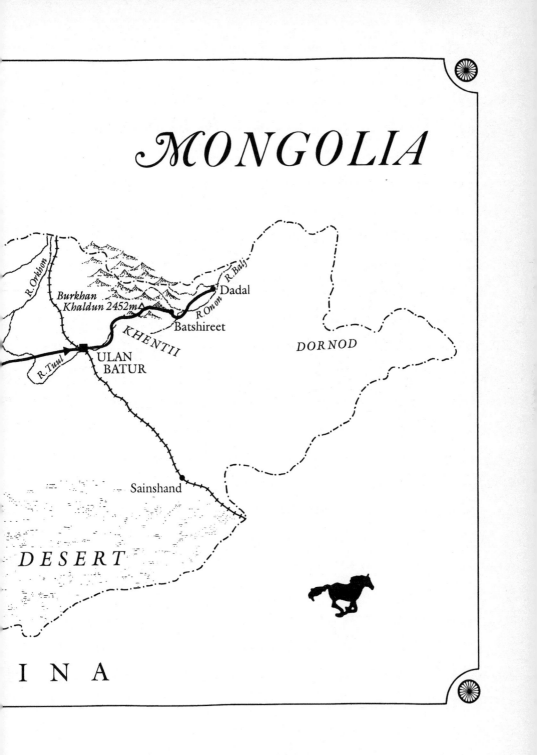

There in the vast steppe, flooded with sunlight, he could see the black tents of the nomads, like dots in the distance. There was freedom . . . there time itself seemed to stand still as though the age of Abraham and his flocks had not passed . . .

Fyodor Dostoyevsky, Crime and Punishment

It is vain to dream of a wilderness distant from ourselves. There is no such. It is the bog in our brains and bowels, the primitive vigour of Nature in us, that inspire that dream.

Henry David Thoreau

Prologue

When I was a child my grandmother used to call me a Mongolian. In memory the word evokes the scent of grass and of fallen leaves, some atmosphere of twilight and of horses.

My grandmother lived at the top of an Irish village with views southwards to the Mountains of Mourne. In the evenings, in the long dusk that my grandmother called 'daylegone', I played on a raised pavement that ran along the churchyard wall, beneath an arch of lime trees. They were solitary and elaborate adventures involving horses and culprits. My stallion pranced through swathes of freshly mown grass and piles of autumn leaves. We leapt the wall in a single bound.

When it grew dark my grandmother would call me home, her voice looping in the lingering twilight like a rope. I resisted as long as I could, galloping between the trees in the thickening gloom, against the tug of her voice. When she stopped calling I sat in thrones of leaves gazing to the south where the Mountains of Mourne shouldered the horizon. The mountains were dark and mesmerizing, the frontier to the wide world of County Down. My father said that beyond the mountains lay the sea.

When the long lasso of my grandmother's voice came again my horse was already melting away between the graves. I turned home, and presented myself in the back hall with skinned knees and leaves in my hair. As my grandmother bent over me to brush and straighten my clothes, she always said the same thing. 'Like a Mongolian,' she sighed. 'Just like a little Mongolian.'

I never heard anyone else speak of the mysterious Mongolians, and I had no idea who they were. I recognized the word was an admonition of sorts but I sensed it also contained a note of praise. I liked its unruliness and its ambiguities, and I wanted to live up to the idea of recklessness that it seemed to imply.

Long before I had any clear sense of Mongolia as a place, the word belonged to those intense adventures played out each evening in the slow descent of an Irish twilight, as I tugged against the mooring of my grandmother's voice calling me home.

It was in Iran, twenty-five years ago, that I first saw nomads. I was part of an expedition looking for the Persian Royal Road. Led by a charming charlatan who was a cross between Rommel and W.C. Fields, our small and happily deluded team spent eighteen months in the field, rattling around Anatolia and the Zagros mountains with a couple of Land Rovers, a leaky tent and a copy of Herodotus. It was the best of journeys. The landscapes were magnificent, the people hospitable and we had the alibi of historical purpose.

In the Marv Dasht plain beneath the ruins of Persepolis the Qashga'i tribes were trooping north to their summer pastures in the mountain valleys around Hanalishah. Skirting fields of new wheat, they passed like a medieval caravan, a whole society set in motion, moving northward to new grass. The layered skirts of the women flashed with gold and silver thread as they ran after straying lambs. Riding slim, leggy horses, the men trotted back and forth along the perimeter of the caravan shouting to one another in a language that had come with them from Central Asia. Camels bearing tent poles and rolled carpets and wide-eyed children swayed through veils of dust. On the edge of the village of Sivand, an old man hoeing vegetables in a walled garden straightened to watch them pass, his face darkening with an ancient antipathy.

I had never seen such glamorous people. They owned not a square inch of land but they strode across the province of Fars towards the mountain passes as if it were their private estate. Passing beneath the stone palaces of Persepolis, they were oblivious to their allure.

Some weeks later we penetrated the mountains around Ardekan where Alexander had defeated the last Achaemenian defences at the Persian Gates on his way to the prize of Persepolis. In these narrow valleys we paid a visit to a Qashga'i chief. It was June, the best month, when the grass was rich and the flocks were fat.

'Nomad tents have big doors,' the khan said as we arrived, referring to Qashga'i hospitality. We sat inside enthroned on splendid kilims and bolsters, looking down over a stony slope where his son was herding goats towards the green line of a river. Piled along the rear wall of the tent were embroidered sacks and chests and saddle-bags, the furniture of nomads. The khan's daughters left their looms at the other end of the tent to bring us glasses of tea and water pipes.

We talked of politics, and the government pressure on the tribes to settle.

'It was always thus,' the khan said. 'The people of the towns, the peoples of the fields, worry they cannot control us. They think of us as barbarians.' He smiled, sensitive to the irony of this, a gracious host with elegant manners, a man whose tribal pedigree went back three centuries. 'They want us to settle in one place. They want to make us part of the life of the towns.'

The canvas walls filled with wind and the tent creaked like a ship. On the tent poles the saddle-bags swayed.

'The tribes were powerful once in Iran. But those days are gone. I do not know what the future holds for nomads. But I fear that we are seeing the end of a way of life.' He gestured to the valley as if the landscape itself was in retreat. 'We have migrated through these mountains for centuries. We came to these lands in the train of Genghis Khan.'

The Qashga'i are a remnant of one of the innumerable nomadic peoples who emigrated from the great grasslands of Central Asia. Iran was a civilization prone to exhaustion and Persian history was shaped by these nomadic incursions. When dynasties weakened, when art became decadent, when the officials grew corrupt and the aristocrats soft and cowardly, they knew the barbarians would soon be coming, a scourge and a salvation.

This pattern of untamed horsemen, bursting forth from the steppes to prey on their more suburban neighbours, was repeated throughout Asia. They came with a bewildering variety of names: the Cimmerians, the Sarmatians, the Tocharians, the Xiongnu, known in Europe as the Huns. Russia was not free of the 'Tartar yoke' until the sixteenth century. In India the great Mughal Empire was founded by a nomadic barbarian from beyond the Oxus. In China, they built the Great Wall in the vain hope that they could keep the nomads at bay.

The high-water mark of nomadic power were the Mongols of the thirteenth century. In the course of a single generation, under the charismatic leadership of Genghis Khan, they rode out of the steppes of Central Asia to forge the largest land empire the world has ever seen. From the South China Seas to the Baltic they stepped from the nightmares of townsfolk onto their doorsteps. Suddenly the Mongols seemed to be everywhere at once, threatening to gatecrash Viennese balls, carrying off princesses in Persia, overthrowing Chinese dynasties, sacking Burmese temples, putting Budapest to the torch, launching seaborne invasions of Japan. Even in a distant England they were front-page news. Matthew Paris, the thirteenth-century chronicler, sounded the last trumpet: the Mongols were coming and the End was nigh. Hysterical congregations crowded into their parish churches to pray for deliverance.

The folk traditions of the Qashga'i insist on their connection to the Mongols and the great figure of Genghis Khan as village chiefs in remote corners of northern Pakistan insist on their descent from Alexander the Great.

'The Mongols were a race of heroes,' the khan said. 'Nomads who ruled the world. And what has become of them? Vanished like all the others.'

'They have gone home to Mongolia,' I said.

The khan looked at me quizzically. With their legendary aura it had not occurred to him that they were a real people with a real homeland.

'Where is Mongolia?' he asked after a time.

'Beyond China,' I said.

'Have you been there?'

'I haven't,' I said.

In the early evening air the whistling calls of shepherds driving the flocks towards the tents drifted from the opposite slopes like birdsong. The women had left their looms and were heading out to the milking with pails and goatskins.

'What do you think Mongolia is like now?' the khan asked.

'They are still nomads,' I said. 'Not like here where most people are settled. Mongolia is a nation of nomads, the last in Asia.'

The khan weighed this news carefully.

'I would like to go to Mongolia,' he announced at last. 'To see the people of Genghis Khan. To see their tents and their flocks, to see the way they are living.' He was seized by the idea and the camaraderie of our shared interest. 'We will go together,' he declared. 'It will be good for you – a man with no wife and no sheep. We will go to Mongolia together and visit the sons of Genghis Khan.'

Basking in the glow of this mythical expedition we shared bowls of lamb stew flavoured with apricots and talked long into the twilight about horses. In the morning the khan hitched a lift with us to Shiraz. He was going to visit the district commissioner to put the tribe's case in a dispute about winter pastures. 'This is how things are now,' he sighed. 'We must plead for what is ours, the grass on which we have pastured our flocks for generations, with a government bureaucrat.'

He had already forgotten about the journey to Mongolia.

But I had not forgotten. I have nurtured the idea of Outer Mongolia for twenty-five years. I longed to travel the width of Asia to this last domain of nomads. I saw it as a journey across the uneasy frontiers between the sedentary and pastoral worlds, between the builders of walls and the inhabitants of what the Chinese called 'a moveable country', people for whom settlement and the commitment of cities was a kind of betrayal. I longed to travel to Mongolia, and once there, I wanted to cross the country by horse, a ride of a thousand miles.

This ride was the central ambition of the journey. In Mongolia children learn to ride before they can walk, and the country offered the rare opportunity to make a journey by horse without feeling you were engaging in some unnecessary eccentricity. It was a question of loyalty, to the careless boy in the Irish twilight. This was the journey of his choosing.

Swept up by these grand designs, I had rather overlooked the fact that I had only ever ridden a horse once in my life. It was in Wyoming where a perceptive rancher had given me a horse so quiet it tended to fall asleep in mid-stride. It was enough to convince me that I was a horseman. Occasionally well-meaning friends would touch upon the question of my riding experience. Gently they tried to point out the difference between a ranch holiday and a thousand miles of Mongolia, but I didn't let them put me off.

In the hurried days before departure I decided to buy my own saddle. Mongolians ride on wooden saddles, and I felt that was probably a technique that you needed to start young to have any hope of surviving. I decided on a Western saddle, with a reassuring pommel to hang onto should the horses prove frisky. In Hereford-shire in a splendid equestrian supplier's I spent a happy afternoon choosing my rig. In the horsey atmosphere of the place I got rather carried away and bought a confusing array of ropes, a halter, a grooming brush, a splendid hoof pick, a felt pad, saddle-bags, a pair of spurs, a hip flask, stirrup leathers, a pair of chaps, and a curious tool rather like a cheese knife whose purpose I never discovered. My pleasure was spoiled only by the scepticism of the young assistant who was obviously struggling to square the challenge of my proposed expedition with the naiveté of my questions.

On the way back to London I stopped at Hereford Cathedral to see the Mappa Mundi. The map hangs in a modern suite of exhibition rooms whose subdued light, after the bright slabs of sun in the cloisters, felt like the dim uncertainties of the past. It dates from the late thirteenth century when the Mongol Empire was at its height.

Over the centuries most of the original surface pigment has flaked away – the bright green seas, the blue rivers – leaving only its weathered base, the colour of old leather. In the religious hush of this place, it felt like a ritual artefact, a piece of ancient hide covered with symbols and obscure passages of text, a geography of spells and wonders.

In thirteenth-century Europe geographical knowledge had sunk to its lowest ebb, and the Mappa Mundi is not so much cartography as storytelling, a compendium of all the tales and marvels gathered from the Bible, from classical authors and from medieval myths, deployed across the continents. The alarums of Matthew Paris, penned just over forty years before, found their unreliable echo here in the frights of Asia. While Europe is full of reassuring cities represented as small line drawings of castles and spires, the rest of the world is portrayed as a landscape of fabulous characters. It was a rattle-bag of tall tales and obsessions, of hopes and fears about the dark beyond one's own borders.

In Africa there are unicorns and men who ride crocodiles like horses. In the exhilarating provinces of the Upper Nile are the Blemyes whose heads were in the middle of their chests. Beyond are the Satyrs, the Hermaphrodites, the Troglodytes, and a splendid race with protruding lower lips which they deploy like umbrellas to shield themselves from the fierce equatorial sun.

With east at the top, according to the convention of the time, Asia occupies the upper half of the map. India was packed with legendary birds like the Alerion and alligators lurking on the banks of the Hydaspes. Dragons swarm across the island of Ceylon while dog-headed men patrol the regions east of the Carpathians.

My journey to Mongolia lay past the eastern end of the Black Sea where Jason's Golden Fleece was pegged out like a drying hide. To the north lay Scythia, the barbarian hinterland of the ancient Greeks, where two rather belligerent looking fellows could be seen threatening one another with knives. To the west are the Grifones, part of the nomadic traditions of these regions. They were said to use the bodies of their enemies as horse-trappings; a human skin can be seen thrown over a stallion as a saddle. Beyond the Oxus lies Samarkand, a rare city in these parts, looking like an Elizabethan sketch for the Globe Theatre. On the far bank of the Jaxartes are the Essedenes respectfully devouring their deceased parents, a practice they believed preferable to leaving them for the worms to eat. On a blunt peninsula enclosed by a turreted wall, a long and rather garbled account in dog Latin identifies it as the place where Alexander imprisoned the sons of Cain, a fearsome tribe who will break out at the time of the Antichrist. Not far away, on the island of Terraconta, was the race descended from Gog and Magog, 'a monstrous brood', the enemies of God, who would one day invade his kingdom.

I stood on tiptoes to examine my destination on the outer edges of Asia. In the top left corner of the map, at the furthest extremities of the known world, where Mongolia should be, between the borders of China and the dark Outer Ocean, the parchment grew darker and the figures fainter in zones that seemed to fade into twilight. A sketch showed men with horses' hooves: the land of the Hippopodes.

Since the days of ancient Greece it has been the conceit of settled people confronted with the horsemen of the steppes that their extraordinary equestrian prowess was not quite human, that the riders were in fact part horse. If any rumour of the Mongols had reached the map-makers perhaps it was here with a race so fleet, so unruly and reckless, that they pranced like horses.

That was my destination, pale markings at the far end of Asia, on an atlas of the imagination.

Chapter One

OUR LADY OF THE MONGOLS

On the evening flight to Istanbul the plane bucked in rogue winds. Dark clouds piled up from the east. Tipping beneath the wings, Asia looked black and thunderous.

By the time I got into the city it was past midnight. Istanbul seemed deserted. In the dark I was struck by how European the steep lanes of Sultan Ahmet looked – the tall narrow houses, the fanlights above the doors, the wrought-iron balconies, the curtained windows. I crossed the empty gardens of the old Augustaeum where the two great rivals of Istanbul, the Sultan Ahmet Mosque and Haghia Sophia, the victor and the vanquished, face one another across the rose beds. Sultan Ahmet was all grace and delicacy, an architectural dancer poised on the balls of its feet. Birds swam around the minarets in tall currents of light. At the other end of the square Haghia Sophia, once the greatest church in Christendom, sulked in the embrace of old plane trees.

I found the hotel in the tangle of cobbled streets falling towards the walls of Byzantium and the Sea of Marmara. I woke the *bekçi*, asleep on a bench in the lobby, by knocking on the window. A tall lugubrious fellow, he led me silently upstairs, showed me the room with a slow melodramatic sweep of his arm, then drew the door carefully behind him as if he was closing the lid of some precious box.

The first night is always the strangest. I went to the window and looked down on the Turkish streets. Among the litter opposite, a cat was marking its territory. Raising my gaze, above the rooftops, I could see ships lying at anchor where the Sea of Marmara narrows to the mouth of the Bosphorus. I wondered if any of them were Russian; I hoped to find a Russian freighter to take me on the first leg of the journey, across the Black Sea to the Crimea. But my mind was still full of London. I slept fitfully in the narrow bed and dreamt of packing in the familiar rooms of my own house. I woke once with the sudden idea that I needed to remember to put in carrots for the horses. Beyond the ghostly window the muezzins were calling.

I had breakfast on a roof terrace overlooking the sad florid walls of Haghia Sophia. Suddenly London was gone, and the world had a different focus. In the room I spread maps on the bed and telephoned the shipping agents to get the names of boats due to depart in the next week for Sevastopol.

In spite of the fact that Istanbul has been a Muslim city for the past five centuries, Europeans still have a proprietorial feeling about the place. For almost 2000 years it was one of us. Byzantium was a Greek city, and Constantinople, its successor, was the new Rome. In its archaeological museum the splendid Alexander sarcophagus and a relief sculpture of Euripides are the star turns in rooms packed with classical antiquities. It is the only city in the world to bestride two continents, but for a long time its heart was in Europe. Then, when we were busy elsewhere, it slipped out of the European orbit and became Istanbul, a Turkish city ruling an Asian empire, capital to both the Ottoman Sultanate and the Islamic Caliphate. To the European visitor, modern Istanbul can seem like a wayward uncle who wandered off to Araby and returned years later with a beard, a pair of satin trousers, a water-pipe habit, and a young wife dressed in a black sheet.

In antiquity Constantinople's position exaggerated the usual anxieties about nomadic barbarians. Rumours of the mounted Scythians who roamed the Don steppes on the far side of the Black Sea echoed the Greek legends of centaurs, creatures who were half-man, half-horse, whose untamed desires were a threat to civil-ized order. But the city was little troubled by nomadic invasion. By the time the Turks descended on Constantinople in the spring of 1453 their own pastoral origins were all but forgotten. They had picked up Islam, the manners of the Persian court and the habit of cities generations ago.

Though the Mongols never took Constantinople, the city con-tains one curious remnant of the Mongol Empire, a thirteenth-century Byzantine church known as Mouchliotissa, or Our Lady of the Mongols. The church is a unique link to the Greek capital before the Turkish conquest as it is the only Byzantine church that was not converted into a mosque. I had faxed the Patriarchate from London to ask about Mouchliotissa and had received a most courteous reply from the Metropolitan of Laodicea, a city of the Byzantine Empire that was in ruins before Columbus set sail for America. He invited me to call on him when I arrived in Istanbul. He would arrange for a visit to the church. His fax concluded with the blessings of the Patriarch for my journey, and I basked momentarily in the idea that I was setting off for Outer Mongolia with an ecclesiastical blessing more ancient and more grand than that of the Pope.

The Patriarchate of the Greek Orthodox Church, the Vatican of the Eastern Church, remains in Istanbul as if the Turkish conquest of 1453 were a temporary aberration, unlikely to last long enough to make it worth moving house. Though Greeks continued to live and worship in Istanbul for centuries after the Turkish conquest their numbers were in continual decline. In the twentieth century, the fall of the Ottoman Empire, the rise of Turkish nationalism and Muslim fundamentalism have seen a dramatic exodus of Greeks, and today less than 4000 remain in a city with a population of 12 million. Yet the Patriarch continues to inhabit his city as if nothing had happened. Though he presides over a worldwide flock of Orthodox Christians, his congregations here in Istanbul, his own seat, have withered away. This anomaly lends the Patriarchate a curious make-believe air, like the last Emperor in China's Forbidden City, a court ruling over a vanished kingdom.

On a bright morning I hailed an old *hadji* in a woolly cap and a silk waistcoat and took a river taxi up the Golden Horn. The

Patriarchate stands in Fener, once a Greek district, now a poor Turkish quarter with a strong fundamentalist character. Ringed by high walls, and guarded by sentries, it is a place beseiged. Muslim fundamentalists, who have a knack for creating artificial enemies, regularly target the Patriarchate as if its elderly clerics posed some threat to the religious fidelity of a nation of 60 million Muslims. Graffiti are scrawled on its walls, and last year a bomb was thrown into the courtyard from a neighbouring minaret, narrowly missing the fifty-year-old doorman and the 1500-year-old library.

I was welcomed by George, a secretary, who apologized that the Metropolitan was late. Despite the fact that his diocese had been Muslim for over five hundred years, the Metropolitan apparently was run off his feet. I settled down in George's office to wait. A tall heavy-set man, dressed like everyone else inside these ancient walls in long black robes and a thick beard, George looked like an august ecclesiastical dignitary. It was a surprise to learn he was a high-school senior from Minneapolis.

The dramatic decline of the Greek community in Istanbul has made it very difficult for the Patriarchate to fill job vacancies, even within its own walls. Their appeals to the wider Greek world had brought George, a Greek-American boy from Minnesota, to work here in his year off between high school and college. They had got lucky with George's appearance. He had the tall face, the deep-set black eyes and the dark brow of an archbishop. They gave George his robes, he grew a big beard – he looked like the kind of guy who could do this over a weekend – and suddenly he looked more like a patriarch than the Patriarch did. George might have stepped out of an eleventh-century mosaic. But despite the impress-ive air of religious gravitas the high-school senior kept breaking through.

Istanbul was not George's kind of city. Diplomatically he tried to express enthusiasm for the antiquities, for the Bosphorus, for the food, but his American horror at the chaos and the general decrepitude of the place was impossible to keep in check. He was homesick for the Midwest. I asked what he missed most. He chewed his pencil. I was expecting him to opt for the communion of his family or the fellowship of his home church.

'Cheetos,' he said after a time.

'Cheetos?'

'Yeah, you know. Those cheese-flavoured things.'

The Cheetos were not just a blip. In George two distinct person-alities co-existed uneasily. He told me he was planning to be an Orthodox priest then almost in the same breath complained about how difficult it was to meet girls in Istanbul. Candidates for the Orthodox priesthood who are already married are generously allowed to keep their wives, he explained, but those who are unmarried at the time of induction are obliged to remain celibate. In September he would begin three years in an American seminary, not the best place to pick up girls. George was desperate for a love interest. There may have been sound ecclesiastical reasons for this but it tended to come across as the kind of hormone rush common to most nineteen-year-old males.

As delicately as his patriarchal persona would allow he enquired about my time in Istanbul, steering the conversation gently towards social activities. I knew what he was after – where was a good place to pull in Istanbul – but the clerical office, the robes, the icon above his desk, made it difficult to broach the subject openly.

The telephone rang. It was a school friend from America. In an instant the bearded cleric fell into the patois of an American high school.

'Hey, Bobby. How's it going?' said George. 'Hey man, I got to get outta here. It's been nine months. This place is driving me crazy.'

He listened for a time, then he asked, 'How's that girl from St Paul's?'

There was a pause. George was chewing the corners of his beard.

'You know, the one with the halter top. Debbie. We met her at the Dairy Queen.'

There was a much longer pause. George's face darkened as he listened. There had obviously been a few developments in the life of Debbie of the Dairy Queen.

After a time George shrugged. 'Hey, who's worried?' he said. 'There are other girls.'

They chatted for a while about basketball and the Chicago Bulls then George hung up. He seemed to have shrunk a little inside his robes.

'Hayal Kahvesi,' I said. 'It's just off Istiklal Caddesi, near Taksim.'

'What's that?' George's thoughts were still with Debbie's halter top.

'It's a café,' I said. 'You can get a beer, listen to live music. It's a good place to meet people.' The thought of George turning up among the hip modern crowd of this trendy café in his robes flashed through my mind.

'Dress is casual,' I said.

The Metropolitan of Laodicea never arrived. He called from his mobile to apologize that he had been held up and to say that he had arranged for the priest of Mouchliotissa to take me to the church. Father Alexandros turned up presently, out of breath, and dressed like an undertaker. He was a handsome fellow in his mid-forties with dark luxuriant hair, long eyelashes, and the mandatory beard. He had been a pharmacist but when the Patriarch began to run short of priests he prevailed upon Alexandros, a family friend, to give up aspirins and Night Nurse for incense and holy water.

Alexandros used to live in Fener before the Greeks fled the district to safer parts of Istanbul during the anti-Greek riots in 1955. We climbed through the narrow streets of his childhood, packed with nineteenth-century Greek villas squeezed in among old bits of Constantinople: ancient city walls, the ruined vaults of a monastery, the charred shell of the Palace of the Wallachians, the rubble of a Greek school. At the top of a lane so steep it had become stairs, he pointed out his old house, a peeling ochre mansion, divided into tenements and bedecked with laundry. A swarm of children came out through the gate to hold our hands, tugging us through the garden where Alexandros had played as a child, now full of junk and oily puddles, to a view, over a broken wall, of the Golden Horn.

'Clematis,' Alexandros said. 'There used to be clematis on this wall.' He poked his hand into a hole between the old bricks. 'I hid marbles here.' But he brought out only a handful of dust.

Our Lady of the Mongols stood in the next street behind high red walls. The round drum of the dome presided over a courtyard of sun and old roses where a caretaker was sweeping leaves. Alexandros opened the tall west doors and the ancient ecclesiastical odours of incense and candle wax and polished wood came out to envelop us. In the narthex the glass of the framed icon of the Virgin was covered with lipstick kisses.

The church has lost various of its parts over the centuries, and what remains makes for a rather charming confusion of arches and vaults meeting at odd angles. Dusty chandeliers were suspended on long chains from the high ceilings like cast-offs from a medieval banqueting hall. Byzantine icons were deployed about the walls, the faces of saints and prophets peering out from the antique gloom of the paintings. By the icon of St Barbara was a metal crutch, left behind by a lame man who had been miraculously cured. Elsewhere votive miniatures were suspended from threads in front of the more powerful icons, in the hope of a similar miracle. Legs were popular, as were ears and feet. But the faithful did not restrict themselves to requests for new body parts: Toy cars, models of new houses, and little aeroplanes represented prayers for material success and foreign holidays. One hopeful and rather brazen petitioner had hung a photograph, clipped from a glossy magazine, in front of an icon of St George. The photograph showed a shapely young woman in a bikini. I wasn't sure if this represented the aspirations of a man seeking help with his love life or of a woman on a diet.

The church was founded by Princess Maria, an illegitimate daughter of Michael VIII, a Byzantine emperor who tended to dole out daughters to potential allies like subsidies. It was the middle of the thirteenth century, and the Mongols were pressing on his borders. He had already dispatched one daughter to the Mongol khan of the Golden Horde, ruler of the districts to the north of the Black Sea. Maria had been engaged at a tender age to Hulegu, a grandson of Genghis Khan and the governor of another of the four provinces of the Mongol Empire, the Il-Khanate of Persia.

The engagement was a long one and by the time Maria turned up for her wedding in Tabriz, the groom was dead. But Hulegu had graciously left his fiancée in his will to his son, Abaqa, and Maria was duly married to the man she expected to be her stepson. She spent fifteen years as Queen of the Mongols until, in 1281, Abaqa was assassinated by one of his brothers. Carefully side-stepping the advances of the assassin, who saw her as a part of his inheritance, she returned to Constantinople where her father, by now running out of daughters, promptly tried to marry her off again to yet another Mongol khan. For Maria this was one husband too many. Mongol romance had persuaded her of the merits of chastity. She became a nun and founded, or possibly rebuilt, this church sometime in the 1280s.

At the time of the Turkish conquest, some two centuries later, when icons of the Virgin all over the city were said to weep tears, Constantinople's churches were converted to mosques. Even Haghia Sophia, for nine centuries the fairest church in Christendom, had minarets erected round the ancient dome like minders. Only Our Lady of the Mongols escaped this wholesale conversion. No one is quite sure why. It may have been that the parishioners were able to argue that a church built by the wife of a Mongol prince, inspirational figures to their distant cousins the Ottoman Turks, should be left in peace. Whatever the reason the *firman* or decree of Fatih, the Turkish conqueror, granting it unique leave to continue as a church, still hangs inside the west door. Our Lady of the Mongols is the only Byzantine church in the city that has continued its Christian career undisturbed.

While I browsed among the icons, Father Alexandros fussed about the old church like a conscientious housekeeper, straightening candlesticks, emptying the collection boxes, dusting the ledges of the iconostasis. He was very proud of his old church, and delighted that a foreigner was taking an interest in it. He kept breaking off from his chores to show me some detail of the place he was anxious I should not miss. He took my arm and led me across to the beautiful eleventh-century mosaic of the Virgin. 'Theotokos Pammakaristos,' he said, inclining his head as if he was introducing us. Through the grime of centuries the eyes of 'The All-Joyous Mother of God' were sad pools of light. He showed me Fatih's *firman* written in loping Arabic script. Later he led me down a short flight of stairs into the crypt to sprinkle me with holy water from the well. On the fresco on the end wall the Madonna and Child hovered, as faint as ghosts. The church's connection to the Mongols meant nothing to him; the point of Mouchliotissa for the Greek community was its connection to Byzantium.

The Syrian caretaker brought us tea in the courtyard where we sat in a long slab of sun on a ledge along the southern wall. I asked Father Alexandros about the future of the Greek community in Istanbul. 'There is no future,' he said blankly. 'Greeks have been here for almost three millennia but in my lifetime I am seeing the end of it. Most of my friends have emigrated. My children will emigrate, to Athens, possibly to America.' He was stroking the stone of the ledge as he spoke. The ancient mortar crumbled beneath his fingers. 'This city is my home, home to our people, but it has abandoned us. Unless you are a Turk, it is impossible here. Greeks have no future in Constantinople.'

When the first tempest of Mongol conquest appeared to have abated in the middle of the thirteenth century, the princes of Christendom longed to know more about these Eastern apparitions who had come so close to overrunning Europe. A series of missions was dispatched, most led by Franciscan friars, to report on the Mongols and to enquire about the possibility of their conversion to Christianity. From the Pope down, European leaders nurtured the rather bizarre hope that the Mongol horsemen could be harnessed as allies to drive the Muslims from the Holy Land.

Two of these friars wrote accounts of their journeys, John of Plano Carpini and William of Rubruck. The latter produced the more interesting book, full of wry and colourful observations about the Mongol hersdmen who had so suddenly found themselves ruling most of the known world. His mission predates Marco Polo's more famous journey to Cathay by almost twenty years; even Polo's great English commentator, Sir Henry Yule, was obliged to admit that Friar William had written 'a Book of Travels of much higher claims than any one series of Polo's chapters'. But William suffered the fate of many worthy authors: a bad publisher. His book never achieved the circulation of Polo's accounts.

We tend to think of Friar William now as an early explorer, and like the best explorers he had no idea where he was going, how he was going to get there, or what he should do once he arrived. When William left from Istanbul in the spring of 1253, he was setting off, like Jason and the Argonauts, into barbarian darkness.

His journey took him from Istanbul across southern Russia and what is now Kazakhstan to the distant Mongol capital of Qaraqorum. It was the route I wanted to follow and I saw him, across seven centuries, as a travelling companion.

William set sail from Istanbul on one of the trading vessels that carried cotton, silk and spices from Constantinople to the ports on the north shore of the Black Sea. In Karaköy, round a watery corner from the Golden Horn, I found the modern equivalents of William's ship, the Russian and Ukrainian freighters which ply the same route. The fall of Communism has given a new impetus to Black Sea trade, and Turkey has become a conduit for Western goods, from tinned tomatoes to Johnnie Walker whisky. Russians and Ukrainians, now as free to travel as Levi's and Coca-Cola, come to Istanbul to savour the bright lights and to buy in bulk. They travel by freighter, the only kind of vessel able to cope with their excess baggage.

My telephone enquiries had been inconclusive and I had come to the docks to see if I could rustle up a passage. In pole position was a huge cruise liner called the *Marco Polo*. Had William had a more aggressive publisher this floating palace might have been named after him. Beyond Marco's luxurious namesake the shipping degenerated spectacularly. There were a few European freighters, shouldering the docks like naval toughs, then a couple of Turkish ships, painted gunmetal grey. At the far end of the dock I came to the Russian and Ukrainian freighters, the shipping equivalent of MOT failures, held together by rust stains and a grimy coating of oil.

The last ship was the *Mikhail Lomonosov*, an ageing rust-bucket that seemed to be kept afloat by its mooring ropes. It had a limp deflated appearance that one did not like to see in a ship, as if someone had let the air out of its tyres. It listed. It sagged. It exuded black smoke from unpromising quarters, like the portholes.

I called up to a man in a naval smock leaning on the rail at the top of the gangway. He replied that they were sailing for Sevastopol on Monday, in two days' time. He waved me aboard and I stepped gingerly onto the gangway, unsure if the ship could take my weight.

Dimitri introduced himself as the second mate. He had one of those narrow Slavic faces, very pale and very bony, that are perma-

nently knotted in expressions of anxiety. I asked about cabins, and
he summoned the accommodation officer by barking into a pipe
in the bulwark behind him. The accommodation officer took me
below, showed me a cramped cabin full of sacks of onions, which
he assured me would be cleared out, and then took a hundred
dollars off me in exchange for a grubby receipt written on the back
of a beer mat.

The speed and the casualness of the transaction startled me. Back
on deck I lingered by the gangway with the second mate, hoping
to learn more about this ship which now contained such a large
proportion of my publisher's advance. In spite of his dour appearance, he seemed eager to talk. He spoke the casual staccato English
of ships.

'Did you get receipt?' he asked.

I showed him my beer mat. He nodded. Beer mats were obviously accepted currency on the *Mikhail Lomonosov*.

'You can't trust anyone on this ship,' he said. He leaned forward
to spit over the rail. 'This is my last voyage. I can't take it any
more. Do you know how many times I make this trip? Sevastopol,
Istanbul. Istanbul, Sevastopol.'

I told him I had no idea.

'Four hundred forty-seven,' he said. 'It is no life. This is my last
voyage. Four hundred forty-seven. It's enough, I think. It's making
me crazy. If I don't get off this ship, I will kill someone.'

I took what comfort I could from the fact that he had ruled out
murder as a career option.

A bell rang twice from somewhere within the ship, and he turned
to go. 'We sail at six o'clock, Monday evening. Don't be late.'

The following day, a Sunday, I went to morning mass at Our Lady
of the Mongols. I felt a few prayers for the voyage wouldn't go
amiss. When I arrived the service had already begun but Father
Alexandros broke off in mid-chant to usher me personally into a
seat. As I looked uneasily about the church I realized why I had
got the special treatment. I was the congregation. It is a measure
of the decline of this ancient church here in its Patriarchal city that

the only worshipper it could muster on a warm spring Sunday was a lone Irish Presbyterian.

There is not a lot to do in Presbyterian services except doze off in your pew while a flushed preacher warns of the fire and brimstone that awaits you just the other side of retirement. A couple of hymns, the collection plate, and we all went home. For Presbyterians even a common Anglican mass was a complicated affair involving a disturbing degree of participation – responses, collective prayer, not to mention the endless standing and kneeling at unpredictable moments. Now suddenly I was the crucial component of the most arcane ritual that the Christian church has to offer, here in the last remnant of Byzantium.

The only other people present were a neanderthal-looking altar boy who kept peering out at me through a door in the iconostasis as if he had never seen a congregation before and an elderly cantor, a cadaverous figure in a black robe. With a scythe and a grin the cantor could have doubled as the Grim Reaper. He stood to one side at a lectern chanting interminable passages in ancient Greek in a thin beautiful voice. In the pauses where the congregation were obviously meant to respond, he looked across at me from beneath lowered lids. I looked at the floor or examined the dome with a critical intensity. Amen was the only word I understood and whenever I heard it I joined in heartily to make up for all the important stuff I must have been leaving out. Otherwise I signalled my involvement by throwing in as many signs of the cross as I could manage – not exactly a Presbyterian thing, but I had seen people do this in films.

Later in the courtyard the Grim Reaper took his leave with a slow funereal nod while Father Alexandros and I lingered to have coffee with Nadia, the Syrian caretaker, as if it was already an established ritual between us.

I didn't allude to the fact that there had been no congregation. It was like some dysfunction that one politely ignored. With the same courtesy Alexandros didn't mention my own lamentable performance as an Orthodox worshipper.

'How long will you stay in Istanbul?' Alexandros asked.

'I leave tomorrow.'

'Do you fly back to London?'

'No, I am going on to Outer Mongolia,' I said, as if it formed part of some natural tour of the region. As I listed the stages of my route – across the Black Sea, then overland across the Crimea, southern Russia and Kazakhstan – he tried to disguise his shock behind a polite clerical façade.

He put his empty cup down on the ledge between us. 'And what do you hope to find in Mongolia?' he asked. Despite his best efforts, I felt a note of sarcasm had crept into his voice.

I expanded on the fascination of nomads, speaking rather too fast, overdoing the enthusiasm as I tried to convince him. I might have been speaking about the dark side of the moon. Alexandros was the epitome of the polished metropolitan figure: a Greek, a man of the city from the race that had created the city state, a man whose ancestors may have inhabited this city, one of the world's oldest and greatest, since before the birth of Christ. He seemed to shudder involuntarily at the notion of nomads, people who lived in tents, people who built nothing. Confronted by his civilized sophistication, I was struggling to convince even myself that the Mongolians were not barbarians who had taken a historical wrong turn when they decided to stick to sheep rather than join the ranks of the committed settlers determined to create something that would outlast their own lifetime.

'I have little opportunity to travel,' he said at last.

He looked up at the old church. 'I must look after Mouchliotissa. If we don't keep the church alive, the Turks will take it from us. When the church disappears there will be nothing left of Constantinople, or of us.'

It was the irresistible tug of the city, the lasso of his own identity moored among these ancient stones.

When Friar William was invited to preach in Haghia Sophia on Palm Sunday of 1253, the great church was already very old. Built in the 530s by the Byzantine Emperor Justinian the Great, it belongs to the architectural tradition of the Roman basilica, and thus indirectly to the pagan world of the Greek temple.

The brilliance of Haghia Sophia is the transition from the earth-bound exterior to the soaring lightness of its interior. From the outside the great church is monumental and brooding, the original form much confused with buttresses and minarets added after the Turkish conquest when it began a new career as a mosque. Inside it takes flight. It is transfiguration in architecture. You may run your hands over the massive outer walls, a millennium and a half, stained and crumbling beneath your fingers, but the ethereal magic of the nave is less palpable. The air is gold- and rust-coloured, like some exhalation of the old mosaics and the red marble. Moted columns of light fall from the high windows onto the wide expanses of the floor. The walls, the columns, the distant vaults, might have been weightless; the great dome, Procopius wrote over fourteen centuries ago, seems to be suspended from heaven by a golden chain. Robert Byron compared the old basilica to St Peter's in Rome. Haghia Sophia is a church to God, he wrote, St Peter's merely 'a salon for his agents'.

It is a daunting place to begin a journey to the nomadic steppes. I spent hours in Haghia Sophia wandering the upper galleries beneath the conch vaults gazing down into the great canyon of the nave. I had come to see it as my world and I lingered here as a kind of farewell. As the slanting afternoon light crept through the galleries, amid lengthening shadows, I listened to the crescendo of the great city outside as its inhabitants began their journeys home. In the golden embrace of Haghia Sophia, I suddenly saw the journey to Mongolia as a Byzantine might have done, a journey into emptiness, into some fearful void. I understood the ambitions and the richness of cities. The desire to carve the aspirations of the human heart into some permanent form was central to my own world. In Haghia Sophia that impulse had produced sublime transcendance.

On this day at the beginning of June, on the other side of Asia, the Mongolians would be packing up and moving to summer pastures, leaving nothing to mark their passage but the shadows on the spring grass where their tents had stood.

Chapter Two

THE VOYAGE OUT

At the docks my fellow passengers, a queue of burly figures beneath amorphous sacks, were making their up the gangway of the *Mikhail Lomonosov* like newsreel refugees.

Below in the cabin the resident onions had been cleared away leaving a faint astringent odour and a litter of red skins. The accommodation master appeared with my cabin-mate, a fifteen-year-old boy from Sevastopol. Kolya had been visiting his mother who was working in Istanbul. He was a thin boy with a mutinous complexion and an agitated manner. His gangly limbs jerked and rattled with adolescent impatience.

Kolya and I conversed in a bizarre amalgam of English, Turkish and Russian, prompted by various phrase books and a vocabulary of gestures and mime. It made for surprisingly lucid conversation. At first I tried to chat to him about kid's stuff – his age, his school, his mother, ice-hockey – but he brushed these dull enquiries aside. He was keen to know the legal age limit for smoking and drinking in England, what kind of guns the police carried in London, and if the Queen was still in the business of beheading. His Istanbul had been somewhat different from mine. He had never heard of Haghia Sophia but he knew where to buy imitation Rolex watches and could quote the prices in three currencies. Like everyone else on this ship, he was a small trader, bringing home goods to sell in Sevastopol. He showed me his wares, – T-shirts, switchblades, pornographic magazines.

He sat on the edge of his bunk, drumming his legs in a nervous rhythm, blowing smoke rings towards the porthole. Kolya was in a hurry to grow up, to find the fast-track to the adult world of hard currency, illegal trading, and women. I was more than he could have hoped for as a cabin-mate, a representative of the glamorous and decadent West, that happy land of rap stars and Playstations. Hoping to cement our relationship, he looked for a way to make himself useful to me. I was a lone foreigner on a ship of Ukrainians and Russians, and he began to cast himself as my protector.

His mother appeared at the door of the cabin to say goodbye. A tall blonde Venus in a fur-collared coat, she was an exotic dancer making a Ukrainian fortune in one of Istanbul's nightclubs. In the narrow passage Kolya was momentarily tearful – a boy like any other saying goodbye to his mother – but once she was gone he was quick to shake off this unwelcome vulnerability. He began to count the fistful of dollars that she had tucked into his pocket. Then he bolted out the door as if he had another ship to catch. Fifteen minutes later he was back, carrying a shopping bag from the free-port facilities on the quayside. Inside was a hard plastic case. Opening it, he lifted out an automatic pistol.

'A hundred dollars,' he said, breaking the seal on the box of ammunition.

'What is it for?' I asked, ducking as he swung the gun round the cabin.

'Protection,' the boy said. His eyes shone.

He had bought a shoulder-holster as well, and sought my help in buckling it round his thin shoulders. Then he slipped the gun into the new leather, and put on his jacket to hide the weapon. Smiling, the child stood before me, armed and dangerous, ready for the voyage home.

We sailed at nine. Below in the cabin, I felt a series of shudders run through the ship, and went out on deck to find us slipping away from our berth. Swinging about in the entrance to the Golden Horn, where a stream of cars was crossing the Galata Bridge, we turned up the Bosphorus away from the old city. The world's most splendid skyline, that exquisite silhouette of minarets and domes, was darkening on a lemon-coloured sky. Haghia Sophia, round-shouldered above the trees of Gülhane, was the colour of a shell, a delicate shading of pinks and greys. Swaying in the wash of currents, ferries pushed out from the docks at Eminönü, bound for Üsküdar where the lights were coming on along the Asian shore. On the foredeck, I made my way through the cables and the piled crates to stand in the prow of the ship as we slipped northward through the heart of the city.

The austere face of the Dolmabahçe Palace, the nineteenth-century successor to the Topkapi, rose on our left. Its restrained façade belies a kitsch interior, a confection of operatic furnishings too ghastly to detail. It was here that the last Sultans watched their enfeebled empire slither to an ignominious end in the early years of the twentieth century. Much of the palace was given over to the harem, whose membership seemed to grow as the number of imperial provinces declined. Sex, presumably, was some consolation for political impotency.

The Bosphorus is a pilot's nightmare. In the twisting straits ships veer back and forth between the two continents, dodging the powerful currents and each other. We passed so close to the mosque at Ortaköy on the European side that I was able to look down through grilled windows to see a row of neatly synchronized bottoms, upturned in prayer. Half a mile on I could see what was on television in the stylish rooms of the old renovated Ottoman houses on the Asian shore. Accidents are not uncommon, and people tell amusing anecdotes about residents of the waterside villas being awoken in the middle of a foggy winter night to find a Russian freighter parked in the living room. Since the late seventies no less than twelve listed *yalis* or Ottoman houses have been run down by ships, invariably captained by tipsy Russians.

A spring wind had blown up, the *Kozkavuran Firtinasi*, the Wind of the Roasting Walnuts, which comes down to the Bosphorus from the hills of Anatolia. On the Asian shore we passed the twin-spired façade of the Ottoman cavalry school where cadets were taught some shadow of the horsemanship that had brought their ancestors from Central Asia. Beyond I could make out the ragged outline of Rumeli Hisari, its crenellated walls breasting the European hills. On the slopes below is the oldest Turkish cemetery in Istanbul. Both here and at the cemetery at Eyüp, there is a marvellous literature of death, ironic and light-hearted. I had been reading translations of them at breakfast. They are a fine lesson in how to say farewell.

'A pity to good-hearted Ismail Efendi,' reads one epitaph, 'whose death caused great sadness among his friends. Having caught the illness of love at the age of seventy, he took the bit between his teeth and dashed full gallop to paradise.' On another tombstone a relief shows three trees, an almond, a cypress, and a peach; peaches are a Turkish metaphor for a woman's breasts. 'I've planted these trees so that people may know my fate. I loved an almond-eyed, cypress-tall maiden, and bade farewell to this world without savouring her peaches.' As we passed, the cemetery showed only as an area of darkness.

Soon the city was slipping astern. The tiered lights fell away on both shores and Europe and Asia drifted apart as the straits widened. I stood in the bow until we passed Rumeli Feneri and Anadolu Feneri, the lighthouses on the two continents flanking the northern entrance to the Bosphorus, blinking with different rhythms.

In antiquity the Black Sea was a watery frontier. When the Ionian Greeks crossed its wind-driven reaches in search of fish and wheat, they came upon a people on the far shores who might have stepped from one of their own mythologies. The Scythians were a diverse collection of nomadic tribes with a passion for gold and horses. To the Greeks they were barbarians, the repository of their anxieties and their prejudice.

Herodotus gives us a compelling account of them. His descriptions show remarkable similarities with Friar William's account of the Mongols two thousand years later, a reminder if one was needed of the static nature of nomadic society and the pervading anxieties they aroused in settled populations. They were a people without towns or crops, Herodotus tells us, clearly unnerved. They lived on the produce of their herds of cattle and sheep and horses, migrating seasonally in search of fresh pasture. They slaughtered their sheep without spilling blood, drank fermented mare's milk and smoked hemp which made them howl with pleasure. They were shamans who worshipped the elements and the graves of their ancestors. In battle they formed battalions of mounted archers. Their equestrian skills were unrivalled, and they sought the trophies of their enemies' skulls for drinking-cups.

The ship lifted on the sea's swell, its bow rising to the dark void ahead. A new wind was blowing, the *Meltemi*. It was a north-easterly blowing from the Pontic steppe across 500 miles of sea. In Istanbul they say the *Meltemi* is a cleansing wind, dispelling foul airs and bad feelings.

Historically, the people of cities have had an ambivalent response to the unsettled landscapes of the steppe which seem to harbour ideas both of Arcadia and of chaos. Settled peoples were forever torn between the notions that nomads were barbarian monsters who threatened civilized order, and intuitive innocents who retained some elemental virtue that had been lost to them. 'Nomads are closer to the created world of God,' wrote the fourteenth-century Arab historian and philosopher, Ibn Khaldun, 'and removed from the blameworthy customs that have infected the hearts of settlers.' He believed that they alone could escape the cycles of decadence that infected all civilization. Only regular blasts of their cleansing winds allowed civilization to sustain its own virtues.

Kolya came to fetch me from my post in the ship's bow, motioning for me to follow him as if he had something urgent to show me. Downstairs in our cabin he produced a bottle of champagne and four plastic cups. Then he disappeared and returned a moment later with two women.

Anna and Olga were the occupants of the neighbouring cabin. They were a dramatic illustration of the way that Slavic women seem unable to find any middle ground between slim grace and stout coarseness. Anna was a striking figure in tight jeans and a short sleeveless top. Olga, in cardigan and heavy shoes, wouldn't have stood out among a party of dockers. Kolya, already a slave to female beauty, had only invited her to make up the numbers.

He was an energetic host, a fifteen-year-old playing at cocktail party. He poured the champagne, produced packets of American cigarettes and a bag of pistachio nuts, and chatted to everyone, the life of the party. I felt like a debutante being launched into the ship's society. When the women asked about me Kolya explained I was going to visit the Tartars, and that I was a good friend of a priest called William who had been to visit them already.

Olga was silent and morose while Anna did all the talking. She had spent three weeks in Istanbul and was now travelling home to Sevastopol. The purpose of her visit was unclear. She tried to make it sound like a holiday but her cabin, like all the cabins on this boat, was so crowded with canvas sacks and cardboard boxes tied with string she could barely get the door open. The collapse of Communism had made everyone a salesman. But Anna, I suspected, had been trading more than tinned sardines. The Black Sea routes carried a heavy traffic of young women bound for the red-light districts of Istanbul. Many were part-timers making three or four trips a year to boost the family income.

We drank the champagne and when it was finished Kolya fetched another bottle, which I tried in vain to pay for. The boy was our host, magnanimous and expansive. He made toasts, he told dirty jokes that made the girls laugh, he kept his jacket on, buttoned up to conceal the gun. Olga soon drifted away to shift some crates and Anna now basked alone in our attention. She had become flirtatious. With the boy she already enjoyed a maternal familiarity, alternately hugging him and slapping him in mock remonstration, and now she extended the same attentions to me, pinching my shoulder and propping her elbows on my knees.

Kolya was showing off his collection of T-shirts adorned with American slogans. 'California is a State of Mind', one announced. 'Better Dead than in Philadelphia', another said. When he presented one to Anna, she leapt up to try it on. Standing with her back to us in the cramped cabin she removed her top. The boy gazed at her naked back and her bare breasts swelling into view as she stooped to pick up the T-shirt, then he shot a hot questioning glance at me. She swung round to model the gift. It seemed a trifle small. Her nipples pressed through the thin fabric just below a caption that read 'Flying Fuck: the Mile High Club'.

When we had finished the second bottle Kolya took us off to the nightclub. I had not suspected the *Lomonosov* of harbouring a nightclub but Kolya was obviously a veteran clubber on the Black Sea routes. We descended a narrow stairway to a windowless dungeon in the bowels of the ship. Coloured lights in putrid hues of pink and blue glazed the shabby velvet sofas and plastic tables gathered round a small dance floor. The room smelt of stale beer and bilge water. Disco Muzak was leaking out of tinny speakers. Kolya ordered and paid for a round of drinks with umbrellas in them. I had given up trying to restrain him.

Throwing back her cocktails, Anna was now in full party mode. A tall bearded Russian, billed as Rasputin, had taken to the tiny stage with a synthesizer that replicated every instrument known to lounge lizards. She insisted I dance with her, tugging me by the arm out onto the empty dance floor. She had two basic steps, neither related to the music. The first was licentious: she ground her hips provocatively against me, insinuating one of her legs between mine. The other was a cross between the Moulin Rouge chorus line and a kung-fu exercise with a series of high kicks and spectacular twirls. It was a nerve-wracking business. The transition from simulated sex to the martial arts was so drunkenly abrupt that I was in real danger of having my head kicked in between romantic clinches.

All the following day at sea, Kolya followed me around the ship like a pint-sized bodyguard, his jacket bulging. Below in the cabin he spent most of his time loading and unloading the pistol. I tried to keep myself out of the line of fire.

In the dining hall Kolya, Anna and I ate together at a corner table. Meals on the *Mikhail Lomonosov* were dour occasions. Breakfast was an ancient sausage and a sweet cake. Lunch and dinner were indistinguishable – borscht, grey meat, potatoes, hard-boiled eggs. The passengers ate in silence, large pasty figures earnestly shovelling food in a room where the only sound was the awkward undertone of cutlery.

At breakfast we sat together like a dysfunctional family, bickering over cups of tea. We drifted into a curious relationship in which I was cast in the role of the grumpy and distracted *pater*. My failure to respond to Anna's advances had upset them both. She behaved as if I was a shiftless husband who had humiliated her. In a filthy mood, Anna cut short the boy's mediating advances by scolding him for his table manners, for his swearing, for his untucked shirt, for his lack of attention to her. Then she scolded me for not exercising more control over him. I retreated monosyllabically behind newspapers. It hardly seemed credible that we had met only twelve hours before. We chaffed at the confinement of our respective roles as if we had inhabited them for a lifetime.

Though he had conceived some loyalty to me as cabin-mate and foreigner, I was a disappointment to the boy. I knew nothing about rap stars, I lacked the flash accessories he associated with the West, and I took a firm and decidedly negative line about his chief pleasure of the moment: the revolver. With Anna he had a tempestuous and ambivalent relationship, alternately straining at her maternal leash and embracing her bursts of affection. Argument seemed to strengthen some perverse bond between them. When they made up, Kolya brought her bottles of Georgian champagne and fake Rolexes, then snuggled into her lap amid the sacks of cargo in her cabin in some uneasy limbo between a childish cuddle and a lover's embrace.

He took the fact that I had not slept with Anna as a personal slight. When we were alone he would try to convince me that I should have sex with her. His pleas were both an injured innocence and a sordid knowledge beyond his years. At one moment he might have been the whining child of divorced parents, hoping for a reconciliation. At another, he was an underage pimp trying to drum up business.

In spite of Kolya's disapproval of fraternizing with the staff, I had accepted an invitation from Dimitri, the second mate. He inhabited a small cabin on the port side of the ship where he had laid out afternoon tea: slabs of jellied meat, salted herrings, hard-boiled eggs, black bread, and glasses of vodka. Despite his long tenure on the *Lomonosov* the cabin had an anonymous air. There was a hold-all on the bed, two nylon shirts on hangers, and an officer's jacket hanging on the back of the door. He might have been a passenger, uncharacteristically travelling light. His mood had not improved since the first evening I met him when the ship was docked in Istanbul.

'In the Ukraine, in Russia, shipping has no future,' he said, shaking his head. 'There are no opportunities. When I first went to sea, the Soviet Union was a great naval power. Its ships sailed the world. It is unbelievable what has happened to us. You will see in Sevastopol. The great Black Sea Fleet. The naval docks look like a scrap yard.'

He poured the vodka and sank his teeth into a boiled egg.

'Do you know what this ship was?' he asked.

I shook my head. The eggs, like rubber, made speech difficult.

'It was a research vessel,' he said emphatically as if I might contradict him. 'I have been seventeen years on this boat. Before 1990 we used to sail all over the world – the Indian Ocean, South America, Africa. We carried scientists – intelligent people, interesting people, engaged in important research. Professors from Leningrad, from Moscow, from Kiev. You cannot imagine the conversations in the dining room. Philosophy. Genetics. Hydrography. Meteorology. You couldn't pass the door without learning something. And nice people.' His voice softened at the memory of the nice professors. 'Very nice people. Polite. People with manners.'

He crammed a salted herring between small rows of teeth. His expression seemed like an accusation of culpability, as if perhaps I was taking up space that might have been allocated to a wise professorial figure with interesting conversation and good table manners.

'Look what has become of us. Carrying vegetables and what else back and forth across the Black Sea like a tramp boat. It is difficult to believe.'

I didn't ask how this had happened. I knew he was going to tell me anyway.

'Money,' he exploded. 'The country is bankrupt. Oh yes we all wanted freedom. We all wanted the end of Communism. But no one mentioned it would bankrupt the country. There is no money for research any more. There is no money for anything. So here we are.'

His rage subsided long enough for him to refill our glasses. 'I have not been paid in five months,' he said quietly.

I asked how he managed.

'I have a kiosk, in Sevastopol.' His voice had dropped; he was mumbling. He seemed ashamed of this descent into commerce as if it was not worthy of him, a ship's officer. 'We sell whisky and vodka, sweets, tobacco. I bring them from Turkey. Otherwise we would starve.'

In the Ukraine, as in the rest of the constituent parts of the old Union, the quest for a living has become everything. From education to the nuclear defence industry, all the great public institutions are obliged to hustle for things to sell like pensioners flogging the remnants of their attics on street corners in Moscow. For Dimitri any hope of advancement had shrunk with the maritime fleet. He had been second mate on the *Lomonosov* for the last twelve of his seventeen years of service, and still the first mate showed no signs of departure or death.

Economic pressures and the tedium of their endless passages had made the *Mikhail Lomonosov* a ship of malcontents, riven by jealousies and intrigues. The officers all hated one another. Dimitri hated the cargo master, the cargo master hated the chief engineer, the chief engineer hated the first mate, who hated him right back. Everyone hated the captain whose position allowed him access to the lucrative world of corruption.

Dimitri piled more sausage onto my plate. His anger had been spent, and he seemed apologetic about drawing me into his troubles, as if they were a family matter, unseemly to parade before a foreigner.

'Do you know who Mikhail Lomonosov was?' he asked.

I confessed I didn't. I had seen his portrait hanging in the dining hall, an eighteenth-century figure in a powdered wig and a lace shirt.

'You are not a Russian. How would you know? But the passengers on this ship. None of them know who Lomonosov was.' He was beginning to grow agitated again, in spite of himself, chopping the air with his hand. 'He was a great Russian, a scientist, a writer. He founded Moscow University. He set up the first laboratory in Russia. He was also a poet, a very great poet. He wrote about language and science and history. The scientists who travelled on the ship all knew his work. They discussed him. But these people, these traders, they are ignorant. They do not know their own history. They can tell you the price of every grade of vodka but they know nothing about Mikhail Lomonosov. No one cares about these things any more, about science, about poetry. Only about money, and prices in Istanbul.'

In the evening I went to visit him on the bridge during his watch. He was alone. The hushed solitude of the place and the instruments of his profession – charts, radar screens, compasses – had lightened his mood. On the chart table the Black Sea was neatly parcelled by lines of longitude and latitude. Near the bottom Istanbul straddled the Bosphorus. At the top Sevastopol was tucked carefully round a corner on the western shores of the Crimea. A thick smudged pencil line joined the two. Overdrawn countless times, it marked the single unvarying line to which his life had been reduced: 43° NE.

Below in the nightclub Rasputin was singing a Russian version of *My Way*. Despairing of me, Anna had transferred her attentions rather theatrically to the singer, and was now gyrating suggestively in front of the tiny stage. The purple lighting did Rasputin no favours. His eyes and cheeks were malevolent pockets of darkness.

I found Kolya alone at a corner table nursing a double brandy.

'Anna seems to be enjoying herself,' I said taking a seat.

He looked at me without speaking then turned his eyes back to the dance floor and the figure of Rasputin in its purple haze.

'He is not exactly Sinatra,' I said.

'He is a shit,' Kolya said.

The boy seemed to have diminished on his stool, sinking deeper into himself. He simmered with resentment. He felt Rasputin was displacing him in Anna's affections, that the arbitrary tides of the adult world had shifted without any reference to him. He glowered at the singer from his corner table like a child gangster.

I retired and when Kolya arrived later in the cabin, he was sullen and uncommunicative. We played cards in a difficult silence.

Half an hour later, Anna arrived with Rasputin, trailing all the forced merriment of the nightclub. She seemed to need to show off her acquisition to me and to Kolya in some act of petty revenge.

They sat together on the bunk opposite. Anna stroked his thigh. They chattered together in Ukrainian. The boy watched them coldly. Rasputin tried to draw him out with bantering exchanges. The nightclub had closed and the two were trying to press Kolya for his usual hospitality. Anna had delved into one of Kolya's bags and produced a bottle of vodka which she proposed they drink. Rasputin held it up and made to open the screw top, looking teasingly to Kolya for his response. He was laughing open-mouthed, a barking ridicule emerging from between rows of long yellow teeth. Then he closed his mouth suddenly, and his expression changed. Anna and Rasputin were suddenly rigid.

I looked round at Kolya. The boy was pointing his gun at the singer. He swore at him, under his breath, as if he was speaking to himself.

'Put the gun down, Kolya,' I said.

He did not respond. For what seemed like long minutes no one moved. We were transfixed by the gun.

'Put it down, Kolya.' I forced myself to stand up. Kolya's gaze flickered toward me for a second then returned to Rasputin. His face was flushed. I felt my heart pounding and my legs felt watery. I stepped between the two.

'Get out,' I said to Rasputin.

The singer seemed about to protest, but Anna silenced him. She stood up and pulled his arm. I herded them out of the door then closed it after them.

Kolya had lowered the gun. He picked at the barrel absent-mindedly, childishly, with his middle finger. He pursed his lips, affecting a casual expression, as if the sudden terror that still stiffened the air in the room had nothing to do with him.

'You're an idiot,' I told him. I wanted to shout at him; my own tension needed an outlet. He sat chewing his lip, gazing at the floor, then threw the gun on his bunk.

'You'll have to get rid of it,' I told him. He said nothing. 'The singer will tell the Ukrainian customs about the gun. They will search you. He might even be telling the captain now. You need to get rid of it. Immediately.'

He sat staring at the floor. Then with the surly grace of a child who had been ordered to clean his room, he picked up the gun, opened the porthole and dropped it into the sea. Then he lay down on his bunk and sobbed into his pillow.

Perched on the southern shores of the old Soviet Union, Sevastopol was a window on more tolerant worlds. There is a Mediterranean feel about the place, some tang of the south, some promise of escape, a lightness borne on the sea air and reflected in the pinkish hue of the stone façades. Built by Black Sea traders who had seen Naples, it has touches of architectural grandeur and a southern desire for colour. Side streets were full of flower boxes and haughty cats. Flights of stone steps connected avenues of plane trees and trolley buses. Vines trailed between the mulberry trees in walled gardens. In the midday sun cafés spilled onto the pavements, and people grew animated and gregarious.

It is easy to understand why the Crimea was the envy of the rest of the Soviet Union. Dour people from Moscow used to come to Sevastopol and Odessa just to look at the vegetables. In those days the Politburo holidayed on the Black Sea. In this easy southern climate it was a simple matter to believe that things were going well. Every other year the first families of the East, leaving their overcoats and their worries at home, gathered at a resort near Yalta just along the coast – the Brezhnevs, the Honeckers, the Zhivkovs, the Ceausescus, and the Tsendbals – to compare growth rates and grandchildren.

Though virtually unknown outside his own country, Tsendbal's survival eclipsed them all. For forty-four years, as general secretary and then president, this obscure figure ruled the People's Republic of Mongolia, the world's second Communist state and the oldest of Russia's allies. To keep tabs on him, the KGB had managed to marry him off to one of their agents, the boorish Filatova, a Russian from Soviet Central Asia. The Crimea was one of her passions and the Tsendbals came to the Black Sea at least twice a year. If any

folk memories of the Mongol Hordes lurked in the Crimean sub-
conscious, Tsendbal must have confused them. The heir to Genghis
Khan was a small mousy man, the epitome of the faceless bureaucrat, obsequious to his domineering wife and his masters in the
Kremlin.

In the afternoon I wandered through the park where Crimean
War monuments were deployed between the flower beds. Tod-
leben, who organized the defence of Sevastopol in 1855, towered
serenely over strolling naval cadets in hats so ridiculous they might
have been dressed for a children's party. At the far end of the park
a fat man reading a newspaper sold me a ticket for an empty Ferris
wheel.

Ten years ago Sevastopol was the most closed of the Soviet
Union's closed cities, and spies in every Western nation would have
considered a ride on this Ferris wheel as the pinnacle of their careers.
Now the operator hardly cared enough about the presence of the
former enemy to look up from the sports pages. With a series of
creaking shudders I rose above the city. Beneath me, in the long
protected harbour, lay the great Black Sea Fleet. It looked like a vast
naval scrap yard full of rusting hulks. Economic collapse appeared to
have done for the fleet what the naval strategies of Nato failed to
do – keep much of it in harbour. Russia and the Ukraine had
argued over the disposition of the ships when the latter declared
its independence, though neither of them can afford to maintain
its share of the naval loot.

Back at my hotel the lobby was dominated by a flashing sign
that read *El Dorado*. Beneath it a cabal of young venture capitalists
in baseball caps worked the slot machines. Upstairs in my room
the television offered two Russian channels. On the first, old Russia
survived. Rectangular men in grey suits were making interminable
speeches. On the other channel, new Russia was in full cry. Encouraged by a deranged game-show host, housewives were performing
a striptease. The applause levels of the audience determined which
one would win the kind of washing machine I remember my mother
throwing out in the 1960s. It was not difficult to guess which
channel was winning the ratings war.

The finest part of Sevastopol is the esplanade along the seafront
which stages the evening *passeggiata*. A series of neo-classical build-

ings – naval academies, customs houses, municipal offices – lines the long promenade where the inhabitants stroll arm in arm taking the sea air as swallows dive between the rooftops. Like the promenaders most of the buildings appeared to have lost the security of state employment and now struggle to make ends meet. Corner rooms in the old academies have been rented out as bars and restaurants. As the soft southern night fell, noisy discos mushroomed between the Corinthian columns where visiting leaders, including the Tsendbals of Outer Mongolia, once reviewed the naval fleet that was the pride of the Soviet Union.

At this season the Crimea was full of poppies. In the winding defile that climbed towards the interior, the kind of treacherous geography that betrayed the Light Brigade, poppies wreathed the outcrops of pink rock. Above on the plateau, ramparts of poppies enclosed fields where armies of stout women were cutting hay with scythes. Then the bus passed into a country of orchards where poppies trickled down the aisles between the trees to gather in pools among apple-green shadows.

I felt relieved to be on the move, to be consuming landscapes. The boat and its complex relationships had engendered a sense of confinement, some cloying and unsuitable feeling of responsibility. Now I was performing the traveller's trick, the trick of departure, the vanishing act that marks the stages of a journey. For the traveller every encounter is conditioned by departure, by the impending schedule of trains, by the tickets already folded in his pocket, by the promise of new pastures. Departure is the constraint and the liberation of journeys.

On this bright morning fresh landscapes opened in front of me. Gazing out the window of the bus I delighted in the flash of fields and houses, the blur of poppies. I watched whole towns sweep past, adrift among wheat fields, then fall rapidly astern. At Simferopol I would get the train and tomorrow evening I would be on the Volga, seven hundred miles to the east. I felt the elation of movement. On this bus fleeing eastward, I felt I was staging my own disappearance, vanishing into Asia, leaving only a handwritten sign on the window of my former life: 'Gone to Outer Mongolia, please cancel the papers'.

Since the time of the Scythians, the pastures of the Crimean interior had lured successive waves of Asian nomads onto the peninsula from the southern Russian steppes. When the Mongols arrived here in the thirteenth century it became an important component of the western province of the Mongolian Empire known as the Golden Horde whose capital lay at Sarai on the Volga. The Russians mistakenly called these eastern invaders Tatars, one of the many tribes that had been subdued by Genghis Khan in the early years of conquest, and the name stuck. In the west this became Tartar when Louis IX, William's benefactor, transformed it by way of a Latin pun on *ex tartarus*, meaning 'from the regions of hell' recorded in classical legend.

Friar William landed at Sudak on the southern shore of the Crimea on 21 May, 1253. His plan was to visit a Mongol prince, Sartaq, rumoured to be a Christian, whose camp lay three days' ride beyond the River Don. On the advice of the Greek merchants in Sudak he opted to travel by cart, filling one with 'fruits, muscatel wine and dry biscuits' as gifts for the Mongol officials that they would encounter along the way. He set off with four companions: his colleague, Friar Bartholomew, a man whose age and bulk made him even less suited to this epic journey than William himself; Gosset, 'a bearer'; Homo Dei, a Syrian interpreter whose knowledge of any useful language was fairly shaky; and Nicholas, a slave boy that William had rescued in Constantinople.

But William's journey was to take him a good deal further than he had planned. He was embarking on an odyssey that would lead him eventually to the distant Mongol capital of Qaraqorum, at the other end of Asia, well over four thousand miles away. If he had hoped to be back with his fellow monks in time for Christmas, he was to be disappointed.

At Simferopol I found the train to Volgograd guarded by an army of formidable carriage attendants, big-breasted women who stood by the doors like bouncers. They had beehive hairdos, thick necks and the kind of shoulders born of a career spent wrestling baggage and the heavy windows of Russian trains. Even their make-up was intimidating – scarlet lipstick, blue eyelids, raspberry-rouged cheeks, and malevolent bits of mascara gathered at the corners of their eyes. But once the train started, they underwent a transformation, from security guards to matrons. They abandoned their jackboots for carpet slippers, and began to fuss with the curtains. Taking pity on a hapless foreigner, my carriage attendant brought me a mug of tea from her samovar and I spread out a picnic of bananas, smoked cheese, a sausage, and Ukrainian pastries.

I shared my compartment with a burly Russian with mechanic's hands and a simian haircut growing low on his forehead. He lay down on the bunk opposite and was asleep before we cleared the industrial suburbs of Simferopol. He slept with one eye slightly ajar. From beneath its lowered lid it followed me round the compartment. As he fell deeper into his slumbers his limbs began to convulse, like a dog dreaming of chasing rabbits.

On the edges of the Azov Sea we crossed out of Crimea on a littoral of islands. For a time the world was poised uneasily between land, water and sky. Causeways linked narrow tongues of marsh where lone houses stood silhouetted against uncertain horizons. A fisherman passed in a boat no bigger than a bathtub, his head bowed over nets, like a man at prayer. Watery planes tapered beneath landscapes of cloud until the sea and the sky began to merge, the same placid grey, the same boundless horizontals.

Beyond Melitopol we sailed over prairies tilting beneath towering skies. This was nomad country, the Don steppe, traversed by winds blowing out of the heart of Asia. The first Greek traders who ventured across the Black Sea were alarmed to find themselves here on the edge of another sea running north and east on waves of grass. The southern reaches of grasslands that stretch intermittently from Hungary to Manchuria, these prairies lent themselves for millennia to a culture of movement.

Maritime metaphors adhere to these landscapes with the tenacity of barnacles. Chekov grew up at Taganrog east of here along the shores of the Sea of Azov. He remembered as a boy lying among sacks of wheat in the back of an oxcart sailing slowly across the great ocean of the steppe. William wrote in a similar vein. 'When

. . . we finally came across some people,' he wrote, 'we rejoiced like shipwrecked sailors coming into harbour.' Pastoralism survived on these prairies until the beginning of the twentieth century when the fatal combination of the modern age and Communism brought the world of the Scythians to a close. The tents and the horses retreated as lumbering tractors ploughed up the grasslands for wheat, and the prairie was colonized by villages and farmers.

The afternoon was full of country stations and haycocks. Peasant women lined the platforms with metal buckets of fat red cherries which they sold by the bowlful to the passengers through the windows of the train. As we pulled away they slung their buckets on the handlebars of old bicycles and diminished down dirt roads between flat fields of cabbages and banks of cream-coloured blossoms. Pegged like an unruly sheet by a line of telegraph poles, the prairie flapped away into unfathomable distances.

In the early evening I stood in the corridor at an open window, breathing in the country air as we passed through invisible chambers of scent: cut hay, strawberries, wet stagnant ditches, newly-turned earth, wood smoke. In a blue twilight we came to the estuary of the Dneiper, as dark as steel and as wide as a lake. Trails of mist unravelled across its polished surface. Dim yellow lights marked another horizon. It was impossible to tell if they were houses or ships.

All that remains of the great nomadic cultures that once roamed these regions are the tombs of their ancestors. William describes the landscape as being composed of three elements: heaven, earth and tombs. Scythians tombs, known as *kurgans*, litter these steppes like humpbacked whales riding seas of wheat. Beneath great mounds of stone and earth their chiefs were buried with their horses and their gold, their servants and their wives. The tombs were the only permanent habitation they ever built. Grave robbers have plundered the tall barrows for centuries, carrying off the spectacular loot of Scythian gold – ornaments, jewellery, weapons, horse trappings, all decorated in an 'animal style' with parades of ibex and stags, eagles and griffons, lions and serpents. But it was horses not gold that were the most compelling feature of these burials.

Horses attain a mythical status in nomadic cultures, and have always been crucial to their burials and their notions of immortality.

Sacrificed at the funerary rites, they joined their masters in order to carry them to the next world. In a famous passage Herodotus described the mounted attendants placed round the Scythian tomb chambers. An entire cavalry of horses and riders had been strangled, disembowelled, stuffed with straw and impaled upon poles in an enclosing circle ready to accompany the dead king on his last ride. For centuries it was treated as just another of Herodotus' tall tales until the Russian archaeologist N.I. Veselovsky opened the Ulskii mound in the nineteenth century and found the remains of three hundred and sixty horses tethered on stakes in a ring about the mound, their hooves pawing the air in flight.

The nomadic association of horses with immortality had even reached China, beyond the eastern shores of the grass sea, as early as the second century BC. In the mind of the Chinese emperor Wu-ti, military humiliations at the hands of the Xiongnu, the Huns of Western records, and fears about his own immortality had become strangely entwined. He seemed to embrace the convictions of the nomads who threatened his frontiers. From behind the claustrophobic walls of imperial China, he envied them their sudden arrivals, their fleet departures. Their horses, he believed, would be his salvation, and he set his heart on acquiring the fabled steeds of far-off Fergana in Central Asia. Known to the Chinese as the Heavenly Horses, they were said to sweat blood and to be able to carry their riders into the celestial arms of their ancestors.

Throughout his reign, Wu-ti lavished enormous expense and countless lives on expeditions to bring thirty breeding pairs of these divine steeds home to China. Only when they finally arrived was he at peace. He watched them from the windows of his palace like a smitten lover, tall beautiful horses grazing on pastures of alfalfa, their flanks shining, their fine heads lifting in unison to scent the air. 'They will draw me up', he wrote in a poem, 'and carry me to the Holy Mountain. (On their backs) I shall reach the Jade Terrace.'

Chapter Three

THE KAZAKHSTAN EXPRESS

In Volgograd the lobby of the hotel was steeped in gloom. A clock ticked somewhere. Blades of blue light from the street lamps outside cut across the Caucasian carpets and struck the faces of the marble pillars. A grand staircase ascended into vaults of darkness. In the square a car passed and the sweep of headlamps illuminated statues of naked figures like startled guests caught unawares between the old sofas and the potted palms. It was only ten o'clock in the evening, but the hotel was so quiet it might have been abandoned.

When I rang the bell at the reception desk, a woman I had not seen lifted her head. She had been asleep. A mark creased her cheek where it had been pressed against a ledger. She gazed at me in silence for a long moment as she disentangled herself from her dreams.

'Passport?' she whispered hoarsely, as if that might hold a useful clue to where she was.

My room was on the fifth floor. I was struggling with the gates of the antique lift when an ancient attendant appeared silently from a side doorway. He wore a pair of enormous carpet slippers and a silk scarf which bound his trousers like a belt. From a vast bunch of keys, he unlocked the lift and together we rose through the empty hotel, to the slow clicking of wheels and pulleys, arriving on the fifth floor with a series of violent shudders. When I stepped out into a dark hall, the gates of the lift clanged behind me, and the ghoulish operator floated slowly downwards again in a tiny halo of light, past my feet and out of sight. I stood for a moment listening to the sighs and creaks and mysterious exhalations of the hotel, and wondered if I was the only guest.

My room had once been grand. You could have ridden a horse through the doorway. The ceiling mouldings, twenty feet above my head, were weighted with baroque swags of fruit. The plumbing was baronial. The furnishings, however, appeared to have come from a car-boot sale in Minsk. There was a Formica coffee table with a broken leg and a chest of drawers painted in khaki camouflage. The bed was made of chipboard and chintz; when I sat tentatively on the edge, it swayed alarmingly. A vast refrigerator, standing between the windows, roared like an aeroplane waiting for takeoff.

I was tired, and in want of a bath. There appeared to be no plug but by some miracle of lateral thinking I discovered that the metal weight attached to the room key doubled as the bath plug. As I turned on the water, there was a loud knock at the door.

Outside in the passage stood a stout woman in a low-cut dress, a pair of fishnet stockings, and a tall precarious hairdo. But for her apparel she might have been one of those Russian tractor drivers of the 1960s, a heroine of the collective farm, muscular, square-jawed, willing to lay down her life for a good harvest. In her hand, where one might have expected a spanner, she carried only a dainty white handbag.

She smiled. Her teeth were smeared with lipstick.

'You want massage?' she said in English. 'Sex? Very good.'

Prostitution is the only room service that most Russian hotels provide, and the speed with which it arrives at your door, unsolicited, is startling in a nation where so many essential services involve queuing. There was some lesson here about market forces.

The woman smiled and nodded. I smiled back and shook my head.

'No thank you,' I said.

But Olga didn't get where she was by taking no for an answer. 'Massage very good. I come back later. I bring other girls.' She was taking a mobile telephone out of her bag. 'What you want? Blondes? I have very nice blondes. How many blondes you want?'

She had begun to dial a number, presumably the Blonde Hot Line. I had a vision of fair-haired tractor drivers marching towards us from the four corners of Volgograd.

'No, no,' I said. 'No, thank you. No massage. No sex. No blondes.'

I was closing the door. The woman's bright commercial manner had slipped like a bad wig. In the gloom of the passage she suddenly looked old and defeated. I felt sorry for her, and for Russia, reduced to selling blondes to cash-rich foreigners.

'Good luck,' I said. 'I hope you find someone else to massage.'

'Old soldiers.' She shrugged. 'Only war veterans come here. It's not good for business. They are too old for blondes. And they are always with the wives.'

I commiserated with her about this unseemly outbreak of marital fidelity.

'Where you from?' she asked. She brightened at the mention of London.

'Charles Dickens,' she cried. Her face suddenly shed years. Dickens, with his portrayals of London's poor, had been a part of every child's education in Russia under the old regime. 'David Copperfield. Oliver Twiski, Nikolai Nickelovitch. I am in love with Charles Dickens. Do you know Malinki Nell. Ooooh. So sad.'

Suddenly I heard the sound of the bath-water. I rushed into the bathroom and closed the taps just as the water was reaching the rim.

'What is your name?' Olga was inside the vestibule. She seemed disappointed with an unDickensian Stanley. 'You should be David. David Copperfield. In Russia they make a film of David Copperfield. He look like you. Tall, a little hungry, and the same trouble with the hair.'

'What's wrong with my hair?' I asked.

'No. Very nice hair. But you should comb.' She was looking over my shoulder at the room. 'They give you room with no balcony. Next door, the same price, a better room with balcony. They are lazy. Hotel is empty. What does it matter?'

When I turned to glance at the room myself, she teetered past me on her high heels and sat on the only chair. She seemed relieved to have the weight off her feet.

I stood in the doorway for a moment then decided I didn't have the heart to throw her out. Dickens had already made us comrades.

'Have a glass of vodka,' I said.

I unpacked my food from the train and she took charge of it, pushing aside my Swiss army knife and fetching a switchblade out of her bag. She kicked off her shoes and carved the sausage, the dark bread, and the cheese, peeled the oranges and the hard-boiled eggs and poured out two small glasses of vodka.

We talked about Dickens and Russia. For seventy years Russians had read Dickens as a portrait of the evils of Western capitalism. Now that they had capitalism themselves, the kind of raw nineteenth-century capitalism that the revolution had interrupted, Dickens had come to Russia. The country was awash with urchins, impostors, fast-talking charlatans, scar-faced criminals, rapacious lawyers, deaf judges, browbeaten clerks, ageing prostitutes, impoverished kind-hearted gentility, people with no past, and people with too much past.

'Russia is a broken country,' Olga sighed, failing to see the Dickensian ingredients of a sprawling Victorian pot-boiler all about her.

Her mobile rang. She grunted into the mouthpiece a few times then put it away again. 'Business,' she said, squeezing her feet back into her scuffed stilettos. She begin to pack up our picnic.

'Don't leave the cheese out,' she said.

She let out a long sigh as she hoisted herself to her feet. 'I am tired,' she said, straightening her dress.

'Goodbye Master Stanley. If there is something you are needing, you see me okay. Ask at reception. They all know me.'

Then she teetered away up the hall into the dark recesses of the hotel.

Russia's tragedies are on a different scale from other nations', as if disaster has found room to expand in its vast distances. Of total losses in World War Two, some fifty million people, over half were Russians. One sixth of the population are said to have perished in what Russians call the Great Patriotic War. Volgograd, under its old name of Stalingrad, was the scene of one of the most horrific battles. In 1942 the German Sixth Army laid siege to the city for four months, bombarding it relentlessly, reducing the city to rubble and its population to cannibalism. In a campaign that speaks more about sheer determination than military sophistication, the Russians turned the Germans and drove them back across the Don. But the cost was staggering. A million Russian soldiers were casualties in the defence of Stalingrad, more than twice the population of the city, and more than all the American casualties in the whole of the Second World War. Their memorial is almost as colossal as their tragedy.

I took the tram to Mother Russia. Her statue overlooks the Volga on the northern outskirts of the city. Long before I reached her, I could see her sword raised above a block of tenements. It vanished for a time then her vast head came floating into view beyond the smokestacks of a derelict factory. Her size confused my sense of distance and scale, and I got down from the tram three stops too soon.

Long slow steps climbed through a succession of stone terraces framed by stone reliefs of grieving citizens. On the last, where a granite soldier with a sub-machine-gun symbolizes the defence of the city, sounds of battle are piped between the trees and a remnant of ruined city wall. To one side stands a rotunda where 7200 names, picked at random from the lists of dead, are inscribed in gold on curving walls of red marble. A tape-loop plays Schumann's *Traü-merei*; the choice is meant to indicate that Russians held no grudge against ordinary Germans.

On the hill above, Mother Russia bestrides the sky. As tall as Nelson's Column, and weighing 8000 tonnes, the statue depicts a young woman, a Russian version of Delacroix's *Liberty Leading the People*, striding into a new world, in too much of a hurry to notice she was still in her nightdress. Her upraised sword is the length of a tennis court. Her feet are the size of a London bus. She is striding eastward, across the Volga, glancing over her shoulder to check that Russia is following.

I reclined on her big toe, warm in the afternoon sun, and gazed across the Volga at an empty lion-coloured prairie beneath a fathomless sky. The city stretches for some 40 miles along the western bank without ever daring to cross the river, as if recognizing that the far bank was another country. There are no bridges. If the Black Sea was the nomadic frontier to the Greeks in antiquity, in modern times in Russia the focus for that uneasy boundary has been the Volga. Within its long embrace lies Mother Russia; beyond was the Wild East, the untamed land of the Tartars. Volgograd was founded in the sixteenth century as a fortress, built to protect Russians settlers from their nomadic incursions. If the Volga is the quintessential Russian river, it is due in part to its character as a frontier, poised between the national contradictions of West and East, of Slav and Tartar.

Scratch a Russian, the old proverb goes, and you will find a Tartar. Over the centuries the Mongol Golden Horde which dominated the Russian princes from their tented capitals here on the Volga became absorbed into Russia's complex ethnicities. The Tatar Autonomous Region lies north along the Volga around its capital Kazan. The Kalmyks, a Mongolian people, have their own region to the south. The Cossacks, another Tartar band, are part of Russian folklore. In these parts every Russian town has its Tartar district where the lanes become narrower, the people louder and life less ordered. Beneath the feet of Mother Russia, brandishing her sword at the eastern steppes, is a Tartar tomb, the Mamaev Kurgan, centuries older than the city.

From Mother Russia's big toe, one is reminded of the political context of the ambivalent relationship between Russian and Tartar. The statue striding towards the Volga is a symbol of the reverse of a historic tide. By the eighteenth century the balance of power had tilted irrevocably away from the peoples who had migrated from Central Asia and who had sapped Russia for centuries with their demands for tribute. By the age of Peter the Great, Russia was coming to dominate the nomadic hordes of the steppes, and had embarked upon an eastward expansion that would eventually reach even distant Mongolia. They built towns, roads, schools and factories; they sought to bring settled civilization to the regions beyond the Volga. Only by controlling these turbulent regions could they feel secure. Marching toward eastern horizons, the colossal statue seeks to mask the scale of Russian anxieties. Their imperial ambitions were a plea for order, for the safe predictability of sedentary life.

Friar William reached the Volga in the middle of August. The problem with his mission was that no one knew what to do with him. Mongol princes to whom he presented himself invariably resorted to handing him on to their superiors. In the Crimea he had been given an audience at the camp of the Mongol governor, Scacatai. When asked what message he brought to the Mongols William replied simply, 'Words of Christian faith.' The governor 'remained silent, but wagged his head', then said he had better speak to Sartaq, a senior figure, camped beyond the River Don.

While William waited on arrangements for his onward travel he had a brief breakthrough on the evangelical front when he persuaded a resident Muslim to convert to Christianity. Apparently the fellow was much taken with the idea of the cleansing of his sins and William's promise of Resurrection from the Dead. The scheme came unstuck at the last moment however when the man insisted on first speaking to his wife who informed him that Christians were not allowed to drink *koumiss*, the fermented mare's milk that is the chief tipple in nomad tents. In spite of William's assurances that this was not the case, the fellow decided he wouldn't risk it.

Sadly the belief, then current in the West, that Sartaq was a Christian turned out to be an ill-founded rumour. He was happy to receive gifts from Christian envoys, William reports on reaching his camp, but when the Muslims turned up with better gifts, they were immediately given precedence. 'In fact,' William confesses, 'my impression is that he makes sport of Christians.' Unsure how to deal with his visitors, Sartaq sent the friars on to his father, Batu, who was encamped on the Volga.

Batu was already migrating toward his winter pastures in the steppes to the east of the Volga, when the friars caught up with him. 'I was struck with awe,' William wrote on seeing his encampment. The vast sea of tents had 'the appearance of a large city . . . with inhabitants scattered around in every direction for a distance of three or four leagues.' At its heart stood the great pavilion of

Batu, its tent flaps open to the sunny and auspicious south.

William's first audience with Batu proved an interesting moment in east-west relations. When they were led inside the tent by their escort they found the grandson of Genghis Khan seated on a broad couch, inlaid with gold, amidst an assembly of attendants and wives. For a moment no one spoke. The friars stood, slightly intimidated by the grandeur of the pavilion, while the Mongols stared. Here were the envoys of the King of the Franks: two fat monks, barefoot, bareheaded, clothed in dusty robes. Itinerant peddlers would have presented a more respectable appearance.

William was not in the best of moods. This was his third Mongol audience in less than three months; each was as inconclusive as the one before. Further irritated by being obliged to kneel before Batu, he waded straight in with the hell and damnation. He would pray for his host, the friar said, but there was really little he could do for him. They were heathens, unbaptized in the Christian Church, and God would condemn them to everlasting fire.

When William had finished his introduction, you could presumably have heard a pin drop. At this point the friar carefully edits his own account and does not record Batu's response. But the reply of the barbarian khan, the harbinger of chaos and darkness, has passed into folklore. We find it in the records of one Giacomo d'Iseo, another Franciscan, who relates the story of the encounter as described by the King of Armenia. It was a lesson to the westerners in a civilized discourse.

Surprised by William's aggressive manner, Batu replied with a parable. 'The nurse,' he said, 'begins first to let drops of milk fall into the infant's mouth, so that the sweet taste may encourage the child to suck; only next does she offer him the nipple. Thus you should first persuade us in simple and reasonable fashion, as (your) teaching seems to us to be altogether foreign. Instead you threaten us at once with everlasting punishment.' His words were greeted with a slow hand-clap by the assembled Mongols.

Despite Batu's disapproval, he invited William to sit by him and served him with a bowl of mare's milk. He wished the friars well and would be happy for them to remain in Mongol territories, he declared, but unfortunately he could not give them the necessary permissions. For this they would have to travel to the court of

Mongke Khan, Lord of all the Mongols, who resided at the capital Qaraqorum in Mongolia itself, almost three thousand miles to the east. William's journey had only just begun.

A month later a guide arrived to escort them eastward. He seemed a trifle tetchy about being assigned two fat foreigners, and was obviously worried that they would not be able to keep up. 'It is a four months journey,' the guide warned them. 'The cold there is so intense that rocks and trees split apart with the frost . . . If you prove unable to bear it I will abandon you on the way.'

By day some life returned to the lobby of the Hotel Volgograd. The receptionist was awake and the ancient lift operator loitered by the door. All they lacked were guests.

The Intourist office located just off the lobby exuded the solid respectability and feminine good sense of a Women's Institute, circa 1957. It was staffed by a phalanx of charming middle-aged matrons, dressed in twinsets and pearls. I dropped by in time for afternoon tea.

In the past most tourists to the city came from the former Communist countries of eastern Europe as well as from West Germany where former Panzer officers were curiously keen to revisit the scene of one of their more spectacular defeats. Few of the former could afford the trip now, and the latter were dying off. In the absence of other tourists, travel information had rather dried up. The planetarium, boat trips on the Volga, Kazakh visas, all were a mystery to the women of Intourist. I asked about train tickets; I had spent much of the morning in the railway station trying to purchase a ticket to Kazakhstan. Offering me a scone, Svetlana, the English speaker, admitted that train travel was beyond their remit. In the genteel atmosphere of the tourist office, beneath posters of Volgograd's factories, my enquiries began to seem impolite, and the conversation turned to a series of Tchaikovsky concerts to which the office had subscribed.

Into this civilized circle Olga descended like a one-woman barbarian horde. I heard my name, a head-turning shriek from the lobby, and suddenly there she was pushing through the glass doors of the office and limping towards us, still in the heels and hooker's uniform of the previous evening.

'Master Stanley,' she called, waving and smiling with the excitement of a fond reunion. Looking up from their tea, the Intourist women gazed at this advancing apparition with horror. Then, as one, they turned their shocked expressions to me. I felt myself blushing, compounding the impression of guilt. There was a moment of dreadful silence as the irrepressible Olga stood before us.

'Hellooo,' I said feebly.

'Master Stanley, I am looking everywhere for you,' Olga said. 'You are not in your room.'

The wide eyes of the Intourist women narrowed as they swung back from my red face to a closer inspection, from the feet up, of Olga – the torn fishnets, the bulging figure in the cheap tight dress, the fat cleavage, the heavy erratic make-up. Then they turned their gaze to one another, a circle of smug disapproval framed by raised eyebrows and pursed lips.

Amidst their condescending censure some instinct for civility finally surfaced in me, and I rose to offer Olga my seat. She did not take it. A change in the set of her shoulders signalled her recognition of the women's disdain.

In the lobby Olga said, 'You want train tickets?' The hotel grapevine had already informed her of my visit to the railway station.

'I am trying to get a ticket on the Kazakhstan Express,' I said.

'I can get for you,' she announced. 'No problem. Don't waste time with Intourist peoples.' She made a face towards the glass doors. She didn't seem to like the company I kept.

🐎

Volgograd was the unlikely setting for an international festival of contemporary dance which coincided with my visit, and in the evening I went along to a performance by the Be Van Vark Kollektivtanz from Berlin. The principal piece, *Orgon II + III*, was based on the work of Willem Reich, the Austrian psychoanalyst, whose guiding principle was that mental health depended upon the frequency of sexual congress. He went so far as to recommend the abolition of the nuclear family which he identified as a deterrent to regular orgasms.

The Berlin avant-garde held no surprises for me since the evening I had taken my mother to a performance of a Handel opera at the Riverside Studios in London. My mother was very fond of Handel and I had booked seats in the front row which at the Riverside meant that you were more or less part of the action. I had not registered that the visiting company came from the cutting edge of German performance art. It was Handel all right, but not as we knew it. When the cast fluttered onto the stage after a lilting overture I was startled to see that they wore nothing more than one or two strategic fig leaves. The performance was in the Reichian mode and for the next two hours and forty-three minutes, unrelieved by anything so old-fashioned as an interval, the cast members cavorted carnally and orgasmically in our laps. I remember it as one of the worst evenings of my life, and cursed myself for balking at the ticket prices at Covent Garden. My mother however was delighted, and never tired of telling people about the production. 'Such energetic performances,' she would say.

The soundtrack of *Orgon II + III*, so far as one could tell, was of frogs mating. The dance itself was a frenzied affair with some brilliant and very physical performances. The dancers kept their clothes on and the orgasms, if there were any, were difficult to distinguish from the triple pirouettes. The audience however seemed rather stunned. Presumably *Orgon II + III* was a bit much for people emerging from seventy years of social realism, when culture was devoted to happy peasants striding into a golden future of social justice, international peace and good harvests.

I walked back to the hotel through a park where orgasmically dysfunctional families were sharing ice-creams. Young people loitered around the ubiquitous kiosks which sold beer and snacks, and shoals of drunks floated between the park benches. Someone suggested after the war that the smouldering ruins of Stalingrad should be left as a monument to the defeat of Fascism. But Stalin understandably did not like the idea of his name being associated with a pile of rubble, so large sums were diverted to the city's reconstruction. The results are pleasant if uninspiring. The town is given to wide avenues interrupted by parks and war memorials.

There are red sandstone apartments with balustraded balconies, built in the fifties as a reconstruction of the past, which look like they will last for ever, and yellow concrete tenements with damp stains, built in the sixties as a vision of the future, which look like they might not see the weekend.

I went for dinner in the grandiose restaurant in the hotel. In Stalin's day it had presumably hosted power lunches of the Party hierarchy. These days it is as spectacular and as empty as a mausoleum. I sat by a tall window overlooking the square. The service left plenty of time to admire the marble columns, the gilt chandeliers, the vast ornate mirrors, and the tables laid with silver and fine linen. The waiter appeared to be the lift operator's elder brother. It took him five minutes to cross the vast hardwood floor with a glass of rust-coloured water on a silver tray. He was deaf and I had to write the order in large letters on a napkin. He scrutinized this for some time, then, turning away without a word, embarked on the long journey towards the kitchen.

I was savouring the pleasure of dining alone when Olga appeared from beyond a fat pillar and sank into the seat opposite.

'I have ticket,' she said, lifting the precious article from her bag. 'You go Saratov on the morning train, then changing for Almaty train.'

I thanked her enthusiastically but she waved her hand.

'I wish I was going with you,' she said, propping her elbows on the table and searching her molars, with a toothpick, for some remnant of her dinner.

'To Kazakhstan?' I asked. It was not a destination beloved of many Russians.

'To Saratov. My village is there. On the other side of the river.'

I had not thought of her as coming from elsewhere, especially a village. She seemed so ingrained in this city with its opportunities for compromise and anonymity.

'What is it like, your village?' I asked.

'*Krasivoje*,' she said. 'Beautiful. The apple trees have the flowers now. There is the Volga. It is like a . . .' she searched for the word, pointing at the ceiling.

'A chandelier?' I suggested.

She shook her head impatiently.

'A tobacco-stained ceiling?'

She frowned. 'No, no.' She flipped her hand to indicate something further.

'The sky? Ah-ha. Paradise.'

'Like paradise,' she said. Her face had softened. 'My son is there, with his *babushka*.'

She looked at me and I realized I had been promoted. A son was not an admission for potential clients.

'How old is he? I asked.

'Eight,' she said. 'I send money. But I will not bring him to Volgograd. Never to this city.' She shook her head emphatically as if it was the city and not the human heart that was responsible for her downfall.

The advance notices for the Kazakhstan Express had not been encouraging. Everything I had heard or read about this train described it as a nightmare. The Intourist women in the Hotel Volgograd politely changed the subject when I mentioned it. The guidebook to Russian railways pleaded with readers to avoid it altogether. Even Olga was uneasy about the Kazakhstan Express.

Prostitutes, pimps, drug-pushers and thieves were said to have all the best seats; the sixty-hour journey to Almaty was standing room only for those without underworld connections. The passengers were described as drunk and belligerent, and the conductors locked themselves in the guard vans to avoid the knife fights. Robbery apparently was more common than ticket collecting. Passengers, it was said, were regularly gassed in their sleep and stripped of their possessions. Reports of the Mongol hordes in thirteenth-century Europe could hardly compete with the reputation of the Kazakhstan Express.

Arriving from Moscow, the Kazakhstan Express crept into Saratov station a couple of hours late, a shabby exhausted-looking train with windows too grimy to allow any view of the interior. The reassuring women attendants of Russian trains clocked off at the end of their shift and were replaced by Kazakh conductors, short stocky men with tattoos and pencil moustaches.

First impressions were encouraging: I boarded and passed down the corridor without a single confrontation with a knife-wielding thug. Predictably my bunk was already occupied by someone else who had paid a bribe to the conductor but after some negotiation I managed to secure a place in another compartment at the end of the carriage. It had the air of a bordello. Scarves had been hung over the windows flooding the place with a subdued reddish light. Women's undergarments were strewn about like decoration. There was a heavy odour of cheap scent and the table was crowded with hairpins, combs, make-up, cigarettes and two empty bottles of Georgian wine. Amidst the debris three women lay on the bunks, slumbering odalisques, snoring gently in the sprawling postures of sleep.

I climbed onto one of the upper bunks and set about secreting my valuables about my person. The limited banking facilities on the journey ahead meant that I was carrying bundles of cash. I lashed thick wedges of roubles around my midriff and filled my boxer shorts with American dollars. The reputation of the train and the atmosphere of the compartment reminded me of a story that I had heard recently about the Trans-Siberian Express. A friend had been obliged to share his compartment with a demure-looking woman who was a librarian by day and a hooker by night. From Moscow to Vladivostok, she had entertained a succession of clients on the upper bunk. I peered over the edge of my bunk at my travelling companions. With their scarlet lipstick and false eyelashes, they had obviously dispensed with the librarian disguise. I wondered briefly if Russia was turning me into a deranged puritan, seeing debauchery at every turn.

We rattled across the Volga and rode away into the late afternoon through an endless plain of wild flowers. Lines of telegraph poles shrank to nothing where dirt roads tipped over the edge of the flat horizons. Villages marooned in all this space were shambolic entities. Everything looked home-made. The houses were made from scavenged planks while the tractors appeared to be assembled from wheelbarrows and old sewing machines. A town hove into view, announced by box cars and grain silos. Ancient cars lumbered through its streets, raising slow clouds of dust between concrete tenements and vacant lots. A row of smashed street lamps dangled entrails of loose wires. In these regions public utilities had a short life. Drunks used street lamps for target practice, and young entrepreneurs stole the glass and the bulbs for the black market. Then we were in the country again, turning through bedraggled meadows where brown and white cows lifted their sad heads as the train passed.

The women awoke together at six o'clock as if a bell had rung. Nodding in my direction, they lit cigarettes and set about filing their nails. Precedence among them was denoted by the number of their gold teeth. I wondered if it was the reputation of the train which had persuaded them to deposit their savings in dentistry. The eldest, a butch blonde, had a mouthful while the youngest, a pretty woman in satin trousers and sunglasses, relied on a single gold incisor to ensure her financial security. They settled down to read the Russian tabloids. Devoted to everyday tales of corruption, sex and violence, the gory covers displayed montages of corpses, American dollars, blazing guns, and a man with tattoos thumping a half-naked woman. I glanced over one of their shoulders at an inside page dominated by a photograph of a man's naked bottom with a spear planted deep in the right buttock. Mercifully this was in blurry black and white.

With evening the Kazakhstan Express settled into a swaying domesticity, the antithesis of the dark criminality that the train was rumoured to represent. Up and down our carriage the compartments had been colonized by their passengers. Bags were unpacked, blankets unrolled, shoes stowed beneath the seats, and food, newspapers and general clutter spread over the tables and the seats. The handrail in the corridor had been commandeered as a communal clothes line for towels and flannels. People changed into slippers and old sweaters, lit pipes and opened brown bottles of beer. Reclining on the lower bunks, unbuttoned and unconcerned, they might have been installed on familiar divans in their own homes. An old-fashioned neighbourliness took hold of the carriage with people popping in and out of one another's compartments to share stories and sausages, or standing outside in the passageway like villagers at their front gates, gossiping, admiring the view, sharing cups of tea from the samovar.

Reports of barbarism invariably tend to exaggeration. The evil reputation of the Kazakhstan Express dated from the dark years of 1992 and 1993 when crime in the former Soviet Union surged into the vacuum created by the collapse of government authority. But a railway police force and the stubborn resistance of the ordinary passengers, who had set upon thieves like lynch mobs, had brought an end to this lawless period. Though it still has its problems, I can report that the Kazakhstan Express was a good train of decent people. The three women in my compartment were not prostitutes but traders transporting dresses to Almaty. In the evening they arranged a small fashion show for our immediate neighbours who applauded the latest Moscow fashions with innocent enthusiasm.

Night fell and the lamps came on in the compartments. Somewhere in the past hour or two we had crossed into Kazakhstan untroubled by border inspection. I stood by an open window in the passage and watched the moon sailing in and out of view as the train curved back and forth. A scarf of smoke from the engine flapped away over a great silver emptiness.

The village street of the carriage passageway was almost deserted now. Two windows along an elderly gentleman in heavy cotton pyjamas and slippers was reading a book by one of the carriage lights. He was a tall ramshackle figure with a bony face and unruly thatch of hair. He looked like the village eccentric. In the dim light he pressed his face so close to the page, he might have been smelling the print. He looked up and saw me watching him.

'Pushkin,' he murmured. His nose was a beak, and his hair falling over his brow gave his face a startled appearance.

'Do you know *Eugene Onegin*?' he asked in French.

I said I did, then went on to tell him that I had named my cat Pushkin. The old man's face darkened at this frivolity, and his long hands encircled the book protectively.

'Russia's Shakespeare,' he said under his breath, as some reprimand to my cat.

'Onegin was a traveller,' the man went on. His voice held some note of accusation. He peered at me as if I too was indistinct print he was trying to decipher. There was something strange about his eyes. They looked at me individually, first one then the other. 'He was never satisfied,' the man said. 'He needed always a new horizon.' The clatter of the rails crescendoed as we passed over a stretch of bad track. The train bucked and we swayed in unison against the windows. Over the noise words surfaced like pieces of wreckage – 'Un romantique . . . unable to form attachments . . . a nomad . . . emotional dilettante . . . only wanted what he had lost . . .' – until the roar of the wheels overwhelmed us completely and the man drifted away, still mouthing complaints about the lovelorn Onegin.

I retired to my bunk. The women were already asleep. All night the long whistle of the train echoed through my dreams, a mournful solitary note, a traveller's complaint, trailing uneasy notions of movement and displacement.

The morning brought further emptiness. The landscape had been reduced to cruel simplicities – a white sky and a flat scaly plain over which clouds and their shadows sailed without distraction. In places the tough hide of the desert was softened by a spring glaze of green, a brief interlude between the twin extremities of winter and summer. The only buildings seemed to be government projects which appeared occasionally in the distance, a cluster of tin-roofed cement barns, a collection of silos, yards of antiquated tractors, a ploughed field as big as Wiltshire, then nothing again. How the Mongols must have loved these regions. Riding towards Europe, they could do a thousand miles out here without having to cross a ditch, or deal with the impediment of cities. Friar William was less happy. It took him almost seven weeks to cross the deserts of Kazakhstan.

'The most severe trial,' William reports. 'There was no counting the times we were famished, thirsty, frozen and exhausted.' What little habitation they encountered belonged to Mongols newly arrived in this recently conquered wilderness. All were keen to know about the sheep, cattle and horses in France and whether the Pope was really five hundred years old.

In the next compartment was a Russian family of three lumbering ursine figures – Father Bear, Mother Bear and Little Bear, a girl of eight. Father Bear was a colonel in the army. He took an interest in me, and emerged every time he saw me in the corridor to tell me things in passable English. He told me about the workings of drilling equipment on distant oil wells, about camel breeding, about the navigational systems of space craft, about the train schedules on our line. You name it, Father Bear was an expert on it. Through the open door of the compartment I could hear him droning on to his wife. Marriage to Father Bear had made the long-suffering Mother Bear a professional listener. She listened for hours at a stretch to his interminable discourses as we drifted through this flat emptiness, including a good hour and a half on the subject of baling equipment.

They invited me for lunch. The main course was a three-foot dried fish which they kept beneath one of the seats. Father Bear was telling me about Russian motorcars, of which he had an unaccountably high opinion. We passed a vast factory, one of the government projects abandoned in this bleak place. The empty buildings showed windows of sky.

'Look,' Father Bear said. '*Perestroika*. Gorbachev's restructuring.' And he launched into a lengthy rant about the last Communist leader. The intense hatred for Gorbachev in Russia is a puzzle to most Westerners, particularly in the light of the directionless governments which succeeded him. Having abandoned dictatorship Russians seem to have gone straight for the basest features of democracy. Yeltsin's appeal was based on his image as the man in the street. He reflected the Russian character with all its virtues and faults – tenacious, romantic, put-upon, alcoholic. He was *prostonarodny*, a difficult Russian term to translate, which means earthy or folksy. Gorbachev by contrast was a pedagogue, never happier than when he was lecturing the nation about its shortcomings. Most curious was the universal loathing for Gorbachev's wife, Raisa. Father Bear believed that she was personally to blame for the country's decline. She had dismantled Communism, he said, in order to buy her hats in Paris.

We rattled on across the flat unrelenting steppe. The grass was thinning, revealing patches of earth like pale raw-looking skin. Beyond Celkar the sand started to take over, and the grass was reduced to tufts in the drifting dunes. Bactrian camels strayed listlessly into the middle distance, their humps still sagging after the long winter. Crusted eddies of salt now wound across the baked sand, and the air seemed to have acquired a bitter acrid taste.

'Salt from the Aral Sea,' Father Bear announced, tasting his lips. 'It is dying.'

At midday we passed through Aralsk, once an important fishing port on the Aral Sea. We gazed out at an emaciated town. Many of its bleaker buildings were boarded up and whole districts were abandoned. In the drifts of sand at the far end of empty streets we could see the rusting hulks of fishing boats tipped on their sides beneath the skeletal forms of cranes where the docks had once been.

A monument to the folly of centralized planning, the death of the Aral Sea is one of the great ecological disasters of our age. Like so many Soviet tragedies, it began with Stalin who decreed in the 1920s that the Soviet Union must become self-sufficient in cotton. The vast spaces of Central Asia were to be the arena for this grand project, and in particular the basins of the two great rivers which fed the landlocked Aral Sea, the Amu Dariya and the Syr Dariya, the ancient Oxus and Jaxartes. Vast irrigation networks, constructed to feed King Cotton, bled the rivers into the surrounding desert, and the level of the Aral Sea, the fourth largest lake in the world, began to fall. The problem was compounded as the population of Central Asia grew and the thirst for water increased with modern facilities. The Karakum Canal was constructed, carrying off almost a fifth of the waters of the Amu Dariya, so that southern Turkmenistan could be brought into the cotton belt.

By the 1980s the inflow into the Aral was one tenth of the rate of the 1950s; by 1993 the sea had shrunk to half its original size. It largest port, Muynak in Uzbekistan, was now almost sixty miles from the shore, and the dunes around the town, like those at Aralsk, are littered with the carcasses of dead ships. By 2020, a sea the size of Ireland may have disappeared altogether.

The dying sea has blighted the entire region. The fish stocks have disappeared and an industry that once supported 60,000 people is now dead. The climate of the area has changed dramatically with rainless days multiplying four-fold. Winds have carried the thick salt deposits left on the dry lake-bed hundreds of miles into the surrounding country, devastating agriculture and causing a litany of health problems from respiratory illness to throat cancers. The irrigation methods in the cotton fields, with high levels of evaporation, have led to further salination, while the chemical fertilizers used on the fields have been washed back into the two rivers, the chief source of drinking water for the region.

For millennia the Kazakhs were a nomadic people, moving with their flocks according to the waxing and waning of the thin pastures of their vast land, following a lifestyle perfectly suited to its marginal vegetation and arid climate. The arrival of the Russians spelt the end of pastoralism. The railway brought hordes of settlers, towns were built, and farms disrupted the pasture lands and the delicate patterns of migration. Gradually the Kazakhs abandoned the nomadic life for the lure of cash incomes and permanent houses. The grandsons of herders became employees on state farms, and the proud world of the Kazakh Hordes withered to an unnecessary eccentricity. The ecological disaster of the Aral Sea has been the vengeance of nature on a system of sedentary agriculture that ignored geographical realities.

But Father Bear didn't see it that way. To him the death of the Aral Sea was simply the fault of the Communists. When I mentioned the nomadic traditions of these regions he frowned, and misunderstood my comment as another example of the difficulties Kazakhstan had endured.

'Nomads,' he shrugged. 'People without education. They cannot plan for the future.'

'Perhaps they are satisfied with the present,' I said.

'Where are they now?' he asked, gazing out at the empty prairie, as if the lack of horsemen and sheep out the train window was an argument in itself.

I mentioned Mongolia and the fact that the most of the population there still adhered to a nomadic lifestyle.

'Mongolia,' he snorted. 'Why speak of barbarians?'

Chapter Four

A DETESTABLE NATION OF SATAN

In 1238 the bottom fell out of the herring market in Yarmouth. Ships from the Baltic ports, which normally converged on the port to buy fish, never arrived and the sudden glut sent prices tumbling. Fishermen and merchants went bankrupt, and even in the Midlands you could buy fifty pickled herrings for as little as a shilling.

In the same year a strange mission appeared at the court of Louis IX of France; later they came on to London where they were received by Henry III. They declared themselves the envoys of a mysterious eastern potentate, known to Crusaders as the Old Man of the Mountains. From a fortress in the Elburz Mountains of northern Persia, this reclusive figure dispatched young fanatical disciples to kill his political enemies. The disciples were known as *hashashin*, or hashish eaters, from which our word assassin is derived. With their cloak and dagger methods the Ismaili Assassins had wielded considerable political power throughout the Middle East for almost two centuries. But now suddenly a new threat had arisen, from a people whose leaders were too distant and too unpredictable for assassination squads. The Ismailis had come to Europe to seek alliances against the advancing threat of the Mongols.

It is a measure of the narrowness of European horizons in the early decades of the thirteenth century that they remained in almost total ignorance of the cataclysmic events then unfolding in Asia.

Under the charismatic leadership of Genghis Khan, the Mongols had embarked upon a series of conquests that were taking them across the breadth of the continent. Ancient dynasties collapsed, empires crumbled, great cities were levelled and their inhabitants butchered while Europe slumbered on, unaware that the Mongol horsemen were advancing ever westward.

In a reverse of the usual historical pattern, the history of the Mongol campaigns was written by the vanquished not by the victors. The apocalyptic language that has come down to us reflects the terror and the prejudices of the defeated. Invariably the Mongols are forces of darkness, barbarian hordes, the scourge of God, a pestilence that was destroying civilization. It is this tradition, the stories told by his enemies, that has cast Genghis Khan as one of history's great villains.

To Mongols Genghis was a great and sophisticated leader, disciplined, incorruptible, politically astute. A lawgiver of considerable wisdom and foresight, an efficient administrator and a master of military strategy, he managed to unite the Mongol tribes for the first time in generations. It was this rare unity that allowed them to turn their eyes outward to the rich but degenerate cities that lay beyond their grassy homelands. Early conquests came with surprising ease, and in the terrible momentum that began to build, the Mongol Empire was born.

Genghis Khan could hardly be expected to respect cities or their inhabitants. He was a man of the steppes, a nomad who viewed settled societies from a position of cultural and moral superiority, with suspicion, with horror, and ultimately with pity. To nomads, men and women who lived in cities suffered a kind of debasement, while farmers who spent their lives on their knees tilling the soil were hardly of more regard than a flock of sheep. Their destruction did not bother the Mongols any more than the slaughter of the Incas bothered the Conquistadors, or the fate of Africans troubled the early slave traders. By the standards of medieval Asian warfare Genghis' methods were not especially brutal. His terrible reputation is a measure of his success, and of the monopoly that the vanquished cities have enjoyed over the historical sources.

The tone was set with the siege and destruction of Bukhara. 'They came, they uprooted, they burned, they slew, they despoiled, they departed,' a historian of the period wrote. Yakut, the famous Arab geographer, who fled from the city of Merv as the Mongols advanced, reported that its noble buildings 'were effaced from the earth as lines of writing are effaced from paper'. Pausing only to water and pasture their horses, the Mongols swept onward and one by one the great cities of Transcaspia and Oxiana, of Afghanistan and northern Persia were sacked: Samarkand, Khiva, Balkh, Merv, Herat, Kandahar, Ardebil, Qazvin, Tabriz, Qum. Typical of their fate was that of Nishapur in the Persian province of Khurasan, the home of the poet, Omar Khayyám. Not a dog or cat was spared. The only monuments left standing in the city were pyramids of human skulls.

Pushing westward the Mongols swept through the Caucasus and into the Ukraine and the Crimea. They wintered on the Black Sea, among the mound tombs of their nomadic predecessors, the Scythians, before galloping northward early in 1223 to defeat three Russian armies. Then they rode home, across the width of Asia, as casually as commuters, for a *quriltai*, a great gathering of Mongol chieftains. The world had had its first taste of a military campaign which for speed and mobility was not equalled until the modern mechanized age. The idea that the Mongols were merely a flood of horsemen overrunning entire lands by sheer force of numbers has been rightly debunked. They were a disciplined and highly organized force, usually outnumbered by their enemies by more than two to one, whose success depended on their extraordinary mobility as well as on sophisticated military strategies; both Patton and Rommel studied the tactics of the Mongol general Subedei. Mongols were born in the saddle, and their conquests represent the greatest cavalry campaigns in history. Time and again columns of Mongol horsemen appeared as if from nowhere, having crossed vast distances and impossible natural barriers at speeds that easily outpaced their enemies' intelligence. This was *blitzkrieg*, seven centuries before the invention of the tank or the aeroplane.

In the summer of 1227, in the middle of conquering China, Genghis Khan died after a severe attack of fever. It is believed he was about seventy years of age. On his deathbed he was said to have gathered his sons and to have handed them a bunch of arrows, instructing them to break them. When they could not, he handed them each arrow separately. His lesson was that they must remain united. Separately, like the arrows, they were weak. He bequeathed his empire to Ogedei, his third son, who would rule as Great Khan. Under him, his second son, Chaghadai, would govern Central Asia; Batu, his grandson, whom Friar William met on the Volga, would rule the Russian steppes which became known as the Golden Horde, and his youngest son, Tolui, was given the Mongol homelands. Thus all of Asia was parcelled out like a series of pastures in accordance with traditional Mongol grazing rights. The eldest son (in this case grandson, as Genghis's first son had predeceased him) received the pastures furthest from home while the youngest was granted the 'heartlands'.

The body of the Great Khan was taken home to Mongolia and buried in the Khentii Mountains near the place of his birth at a spot he had chosen himself. All of the bearers of the funeral cortege, and all those who encountered it on its way, were put to death to guard the secret of its location. To this day no one knows where his tomb lies.

At the time of his death, Genghis' empire was four times the size of Alexander's and twice the size of the Roman Empire. But the Mongols were still far from their zenith and under the new khan, Ogedei, the campaigns of conquest continued apace. By 1234 the whole of northern China had been subdued. Famously and no doubt apocryphally, Ogedei had considered massacring the entire Chinese population, some forty-five million people. 'They are of no use to us,' a Chinese historian reported him as saying. 'It would be better to exterminate them entirely, and let the grass grow so we can have grazing for our horses.' Wiser counsel prevailed when they were reminded of the taxes they might expect from all those hardworking Chinese.

Having dealt with the traditional enemy, the Mongols now turned westward once more to new horizons, intending to push the frontiers of the empire well into Europe. In the winter of 1237–8 they crossed the frozen Volga and launched what would prove to be the only successful winter invasion of Russia, a campaign that so alarmed the people of the Baltic that they cancelled their annual trip to Yarmouth with dire consequences for the English herring market.

The summer found the Mongol armies resting in the Don steppes. Reinforcements were enlisted and fresh supplies of horses were sent out from Mongolia almost three thousand miles away. Meanwhile on the other side of Europe the Assassin envoys were setting out across a choppy Channel to warn the English king of the coming threat. They described 'a monstrous and inhuman race of men' who had burst forth from the northern mountains to devastate the lands of the East. 'Threatening letters had come with dreadful emissaries', the Middle Eastern envoys warned, 'and if they themselves could not withstand the attacks of such people, nothing remained to prevent them devastating the countries of the West.'

Their entreaties fell on deaf ears. The Bishop of Winchester, attendant at the English audience, found the idea of assisting infidels absurd. Crusaders had been at war against the Muslims of the Middle East for centuries, and he saw no reason to help them out of their present difficulties. 'Let us leave these dogs to devour one another,' he counselled, 'that they might be consumed and perish; and we, when we proceed against the enemies of Christ who remain, will slay them and cleanse the earth.' To most of Europe, the Mongols were still barely a rumour. Events of the next two years would make them a grim reality.

By the spring of 1240 the Mongol forces were ready for the great push into Europe. They descended first on Kiev, at the time the religious and political centre of Russia. Residents in the city reported that the thundering hooves and the war cries of the approaching Mongols were so loud that those within the city walls had to shout to make themselves heard. The eastern invaders levelled the city, sparing only the Cathedral of St Sophia. Dividing the army into separate detachments one division now broke through the Carpathian passes into Hungary while another galloped across the plains of Poland. Before the end of March the latter force had razed Cracow and Breslau. At Liegnitz, they defeated a massed army of Poles and Teutonic knights, filling nine sacks with the ears of the enemy dead. Meanwhile in Hungary the second force were sweeping through Moldavia, Wallachia, and Transylvania, laying waste all before them. On the banks of the river Sajo they defeated an army of 100,000 cavalrymen, put Pest to the torch and took control of the vast Hungarian plains. The sons and grandsons of

Genghis were at the height of their powers. From the borders of Poland to the Yellow Sea, 'scarcely a dog might bark without Mongol leave'. No power it seemed could now stop them from reaching the Atlantic Ocean.

In the beginning Europeans had sought to identify the strange figures swarming out of the east with the armies of Prester John, the legendary Christian king, a descendant of one of the Magi ruling over Eastern lands, whose arrival Europeans were yearly expecting to help them sort out the Muslims in the Holy Land. Thus the first hazy reports of Genghis were seen as a prophecy of salvation rather than a warning of coming disaster. The idea of Prester John was remarkably tenacious. Even as the Mongol armies swept through Georgia and Russia in 1223, reportedly killing 200,000 people, Europeans remained convinced, on the basis that the dead had been Orthodox Christians and not Catholics, that this might still be the benevolent Christian king coming to dislodge the infidels.

The devastating campaigns in Poland and Hungary seemed at last to have awoken the rest of Europe to the idea that the Mongols were foes not friends. Still stuck with medieval legend, they now speculated that the Mongols might be Gog and Magog, the two foul monsters whom the Book of Revelations foretold would be released from Eastern imprisonment by Satan to herald the Apocalypse. European princes beseeched one another to throw aside their differences and unite in defence of Christendom. Count Henry of Lorraine wrote to his father-in-law:

> The dangers foretold long ago in Holy Scripture are now, owing to our sins, springing up and erupting. A cruel tribe of people beyond number, lawless and savage, is now invading and occupying our borders . . . after roaming through many other lands and exterminating the people.

The Landgrove of Thüringia tried to rouse the Duke of Boulogne to arms. 'The Day of the Lord is come . . . (the Tartars) of unbounded wickedness . . . from the East even to the frontiers of our own dominion, have utterly destroyed the whole earth.' King Louis of France was philosophical. 'We have the heavenly consolation,' he wrote to his mother, 'that, should these Tartars come, We shall either be able to send them back to Hell whence they have emerged, or else shall Ourselves enter Heaven to enjoy the rapture that awaits the select.'

Even in England, where the Bishop of Winchester was busy eating his words, the alarm was sounded. 'A detestable race of Satan,' wrote Matthew Paris in his chronicles,

> to wit the countless armies of the Tartars . . . poured forth like devils from the Tartarus . . . Swarming like locusts over the face of the earth, they have brought terrible devastation to the eastern parts, laying it waste with fire and carnage. For they are inhuman and beastly, more like monsters than men, thirsting for and drinking blood, tearing and devouring the flesh of dogs and men. They are short, stout, thickset, strong, invincible, indefatigable . . . they drink with delight the blood of their flocks . . . They are without human laws, know no comforts, are more ferocious than lions or bears . . . They are wonderful archers . . . They know no other language than their own, which no one else knows, for until now there had been no access to them . . . They roam with their flocks and their wives . . . And so they came with the swiftness of lightning to the confines of Christendom, ravaging and slaughtering, striking everyone with terror and incomparable horror . . .

In the grip of the Mongol horror, Matthew confidently predicted the world would end in 1250. All over northern Europe flagellants roamed the country towns with predictions of Armageddon. In Germany they rounded up the usual suspects, slaughtering large numbers of Jews, on the ridiculous suspicion that they must be smuggling weapons to the Mongols.

With the coming winter of 1241–2 the Mongols were already preparing the next stage of the European campaign. On Christmas Day, Batu led his forces across the frozen Danube and sacked Buda and the ecclesiastical centre of Gran. An advance force of 10,000 men was despatched into Austria ravaging the countryside as far as Weiner Neustadt. Another force, after sacking Zagreb, was sweeping along the Dalmatian Coast to Split in hot pursuit of the

Hungarian king. By the spring, Mongol reconnaissance patrols were spotted at Udine only sixty miles from Venice, while to the north in Austria Mongol scouts were seen in the outskirts of Vienna. Armageddon, it seemed, was indeed at hand. All Europe held its breath awaiting the Last Trumpet.

And then a remarkable thing happened: the Mongols went home. News had reached them of the death of Ogedei, the Great Khan, who had passed his last years in the Mongol homelands in an alcoholic haze. One morning in May the Mongols struck their tents, turned their horses eastward, and set off to ride home, over four thousand miles back across Asia. A great *quriltai* would be held to elect a new Great Khan, and no one could afford to miss the political manoeuvring for the succession. When the dust had settled on Mongol politics, the focus of empire was shifted once again to Asia, and Europe was not threatened by the Mongols again. It was the narrowest of escapes.

On the Kazakhstan Express news of my expedition had spread through the train like village gossip so that people, carriages away, knew about Mongolia and the strange foreigner. When I disembarked at Turkestan the news had mysteriously leaked from the train into the town so that by the time I reached the hotel, the receptionist was expecting me. Upstairs in the restaurant, the manager asked if I thought my French holy man, Friar William, had fathered any children while he was in Mongolia. Apparently he had met a Mongolian woman in Almaty once who only seemed to speak diplomatic French. I was pleased that William was recapturing some minor notoriety in the towns through which he had passed seven centuries before.

Turkestan is a Kazakh town on the northern fringes of the Kizil-kum desert, too remote and too bleak to have attracted Russian settlers. Desert dust cloaks the leaves of the shade trees along the main road. The bazaar was a mean affair of tin huts. At one end butchers were dismembering sheep's carcasses among swarms of flies while at the other a row of elderly fortune tellers squatted by piles of prophetic beans and dog-eared playing cards which held the dormant secrets of their customers' fates. In the roadway outside a company of mountebanks was attracting a large crowd with the promise of jokes and acrobatics.

Turkestan is the unlikely home of the holiest of Kazakh shrines: the mausoleum of the first great Turkic Muslim saint, Sheikh Ahmed Yasavi, the founder of a Sufi order in the twelfth century. Its blue dome rises on the edge of the desert beyond a row of shabby mud houses, the sole survivor of the town's more glamorous past. The shrine was built by Tamerlane, the ruthless fourteenth-century conqueror, who traced his ancestry back to Genghis Khan and styled his empire on the lost glories of the Mongol era. Surrounded by vast battlemented walls that have fallen into toothless ruin, the building stands in splendid defiance of the nomadic traditions of these regions.

Closed during the Khrushchev years, the shrine is now undergoing restoration, funded by the ubiquitous Turks, happy to step into the paternalistic role vacated by Russia, as a way of re-establishing links with their long-lost brethren in Central Asia. The Kazakhs, struggling for national identity in the post-Soviet era, claim the shrine as a magnificent example of Kazakh architecture. No doubt it would be if there was such thing as Kazakh architecture. The building is Persian, part of the Timurid tradition that found its greatest expression in Samarkand.

I approached through half an acre of roses whose petals carpeted the dust paths. The ribbed dome hovered above walls of turquoise and azure tiles. When Tamerlane died the tile work was incomplete, and the workmen lacked the will or possibly the wages to carry on. The stumps of their timber scaffolding still dangle from the towers where they walked off the job six centuries ago. In the cool interior whitewashed *ivans* soared through delicate traceries of arabesque to an unadorned dome. Vaulted corridors led from the central chambers into a labyrinth of tall white rooms whose grilled windows filtered the outside world to a pale wash of light and a filigree of muted sound. Even here on the remotest frontiers of the Muslim world, Islam works its architectural magic. No religion has so caught the longing for a tranquil soul in the arms of stone and masonry.

For the Kazakh pilgrims who trooped into the shrine, the chief interest was an enormous two-tonne bronze water stoup that stood beneath the dome. They queued to kiss its rim and drop coins into its echoing depths. Built by Persian craftsmen, it was a gift from Tamerlane. When it was carried off by the Russians to the Hermitage in 1935, dark rumours, akin to those associated with Tutankhamun's tomb, developed concerning the premature deaths of those involved in its removal. In 1989, the Russians returned it; presumably they had enough trouble on their hands by that stage without having to deal with the curse of Tamerlane.

On the ridge above the shrine was a splendid hammam where marble benches lounged in alcoves beneath a low dome. If the shrine was sanctuary for the soul, the hammam was the palace of the body, committed to sensual pleasure. Their common architectural language of arches, vaults and domes seemed to establish some refreshing connection between the sacred and the profane.

Outside at a stall I examined a pair of horsewhips with decorated handles. The stallholder sidled up beside me.

'Very beautiful whips,' he said. 'I give good price.'

'I don't have a horse,' I shrugged.

He looked me in astonishment. 'They are not for your horse,' he said, taking the whips from me. 'They are for your wife.'

In the morning a driver arrived, and we headed east in his ancient Lada on a blue road. The chipped tarmac shimmered with heat. Away to our left mountains buckled into view, the Karatau range, cupping pools of shadow between their flanks. From their heights streams cut across the fields towards the blighted Jaxartes which curled out of Uzbekistan to the south to be pillaged by a myriad of irrigation channels. Thick blankets of grass lay between the brittle fields while poplars strode along the watercourses. Away to our right, the fields staggered towards the pewter haze of the Kizilkum desert.

I wanted to visit the ruins of the great city of Utrar which lay on the edge of the desert between Turkestan and Chimkent. In the village of Saul'der, a dusty shadeless place a few miles off the main road, we hailed a severe-looking pasha to ask directions. It took him half the length of the main street to bring his mule to a halt. Two women, trotting behind him in sweaty attendance, looked grateful for a breather. The old man waved us towards a small museum at the far end of the town.

Sand had drifted through the doors of the museum to gather in the corners of the vestibule. The ticket clerk was so startled to see me that she fled, leaping up without a word and vanishing up a flight of stairs. Some minutes later she returned with a small man who pumped my hand in welcome. He was the curator and the local archaeologist though one might have mistaken him, in his shabby jacket and broken shoes, for the cleaner. He nodded excitedly when the driver announced that I was travelling to Mongolia. 'Yes, yes,' he said, holding my hand and gazing at me intently. 'Yes, of course. Mongolia.' I had the eerie sensation he had been expecting me – possibly for years.

Nothing in the early career of Genghis Khan had foretold an empire builder. In 1211, when he had crossed the Gobi to launch attacks on China, they were only raids, the usual nomadic business of loot and retreat, an expedition bent on plunder not on conquest. It was the confrontation with the Turkish Khwarazm Empire, his great western neighbour, that led to imperial aspirations.

Relations were already strained when Genghis sent a large party of merchants into the Khwarazm Empire to trade in 1218. At the frontier city of Utrar they were arrested as spies, no doubt with some justice, and put to death. At first Genghis was conciliatory. He sent three envoys to the Khwarazm Shah in Samarkand to demand reparations. There, further insults awaited the Mongols. One of the envoys was killed and the beards of the other two were shaved off. To the Mongols, sticklers for diplomatic etiquette, this amounted to a declaration of war. Interpretations of the Mongol response vary. The treatment of the Samarkand Three may have turned the course of history. Or it may simply have been the excuse that Genghis had been waiting for.

In the autumn of 1219, 50,000 Mongol horsemen, led by two of Genghis' sons, assembled before the city walls of Utrar to avenge these provocations. Mongol military tactics were hardly suited to investing a city but they were an ingenious people and they had developed a few tricks of siege warfare picked up in China, including catapults which hurled naphtha and burning tar inside the walls, and the ballista, a powerful long-range crossbow. The siege took five months, by Mongol military standards an eternity. When the walls were finally breached the entire garrison, some 80,000 men, along with all of the inhabitants, were slaughtered. Genghis had demanded that the governor and his wife be taken alive. When they fled to the roof of the armoury, the Mongols took the building apart brick by brick. The governor was dispatched to Samarkand, by now in Mongol hands, where molten silver was poured into his ears and eyes. Utrar was burnt to the ground, and the Khwarazm Empire, a vast territory that included Central Asia, Northern Iran, Afghanistan and parts of Pakistan, fell to the Mongols. This sudden acquisition of the rich cities of Asia opened a new vision to Genghis Khan, of conquest and rule. The Mongol Empire was born here at Utrar.

The ruins of the old city lay a few miles from Saul'der among the baking fields. The museum the archaeologist had created was a monument to the city and to that seminal moment when it was overrun by nomads. Visitors were rare, and the archaeologist held my hand as if he had no intention of letting me go. Behind the thick fishbowl lenses of his spectacles, his eyes floated in an aqueous myopia. He had cut himself shaving and a dried trickle of blood had congealed along the slack skin of his neck. A translator materialized mysteriously, a girl from the town.

I asked how long he had been working here. Thirty-five years, he said, holding up a collection of grubby fingers. He had come as a young graduate from Saratov. When I asked about wife or family, he shrugged and said he had devoted his life to Utrar. He bore the marks of solitude: the unkempt clothes, the anxious uneasy manner. The young translator shied nervously from him, as if his reputation for eccentricity unsettled her.

He had excavated for fifteen years, he explained, working on the site in three-month seasons every autumn, until the government funds had run out. I commiserated with him about the interruption to his work but he brushed my concerns aside, impatiently. The real work was interpretation not digging, he said. 'There is so much to catalogue, to examine . . .' He belonged to that school of archaeologists which prefer the neat world of the museum, the cataloguing of finds, to the messy business of excavation and new revelations. His voice bore a note of exasperation. 'Here you cannot find good workers. You cannot excavate a great city with farmhands.'

Like a meticulous prosecutor he led me through the rooms of exhibits, slowly compiling his case, keen that I should miss nothing. There is more to the history of Utrar than the siege of the Mongols but the archaeologist and his museum had focused on this single terrible episode, as if it contained a resonance so overwhelming it had submerged the previous centuries. In these rooms the Mongols were in the dock. Each of the displays documenting the great city was an accusation of guilt. The building was a Holocaust Museum, and the archaeologist was one of those men driven to dredge through the confused detritus of history to establish ancient culpability.

A huge mural, painted to his own drawings, depicted the city on the eve of the Mongol siege, a vision of peaceful and prosperous urban life, busy with the business of cities. Blue domes rose above crenellated walls, an assurance of architectural and religious sophistication. The specializations of settled life were all depicted like a carefully structured argument – crafts and trade, agriculture and scholarship – with its silent reproach about Mongol barbarity. Caravans of merchants were arriving at the city gates. Stallholders hawked bolts of cloth, a workman made bricks while a ploughman attended a water wheel spilling the wet life of the city towards rows of crops. The archaeologist pointed out other characters, introducing them like personal acquaintances: a historian, an astronomer, a bookseller carrying a bundle of new volumes, the thirteenth-century philosopher Abu Nazir Muhammed, bearded and robed by the gates.

We arrived at a map. Utrar lay at its centre with the great trade routes linking the city to a wider world, fanning out across Asia to Kashgar, Samarkand, Tabriz, Sudak where Friar William had landed on the Black Sea, and Constantinople. On the eastern margins of the map Mongolia was an empty space, trackless and cityless. Below the map stood cases of the finds confirming this prosperous trade along the northern arms of the Silk Road, from fragments of Persian porcelain at one end to Chinese pieces at the other. The archaeologist fumbled for keys in his pockets, opened one of the cases and handed me the Iranian piece. From Kashan, he said. It was crowded with blue arabesque. Then he pressed the Chinese sherd into my hand, its decoration more assured, more mature, less dependent on virtuosity.

'Development,' he whispered. 'Development, exchange, progress.' The eyes peered at me. 'There is nothing here from Mongolia. The nomads made no contribution to the culture of this area. Only destruction.' Through the thick lenses the eyes were distorted, swollen, almost inflamed. He was a man obsessed. The prosecution of the Mongols had become his life's crusade.

There were shelves of luxuries, labelled like forensic exhibits – wine vessels and ornate knives, dull mirrors and cosmetic pots, tiles and jars from the bathhouse, still emitting some sense of watery coolness. Another display held agricultural tools. Alone in a corner case was a glazed brick, the elemental component of cities, ensconced on a velvet cloth like a religious artefact. We stood before it in absurd silence.

'All this.' He threw his arms wide. He had graduated to the histrionics of summing up. 'All of it. Destroyed. Overnight. By a people with the narrowest view of human activity.'

I struggled to think of mitigating circumstances. In the face of such damning evidence I felt I should mount some defence of nomads. But what was I to say: that they hated cities? In the end I said nothing, trailing after the archaeologist with silent complicity. In the wider scheme of things his anger was ridiculous. To Utrar and all the cities of the world have gone the victory and the spoils. The great historic conflict between sedentary and pastoral society, between the city and the steppe, has been won. Nomads, not the inhabitants of Utrar, are history's victims; the modern world has rendered their way of life at best anachronistic, at worst fatal. They have become an irrelevance, a curiosity. In Mongolia, nomads still proudly migrate with their flocks, their tents and their horses but to the rest of the world they have the archaic appeal of Amazonian tribes with their blowpipes or Lapps chasing after reindeer. The fact that they had once been powerful only adds to their melancholy charm.

I was surprised when the archaeologist did not come with us to the ruins of Utrar. He seemed so devoted to my visit that I wondered that he would want to miss the climax. But he hesitated in the hallway of the museum, and shook my hand. His Utrar lay inside these dim rooms, the careful construction on which he had spent his life, not out there in the heat and the dust, among the unruly fields.

'Take care,' he said, waving to me from inside the door of his museum.

The road to Utrar was empty but for the occasional cow, slumbering in the white dust. The old city floated above the fields, a long featureless mound breasting waves of corn. Paths led up the steep sides, scaling slopes that had once been walls, to the broken plateau that covered the buried city. Its surface was littered with dry bushes and pottery sherds and bleached bones. Lizards darted between the stones. The midday sun was unrelenting. I waded through its thick heat to the site of one of the digs. As I reached the rim of an excavation pit, hordes of swallows who had colonized its crumbling sides rose in a fluttering cloud, as startling as ghosts.

I climbed down to the bottom of the pit, once the floor of Utrar's chief mosque. All that remained were the shattered bases of its brick columns. In the layers of sediment exposed in the pit walls was a clear line of dark ash: the Mongol era, the city's conflagration. Time had compressed the conflict to this narrow stratum, a few inches wide. I raked my fingers over it and the old ash, the ancient antipathies, crumbled onto my boots.

Later in the car I glanced at my hands; my fingertips were black with the indelible mark of Mongol conquest.

Chapter Five

THE BIRTHDAY PARTY

Marat had a cherub's face and a pale narrow beard like a halo that had slipped. He reminded me of Winnie the Pooh, lumbering through the world with a look of injured innocence, a teddy bear abroad.

Marat lived in a half-made house on the outskirts of Almaty. His street had been dug up two years ago for water pipes that had never arrived. We left his car half a mile away and trekked home through a muddy wilderness of trenches and hillocks of excavated earth. Everything in the former Soviet Union seems to be either in a state of construction or of dereliction. Pavements, roads, houses, government policies, people's lives – all are either half-built or falling apart.

Not the least of the surprises about Marat was that he had a beautiful wife. I arrived for lunch – pickled eggs, salted herrings, and horsemeat. Valentina floated about the kitchen like a dancer, vivacious and compelling. She had a large sensual mouth, dark eyes and a sudden reckless enthusiasm that made Marat seem ponderous. Marat said she was half-gypsy. She looked all gypsy to me.

Marat's own ethnic mix – his mother was Russian and his father was Kazakh – made him a neat reflection of the demographics of Kazakhstan where Russian settlement over the past century has meant that Kazakhs now form only half of the population. To Marat the break-up of the Soviet Union had been as traumatic as parental divorce, and the creation of independent Central Asian republics an unmitigated disaster. His sympathies lay squarely with Mother Russia. He saw himself as a Russian, and like many Russians – there are almost six million in Kazakhstan – he found that his homeland was suddenly an alien country, predicated on someone else's national aspirations.

As a child he had been sent to a Kazakh school against his mother's wishes. He had been very blond and Russian -ooking and when visiting dignitaries arrived, he was trotted out as the school's star turn, the little Russian boy speaking Kazakh, a fine example of the ethnic comradeship of the USSR. When the dignitaries were gone the little Kazakh boys went back to kicking the shit out of him. Marat held a very traditional view, the view that lay behind the fraternal platitudes of the Party, that Russian culture and indus-try had rescued the peoples of Central Asia from their own back-wardness.

He worked as an English-speaking guide, and was to accompany me on a short excursion I had planned into Kirghizstan. I arrived on his birthday, and in the evening the guests, all of them Russians, gathered around his kitchen table, crowded with overlapping plates of food. I braced myself for an evening of heavy drinking and conversations about freedom. Valentina's younger sister, Julia, had been put on my right, much to her embarrassment, to practise her English. 'She is a pianist,' Marat said. 'Talk about Chopin.' A shy ethereal girl, she looked like she would rather die.

At the far end of the table Marat's next-door neighbour was telling dirty jokes. He seemed to have stepped from an American sitcom, a big man in a check shirt, the archetypal Neighbour, always ready with the loan of an electric drill and a mother-in-law joke. On either side of him, two women with fat cleavages, bad teeth and worse lipstick, threw their heads back and barked at his punch lines.

A man whom Marat had introduced as 'the Convert' leaned across the table to ask if I was a Catholic. He was a grave messianic fellow with a dark beard and eyes that seemed to inhabit different personalities. The right was narrowed, searching, a discerning eye. The left was wide and glaring, an eye for dogmas and apocalyptic visions. He had converted from Russian Orthodoxy to Catholicism, a sign of radical modernity in these parts.

The Convert was fascinated by Friar William, and interpreted my journey as a religious pilgrimage conducted in his honour. Over the borscht he began a complicated discussion of Catholic liturgy. He was fascinated by the miracle of transubstantiation, he said. The left eye glowed. Then the right eye focused and he wondered if he could be so indelicate as to ask about my position on Papal Encyclical twenty-three. Marat rescued me with politics, an easier subject for bluffers. He was expounding on the follies of Kazakh nationalism.

'It is a step backwards, to the nineteenth century, to the nation-state. We thought we were past all this narrow nationalism. Now suddenly there are new nations springing everywhere like weeds. Who are the Kazakhs anyway? They have never been a nation. They were nomads until the Russians came. Look at the President. I speak better Kazakh than he does. He was educated the same way as every Kazakh who wanted a good education, at a Russian school.'

'They did not want independence,' said the man on Marat's left. 'The Russians were tired and could no longer afford to support them. Moscow gave them independence, on a plate, and they had no choice but to accept it.'

He was an amiable fellow, whose handsome face was softening into middle age. Marat had introduced him as 'our Casanova', taking me aside to offer a whispered account of his conquests.

'These independence movements,' Marat said, taking up the theme again. 'They are ridiculous. Look at Algeria. They realized their mistake when it was too late. Thirty years ago Algeria was a *département* of France. What more could they want? Now they have independence, and all the Algerians want to emigrate to France.'

He handed me a bowl of beans. 'Everything in Kazakhstan was made by Russians – roads, schools, hospitals, factories,' he said. 'Now the Russians are leaving and the country is ruins.'

'We are the dregs,' said Casanova, charming us with his smile, 'who have been left behind.' He spoke philosophically, without Marat's rancour.

'You see,' Marat said to me. 'He accepts everything. No wonder the women love him. He is a refuge against judgement.'

At the other end of the table the Neighbour was on his feet for a birthday toast. Marat translated it for me.

'A good neighbour is a man who sees nothing and understands everything.' He paused theatrically. 'To Marat, the worst kind of neighbour.' The two women barked and we drained our glasses like a drill team.

Among Russians, freelance sipping of one's drink is deemed to be antisocial. Drinking is meant to be a collective activity; you drink when the others drink, and the others drink only in response to the toasts. These begin at a deceptively quiet pace.

Valentina was carrying more plates of food from the sideboard. She was in high spirits, flirtatious and provocative. She draped her long arms around Marat's neck, kissing the top of his bald head.

'Women are most affectionate,' the Neighbour warned, 'when they are contemplating betrayal.'

Marat drew her into his lap and whispered something in her ear. She laughed, arching her neck, throwing her head back. Marat raised his glass. 'To my wife, who I love more today than I did ten years ago.' We all drank. Blushing, Valentina retreated to the sideboard for another bottle.

At the urging of the other guests Marat produced his guitar.

'Bulat Okudzhava died this morning,' he said. He shook his head. 'On my birthday.'

Okudzhava was a poet and a singer, the voice of Russia's 1960s generation, Marat's generation. He was part of a Russian intelligentsia that had stood aside from politics, trying to carve out private individual spaces away from the ghastly communality of Soviet life. His understated songs, alien to the declamatory style of the age, were the voice of ordinary people determined that the personal should not be merely political. The songs belonged to kitchen tables.

Marat sang one of the early songs, about love and loss, and then without pausing, sang another about departure. A sweet melancholy descended over the table.

'He stopped writing after the collapse of the Soviet Union,' someone said.

'Things are better, that is why,' Valentina said spiritedly. She was a rebel in this comfortable consensus of Slavic despair. 'Okudzhava belonged to another age. His melancholy is irrelevant now. It is a new world. We can live now. We are free.'

Marat sat strumming soft chords on the guitar. No one spoke for a moment. Melancholy came naturally to Russians, and with the exception of Valentina, none of them seemed sure they wanted to abandon it so precipitously. It was familiar. Hope was a risk better left to a younger generation. To people still recovering from the collapse of the last 'new world', the idea of another one was tiring.

'Freedom is relative,' the Convert suggested. The right eye seemed to be in the ascendant. 'Take my friend Sergei. He was a doctor. He trained for six years. Before the fall of Communism he made 100 roubles a month. Not a lot, but enough to live on. Then came the end of the Communist regime, and the beginning of freedom. Within a couple of years he was destitute. A hundred roubles was worthless in the new Russia, and his salary was invariably months behind anyway. So he became a taxi driver, buying a car with his father's life's savings. Now he is back to where he was, able to offer a modest living to his wife and children. His life is full of new freedoms. He is free to own his own taxi and to make his own business. He is free to vote in elections, and he is free to complain about the politicians with his passengers without fear they are informers or KGB. But he has lost one important freedom. He is no longer free to be a doctor.'

'The end of Communism,' the Neighbour boomed from the far end of the table, raising his glass. 'And the beginning of democracy. In another seventy years we might be back to where we began, seventy years ago. Here's to progress.' The two women barked and spluttered as if it was another of his dirty jokes.

'In Russia everything takes time,' Marat said to me. 'We have a saying. "The first five hundred years are always the worst."'

Then Marat sang a Russian drinking song, and the mood swung instantly from reflection to carousal. Everyone clapped and sang. The Neighbour pulled one of the women to her feet to dance. A big heavy-footed couple, they filled the middle of the kitchen. Valentina threw her arms above her head like a flamenco dancer and swung her hips erotically while Casanova shuffled around her.

At this moment the power failed and lights went out. It was a common occurrence in Almaty; electricity was the city's faltering lifeblood. There was a chorus of exclamation in the darkness. Someone knocked over a chair. The dancing woman squealed, the Neighbour seemed to have used the cover of darkness to pinch her bottom. 'Wait a moment,' Marat said. 'I'll find candles.'

We could hear Marat fumbling noisily in the garage next door. From where I sat I could see Valentina silhouetted against the grey square of the kitchen window. She had turned her head. Her neck arched. And then suddenly Casanova was leaning towards her. The dark shadows of their heads came together as they kissed. I felt my pulse racing with the danger of their stolen moment, in the sudden dark, willing them to break it off before the light came again.

A moment later Marat returned, matches were struck and the table and the faces around it re-emerged in the uncertain glow of the candles. Valentina and Casanova had already retaken their seats. They were not looking at one another. The others resumed their animated conversations. I stole a furtive glance at Julia beside me. She was gazing blankly at her half-eaten meal. Her expression had altered. She too must have seen the silhouettes against the window.

Marat gestured across the table to her. '*Nostalgie*,' he said to me, speaking French as if this reflection required a different language. 'She reminds me of my wife when we first met.'

Without speaking, Julia pushed her chair back suddenly and fled upstairs.

Marat looked after her, bewildered. 'The same temperament,' he sighed. 'Like trying to hold a stream in your hands.'

In the soft embrace of the candlelight the mood had deepened. The consonant-littered murmur of Russian ebbed and flowed about the table; no one tried to speak in English now or to translate for my benefit, and I was happy to retreat into mute observation. Valentina and Casanova too had fallen out of the conversation into their private disturbance of passion and guilt. I felt the burden of knowledge I did not wish to have. I had been intrigued by Marat and Valentina's relationship. Now suddenly my curiosity had curdled. I already knew too much. In the room above, Julia was playing the piano. The restrained passions of a Chopin sonata tumbled down the stairs.

I retreated before the endless toasts, and climbed towards the music. Upstairs the windows were open and breaths of fresh night air rushed into the dark room on shafts of moonlight. Julia sat at the piano, her narrow back turned slightly in response to a rising line of notes. I stood in the doorway listening: the tumultuous emotions of the sonata filled the room. The girl poured herself into the music, fleeing the melancholy disorder of the dinner, with its revelation of betrayal. I felt overwhelmed, and suddenly tearful. It was not the sad figure of Marat, still oblivious to his own heartbreak, but the girl, in the arms of the music, oblivious to hers.

All week the Mountains of Heaven had loomed above Almaty, promising escape. The city had been full of petty city hassles: queues, overcrowded buses, Mafia shootings, banks that disappeared overnight. In the midday heat the crowds in the big boulevards seemed to move in slow motion, like people wading through treacle. When I lifted my eyes unto the heavens I saw the white flanks of the Tian Shan mountains shining among the clouds. The vision made me giddy with longing.

Marat was less certain. 'I need to get away,' he admitted, packing the jeep with jars of honey. 'Breathe the good air and all that. But the people.' He shook his head. 'They are barbarians.'

We took the road to Bishkek through velvet foothills. Gangs of haymakers were out in the fields with pitchforks and scythes. On the far side of a pass of poplars and rose-coloured rocks, waves of sheep rolled out of clouds of dust, tended by horsemen cracking long whips.

Marat gazed at them uneasily. He saw our expedition as a heart of darkness thing, away from the civilising influences of Russia to vertiginous places where home was a felt tent and lunch was a bowl of sheep's testicles.

'I spent three months every summer with my father's family near Tekell. Until I was nine,' Marat shuddered. 'Then I refused to go any more. My father beat me, but I did not care, so my mother kept me back in Almaty. She was glad to stay in the city too.'

'What did you dislike about it?' I asked.

'Everything,' Marat said. 'The yurt. The food. The insects. My cousins.'

'Your cousins?' I said.

'I was a city boy. I was afraid of horses.' Some shadow of childhood trauma passed across his face. 'My cousins tormented me.'
He changed the subject, taking up the miserable plight of Kirghizstan since independence, and the problems they faced trying to
persuade their Russian population, largely professional and technical people, to remain. Somewhere during the course of his monologue we crossed the unmarked border into the new state.
Independence was a romantic notion. No one cared to bother much
with the more petty business of nationhood, like border formalities.

Bishkek, the capital of Kirghizstan, was a sweet provincial place
of tree-lined streets. The main avenue was called Silk Road Street.
There was a champagne factory with a suitably grand façade, and
an over enthusiastic Russian cathedral like a refugee from Disney-
land. At the presidential palace two boys were climbing over the
high walls to steal apricots.

The road to Issyk-kul, the great lake that lies in the arms of
the Mountains of Heaven, ran through alpine meadows full of wild
flowers. We passed the eleventh-century Burana Tower, a lighthouse
of the Silk Road, marooned now in slopes of edelweiss. In the Boum
gorge, above a grape-coloured river, a Kirghiz boy, bareback on a
chestnut mare, watched us from the heights. We passed a road to the
Torugart Pass which led through the mountains to Kashgar, only 300
miles away. It seemed odd to think that I could be in one of my
favourite hotels in China – the Hotel Semen – by dinner time.

We came down to the lake in mid-afternoon, a glassy expanse
twice the size of Kent, reflecting snow peaks and wind-torn clouds.
The Silk Road had skirted its northern edges, Mongol armies had
once wintered along its shores, and Tamerlane exiled prisoners here.
The Chinese always coveted the lake but never managed to breach
the ramparts of the Tian Shan which guard its eastern approaches.

Halfway along the north shore we passed Cholpon-Ata, the
fashionable place to take the waters during the Communist era.
Brezhnev came here every spring to give his pallid corpulence a
spring clean, inside and out, at a sanatorium built rather unconvinc-
ingly in the shape of the cruiser *Aurora*, whose guns sparked the
October Revolution. Since the fall of Communism, business has
fallen off somewhat. The new emperors of Russia, the free-market
millionaires, prefer Florida.

We rumbled on through gingerbread villages where Russian cottages with pretty blue shutters peeked over picket fences. A family went by in a wagon, the patriarch in a tall felt hat, reclining on bolsters of new hay among a tribe of daughters. Red clover, yellow gentians, blue forget-me-nots draped thick blankets of colour across the meadows. At the end of the lake we descended through apple orchards to Karakol.

The town of Karakol was the last frontier for the Russian settlers, the furthest extent of their penetration of Central Asia. China was less than a hundred miles away. Its straight leafy streets have an oddly cosmopolitan air. Blond Russian schoolchildren were trailing home past old wooden houses. Uighurs from Xinjiang, in their pretty embroidered caps, had laid out cheap Chinese imports at makeshift stalls in the main square. In the market Uzbek butchers were dismembering cows with huge axes. Kazakh men rode by on tall horses. On shady street corners elderly Kirghiz gentlemen, waggling their wispy beards, gossiped on benches, while their glamorous granddaughters promenaded in sunglasses and miniskirts for the approval of thuggish-looking young men in flat caps and baggy trousers.

In Soviet times the town was called Przhevalsk after the great nineteenth-century Russian explorer whose epic journeys through Central Asia did so much to alarm the British administrators in India, fearful of Russian intentions in the lands to the north. Charismatic, imperious, puritanical, and equipped with astonishing reserves of physical stamina, he conducted a series of expeditions through Xinjiang, Tibet, China and Mongolia in the 1870s and 1880s. He was the first European to write a scholarly account of Lhasa, he crossed the Gobi twice and he 'discovered' the wild horse that bears his name and which survives now only in captivity. He was honoured by the Russian Geographical Society and the Royal Geographical Society who in spite of British concerns about his political motives awarded him their highest accolade, the Gold Medal.

Przhevalsky died here in 1888 of typhus, at the age of forty-nine. He was buried above the lake in his explorer's clothes. At his own insistence the inscription on the gravestone omitted all mention of his many military, academic and scientific honours, and bore only the single word: Traveller.

An elderly Kirghiz woman in a red cardigan showed us round the museum and memorial which mark the site. A map showed the journeys of Przhevalsky's three great predecessors, explorers who had crossed these regions six centuries before: John of Plano Carpini, Marco Polo, and our Friar William. The exhibits were an impressionistic collage of nineteenth-century travel in Mongolia and the remoter regions of Central Asia – drawings of yaks, a Chinese visa, a telegram from St Petersburg, a model of a yurt, a stuffed snow leopard, photographs of sinister-looking local rulers in fur-lined robes. There was a sepia photograph of Urga, the forerunner of Ulan Batur, and the only permanent settlement in Mongolia. It showed a rather flamboyant Buddhist monastery in a sea of shabby tents. Another photograph, pockmarked with age, showed a Mongolian noblewoman, seated on a high-backed chair. The upturned toes of a pair of tiny shoes protruded from beneath the skirts of her heavily-brocaded robes. There were rings on each of her ten fingers and two moles painted on her cheeks. She looked choleric. Nearby were photographs of Mongolian landscapes. I peered at them through the glass of the cases. In muddy black and white, the vastness of the sky and the steppe seemed indistinguishable.

'He never married,' the woman said, leaning over my shoulder. 'There are no descendants. He died alone here.' In these cultures there could be no greater tragedy than the lack of children to honour his memory. She stretched her arms. 'We are his family,' she said.

On the way out I signed the visitor's book. The preceding entry had been made almost two months before. It was a Japanese visitor. He had written in English: 'After forty years of respect, I finally bow at this shrine to the great Przhevalsky.'

The next morning we took up the trail of Tamerlane, heading east into the mountains. To Marat, this great figure of Central Asian history was just another nomad chief without the benefit of a Russian education. Like most ambitious men in these regions, Tamerlane claimed descent from Genghis Khan, and much of his career was an effort to live up to his remarkable ancestor. His fourteenth-century empire never matched that of his Mongol predecessor but in the butchery stakes Tamerlane had few rivals. In Samarkand, his capital, he left one of the world's most beautiful ensembles of Islamic buildings, a model of architectural delicacy and sophistication. Everywhere else, from Baghdad to Delhi, he left vast piles of skulls.

All day the world of agriculture fell away, the hay fields, the wagons, the old harvesters like giant yellow insects, the pretty Russian cottages. We rose into high valleys of grass and nomads. Away to the right silver clouds parted to reveal a host of white summits tumbling towards us. Through the open windows we could smell them, the thin scent of snow and pine and mountain air.

On the far side of a narrow pass we dropped down to the valley of Kakhara. In the evening light it was empty and pristine and full of birdsong. Mountain streams sparkled among horse-high grass. The valley rose majestically to a distant skyline that might have marked the edge of the world. As a prelude to Mongolia, few places could be so promising.

Halfway along the valley floor we came to the *kurgan* of San Tash, a vast pile of boulders. The stones mark the grave of a unknown Turkic nomad chief; his plundered tomb lay nearby, surrounded by the votive rags of local people to whom this spot was still sacred. But legend has assigned the *kurgan* another history. It is said that Tamerlane, on an eastern campaign, had ordered all his soldiers to place a stone on the pile as they marched up this valley towards China. On their way back from the wars, each soldier took a stone away again. In this way Tamerlane could calculate his losses. The tall mound of remaining stones, numbering in their tens of thousands, was a cenotaph erected by the fallen to their own memory.

I climbed to the top. The rocks slipped and rumbled beneath my feet like old bones. Time subdues war, gradually shifting the emphasis from horror to melodrama. But here at San Tash the numbing casualty figures that litter the annals of Central Asian history re-asserted themselves as individual men. Each rock beneath my feet was a death. In the descending twilight, the 'daylegone' of this remote valley, the terrible tragedy of these colossal losses, the young dead, the grieving families, the bitter sorrow, pressed in upon me.

Marat had grown silent and uneasy. He was anxious to find a place to spend the night. We followed a pitted track up the valley through the last light. As we climbed, great snow peaks were emerging on all sides, looming over the shoulders of the valley's grassy slopes. Away to our left a herd of untended horses was trotting through blue twilight.

In this desolate place we arrived at a group of yurts on a bluff above a dark river. In the dusk flocks of sheep were drifting homewards shepherded by the calls and whistles of children. An old man rode up on a white horse. He wore tall leather boots and a hat such as might have been issued to an Australian park ranger in 1937. From his saddle, he was as imperious as Tamerlane. With a jerk of his head, he invited us to dinner.

A domed tent made of grey felt, his yurt was as snug as a womb. We took our place with our host, sprawled on rugs, on a raised platform. Bowls of milky tea laced with butter were handed round and a great plate of petrified cheese was set before us.

The old man's flat Kazakh face was the colour of leather and his white beard had yellowed at the edges. He gazed at us without speaking, as if he was assessing our fate. Then he set about eating. His table manners would have seemed a trifle rough at a medieval orgy. He chomped his way through the bread and cheese with a series of deep throaty growls, like a bull elephant on rut. Eventually he threw himself back onto the pillows with a great belch and began to pick his teeth with his knife. Marat, nibbling on the petrified cheese, was making polite enquiries about his flocks. But the old man wasn't looking at Marat. He was looking at me. I felt myself shrinking under his fearful gaze.

'ENGLISH,' he bellowed suddenly. I'm not English but it didn't seem the moment to quibble about details. 'ENGLISH, WHERE IS YOUR WIFE?'

I thought for a moment he knew something about my wife that I didn't. Then I remembered I didn't have a wife.

'No wife,' I stammered, relieved.

He made a pantomime expression of surprise. His eyes, the colour of tea, widened to saucers.

'NO WIFE,' he bellowed. Then his voice dropped to pianissimo. 'English, are you circumcised?'

Marat's translation foundered for a moment. 'Circumcised,' he muttered. 'You know.' He made a vague chopping gesture. As Muslims, Kazakh men were all circumcised. Russians, to their horror, were not.

I said I was, and the old man's face lit up. 'CIRCUMCISED,' he bellowed to his wife. A quiet woman in a headscarf, she smiled and nodded at me in an encouraging fashion. 'Don't worry, English, you will find a wife.' And fetching a rogue bit of cheese from his rear molars with his twelve-inch blade, he told me how to get a wife in the Kazakh manner.

Kazakhs tend to cut to the chase when it comes to courtship. A single man in possession of numerous sheep and in want of a wife, simply kidnaps the woman of his dreams, and then through intermediaries, usually his own father, he makes her family an offer they can't refuse. When the ransom has been agreed – quantities of sheep generally need to change hands – they set a date, and the young man and his fiancée emerge from hiding to a welcome from both families.

The old man sat back, spreading his hands wide. 'That's the only way to get a decent wife,' he said. His own wife, and former hostage, beamed with approval.

Later, outside the yurt, Marat shrugged. 'You see what these people are like. Impossible.' He retreated to the jeep where he had decided to sleep, waddling slightly, his arms sticking out at his sides. In the moonlight I saw him unpacking a midnight feast of bread and honey.

On the way home to Almaty we paused to visit a monastery in the Zailiysky Alatau Mountains to the south of the city. A road of red earth led up the Aksay Gorge, a favourite picnic spot where city families had spread themselves out on blankets in the afternoon sun amidst bowls of potato salad, slabs of dark bread and bottles of vodka. A party of boys was swimming in the fast creamy river. Jerry-built dachas peered through the pine trees from the steep slopes above.

We left the car and walked, climbing through the scented woods, past thickets of blueberries and sloping meadows charged with tall yellow flowers. When the pine forests deepened and the way grew muddy and steep, the roots that braided the path acted as ladders. Above us we could hear cuckoos calling.

After a couple of hours we emerged in the sunlight of a high alpine meadow. The summits of verdurous mountains fell away southward. Two women, gathering flowers for monks killed seventy years ago by Bolsheviks, led us down through the trees to the monastery, a tiny collection of wood cabins set in a piny gloom on carpets of dry needles. Seated at a long table, beneath the thatched canopy of an open-air refectory, were two young monks. They rose to greet us and the women went forward to kiss their hands.

The monks had the air of medieval pilgrims: unruly hair, dusty cassocks and worn leather sandals. Their names seemed as mythological as the setting. Seraphim, the abbot, might have been Christ's younger brother. He was tall and lean with blue eyes and a pale beard. Artemis was the Friar Tuck of these forests: short and fat with long-lashed green eyes and a black beard. The two were the only monks of this bucolic monastery. Their tiny community was completed by a couple of adolescent novices, and a gangly cook who was stirring a huge pot over an open fire.

We sat at the table and Artemis poured mugs of tea made from fruits of the forest. I asked about their rites and they explained they took three vows: obedience, abstinence, and celibacy. They were unconcerned by solitude, they said. They seemed to take pride in the fact that they were only two, as if it was a testament to their devotion.

'We have many visitors,' Seraphim said simply. He gestured to the women, who were sweeping the bare earth in front of one of the cabins. They were plain women in heavy skirts and headscarves, clearly enamoured of the two young monks so far from maternal concern.

In their remote eyrie the monks seemed to be hurtling into the twelfth century. They inhabited a medieval world still obsessed with all the petty formularies of the early Church: the fourth-century heresies of Arius and the schisms of the Council of Chalcedon in

451. I mentioned a visit to the Coptic monasteries in Egypt and they exchanged knowing glances. 'Ah, yes, the Monophysites,' Artemis said with a note of disapproval, referring to theological arguments that had divided the Church fifteen centuries ago. When I mentioned Boris Yeltsin they looked at me with blank indifference. But when I said I had visited Haghia Sophia in Istanbul, a world away from these pine forests, they talked animatedly and knowledgeably about the Emperors Constantine and Julian as if they were contemporary figures. I thought they might be interested in Friar William who passed within a day's ride of this place on his way to Mongolia. But if the Monophysites were heretics, Catholics were no more than a deluded cult. To these men the Pope was an embarrassing renegade, with all the authority and dignity of a fairground preacher.

Artemis mentioned that he had been to Jerusalem. I pictured him in the William mode, a footsore pilgrim crossing the Caucasus where he would have been obliged to spurn the hospitality of the Armenians on the grounds of their heretical views about icons. But he confessed he had found a cheap return fare with a charter airline based in Almaty. Having touched down briefly in the twentieth century, he immediately veered back into the Middle Ages. In Jerusalem, he informed me, the Orthodox Patriarch was able to produce fire miraculously at the altar of the Church of the Holy Sepulchre. It would be a cold day in Hell before the Pope would be capable of such miracles.

Artemis talked in parables, not the clear concrete parables of the gospels, but a collection of fabulous tales, packed with the kind of outlandish miracles for which he had a childish fascination. His was a primitive God whose persuasiveness was based on an ability to transcend the mundane physical realities of this world. In his slow measured tones Artemis told stories about the Emperor Julian and flying demons, about walls of divine fire that had protected the Byzantines from the Persians, about icons that wept real tears and pieces of the True Cross that had magically appeared among the baggage of pilgrims, allowing them to pass unmolested through the valley of death.

The light was falling. A chill crept between the trees and we rose to take our leave.

'Blessing for your journey,' Seraphim said. 'How far are you going?'

'To Mongolia,' I said. 'To the land of the horse-footed men.'

The monks nodded solemnly.

We descended through slanting channels of light and shadow. The two monks stood watching us for a time, their robed figures darkening above us among the pine trees.

When I looked again they had vanished.

Chapter Six

SOME OTHER WORLD

From the air, Mongolia looks like God's preliminary sketch for Earth, not so much a country as the ingredients out of which countries are made: grass, rock, water, and wind. Undulating hills, smooth as felt, rolled away into grassy infinities. A river spilled a silver lace work of water across soft downs. The emptiness was startling. Mongolia made the sky, with its baroque clouds, seem crowded and fussy. A few trees appeared. Having stumbled into the wrong landscape, they clustered together in the lee of a hill, trying to keep out of the wind. For miles there were no fields, no roads, no towns, no buildings. The only signs of habitation were the occasional encampments of round white tents, which sprouted suddenly and mysteriously in the grass below like mushrooms.

My neighbour, an ancient woman in a battered trilby, sprawled across my lap for a glimpse of home. She smelt of butter and dung fires. Gripping my knees for leverage, she craned her neck to catch sight of the encampments below. When she spotted them she made a sucking sound, a note of approval on a sharp intake of breath.

Over the in-flight service – two boiled sweets and a glass of sticky lemonade – she asked about my journey. I told her that I would be travelling by horse, that I hoped to ride from Bayan Ölgii to Dadal, over a thousand miles to the east.

She made the sucking sound which I took for encouragement.

'The Mongol horses are strong,' she assured me. 'They will take you.'

The plane had been a compromise. I had hoped to continue overland from Almaty, curving northwards through Kazakhstan into the Altay Mountains and a corner of Russia, and thence into Mongolia. But my informants told me that the Mongolian land borders were closed in these western regions, and it seemed a long way to go to – over eight hundred miles – for an unproductive argument with a border official.

Instead I had discovered this flight, a little known service between Almaty and Bayan Ölgii in western Mongolia. It was one of the many private concerns that have sprung up in the former Soviet Union now that deregulation and privatization have broken the monopoly of Aeroflot. My airline, whose fleet did not extend beyond this single plane, was so deregulated that it verged on the illegal; apparently it operated without the sanction of the aviation authorities who were paid to look the other way. I had bought a ticket from a man called Boris who operated what purported to be a dry-cleaning business from a tin shed behind the Museum of Kazakh Culture. The following morning under the cover of darkness I boarded an antique Soviet Antonov with a scrum of Mongolians returning home with consumer goods. Their boxed stereo systems had all the best seats.

Beyond Lake Balkash, glittering in desert expanses, the Altay Mountains had surged into Asia's navel where frontiers of China, Kazakhstan, Russia and Mongolia converge. Their summits looked ancient and crumpled, their bony spines protruded from desolate flanks. As we banked eastward Mongolia stretched away like some vast vacant lot grown wild on the edge of the world. The size of western Europe, it has a population of just over two million people, a quarter of whom live in the distant capital, Ulan Batur. As the plane descended, I gazed down on an empire of grass tipping away to empty horizons. Chased by the tiny shadow of our plane, a herd of horses wheeled across water meadows. Then a town appeared, a smudge of grubby buildings in a dust-coloured plain.

We bounced to earth on a runway of red dirt, and came to a

halt in Asia's last nomad domain. The old woman smiled toothlessly at me. 'Home,' she whispered.

Mongolians are not very good at towns and Ölgii was no exception. The capital of an *aimag* or province the size of Holland, it felt like an abandoned outpost at world's end. It had an apocalyptic air, as if only a recent catastrophe could possibly explain such bleakness.

Mongolia's few towns are administrative gestures, state projects, built within the past fifty years, to provide the facilities of modern life – education, health, and wrestling arenas – for sceptical herdsmen. They are all composed of the same ingredients, as if officials, unfamiliar with towns, were working to a check list: a barren-looking square, a town hall, a theatre, a museum, a school, a hospital, a sports stadium. In their cement drabness the buildings are barely distinguishable from one another. Mix in a few potholes, add a lot of waste ground and a handful of Russian-style tenements in an advanced state of dilapidation, and the desolation is complete.

Flats in the tenements were much sought after by the urban elite for their futuristic facilities like light fittings and flush toilets, though the erratic supply of electricity and mains water made these largely redundant. Most of the population remained unconvinced by the idea of buildings and lived in sprawling suburbs of tents, the round felt *yurts* of Central Asia known in Mongolia as *gers*. At this season the bleakness of Ölgii was exaggerated by the fact that much of the population had packed up their *gers* and departed for the summer pastures. The municipal buildings were shuttered and closed, and dead things littered the town: the carcasses of jeeps, the hooves of deceased horses and the bones of butchered sheep. A bitter wind blew relentlessly between the buildings, banging loose doors, hurling scraps of paper into the air and bending the stray pedestrian figures like saplings.

The hotel offered little comfort. A surly caretaker lived in a small anteroom off the lobby like a squatter with his Thermos and his cot. On the stairway murals of Mongolian landscapes were flaking onto the burgundy runners. The door of my room had been smashed open so often that it no longer closed; this was not crime but simply people unused to the idea of locks and keys. The nagging wind whistled through a broken window pane. As the sun set a winter chill settled on the town. It was the end of June but it felt like November. After the vistas of noble grasslands glimpsed from the aeroplane, Ölgii was a bitter arrival, a town built by people who hated towns.

The following day Bold arrived from Ulan Batur in the hold of a cargo plane. Bold was the interpreter whom Mongolian friends had enlisted for me, now destined to accompany me for five weeks through the wilds of western Mongolia. He came with the two boxes that I had shipped from London, which contained all the paraphernalia for our expedition including my splendid saddle. I was delighted to see them, still sealed with the anxious layers of packing tape I had applied in my house, half a world away.

Bold was more of a worry. He didn't strike me as horseman material. The immediate impression was of fraility. He was forty though he looked ten years older. His face was flat and sad and rather feminine with a down-turned mouth and a mop-top haircut, circa 1965. Everything about him was thin, his shoulders, his wrists, his narrow ankles beneath trousers that were too short. I had spoken to him once on the telephone. On a bad line from Almaty I could sense his alarm as I had outlined my plans to travel by horse. Bold was a teacher in Ulan Batur, 'a city man' in his own words. Horses and open steppe and sleeping under the stars were not really his kind of thing.

Bold had brought the name of a horseman, a relation of someone in Ulan Batur, who might be able to act as our guide for the first stage of the journey. The directions had the virtue of simplicity. Drive to the Namarjin valley, a summer pasture the size of Hertford-shire, and ask for Batur.

We skipped town in a jeep clinging to its last weeks of life. The driver was an impressively taciturn fellow in a straw fedora with a hat band advertising the 1974 World Cup. In a land where the internal combustion engine is seen as the coming thing, jeep drivers are prestigious, even heroic, figures. The acquisition of a driving permit is a celebrated event akin to university graduation, and mothers are proud to introduce 'my son, the driver'. Tradition dictates that Mongolian jeeps, like horses, should only be boarded from one side, in their case the right. The handles on the left-side doors have been thoughtfully removed to remind the unwary.

We followed the Hovd river out of town, along grassy tracks shadowed by low hills shot with pink and purple rock. After an hour or so we struck across empty gravel plains, the winter pastures of families who were now in the mountains. At this season the only sign of their passage were tufts of sheep fleece snagged on the thorn bushes. From a low ridge we came down to the Khatu river bubbling over boulders, then climbed passes to Khos Tereg, or Two Trees, where a pair of lonely poplars stood in the middle of wide summer pastures. Here we encountered the first people we had seen since leaving Ölgii two hours before. They had just arrived and were still unpacking. They waved to us from amidst a jumble of kneeling camels and cooking pots and half-built *gers*.

We swung towards the south-east, sailing across the smooth grass along a rising valley. After another hour we came to a nameless river of fast grey water where a passing horseman directed us downstream to the ford. On the far bank we climbed over a wind-blown pass and came down in the late afternoon into the high wide valley of Namarjin beneath the white flanks of Tsast Uul. Scores of *gers* were spread across the spring grass. With the late sun raking the valley, it was like a tableau of the American plains before the arrival of Europeans: white tents, tethered horses, pillars of camp smoke.

'When I came among them,' Friar William wrote, 'I felt as if I was entering some other world.' Genghis Khan would not have seen anything amiss in this valley bar our own jeep. This is Asia's secret, I thought, a vast medieval world of nomads, slumbering in the heart of the continent, traversed by winds and clouds and caravans of camels, apparently undisturbed since 1200. It was irresistible and strangely familiar.

We stopped at various *gers* to ask for Batur; Mongolians only have one name, a given name. It was like asking for Paddy in Dublin's O'Connell Street. Every enquiry brought a new reply. He was just over the low hills to the east, he was on the other side of the river, he was back in Bayan Ölgii, he had left his wife and gone to Russia, he had been dead for twenty years. In the end the Batur we wanted found us, riding up on a white horse, an elderly patriarch with a closely shaven walnut-coloured head and a wisp of beard beneath his lower lip. News travels mysteriously in the huge spaces of Mongolia, and he seemed to be expecting us. He took us home to his *ger*, set on a slight rise half a mile away. Horses were tethered outside and a flock of sheep of Biblical proportions was converging on his front door.

Inside formal introductions were made. The Mongolians had some difficulty with my name – the 'st' was troublesome, and the 'ley' was unpronounceable – but eventually it emerged as 'Stalin' which seemed to please everyone except me. Batur's wife handed us bowls of steaming milk tea and we slurped noisily. Everyone wore tall riding boots and a *del*, the traditional quilted Mongolian robe, side-buttoned and bound at the waist with a brightly-coloured sash.

Batur and I exchanged snuff bottles. Mongolia is the last refuge of the snuff-taker. Exchanging snuff bottles with a new acquaintance, to sample one another's blend, is as essential a part of polite society as the handshake. I had come to Mongolia equipped with George IV Blend from an old tobacconist's shop in the Charing Cross Road. Batur was clearly impressed.

Grubby felt mats covered the floor of the *ger*, and at our backs round the curving walls were metal cots and stacks of eiderdowns and low chests. Behind Batur was a bureau painted a traditional garish orange on which the family photographs were displayed – black and white mug shots of unsmiling ancestors. Rounds of cheese hung from the roof, a couple of saddles and bridles lay just inside the door beneath a fat sweating goatskin, suspended from the wall, which held the family's supply of *koumiss*, the fermented mare's milk known in Mongolia as *airag*.

Cool in summer, warm in winter, and capable of being dismantled and loaded onto the back of a single camel in the course of an hour, the Mongolian *ger* is a triumph of nomad technology, perfectly tailored to a mobile life in a difficult climate. It is also the ultimate symbol of the innate conservatism of nomadic society. It has not changed in a thousand years or more. Bar the innovation of a wooden door, William's description of the layout, penned in the 1250s, could serve for every *ger* in modern Mongolia. Even the position of the door is dictated by tradition; it always faces the auspicious south.

Inside, everything has its appointed place. Batur sat at the centre of the back wall, opposite the door, the traditional seat of honour for the man of the *ger*. As his guests we sat on the floor on his right, in order of precedence according to age and status. For the next three months, in countless *gers* across Mongolia, I would always sit in exactly the same place. It had the odd effect of making strangers' homes feel familiar. The stove, fuelled by animal dung, was at the centre of the *ger*; its chimney disappeared through a hole in the roof. On the women's side were the cooking pots and the children's cots. On the men's, the *airag*, the saddles and the guests.

Batur was like an old lion settling into his den. He sucked the hot tea and ran a huge paw over his great bald head. A trio of grandchildren, squirming out from beneath the cot opposite, clambered over his legs like cubs. One disappeared inside the folds of his *del*, only to re-emerge peering out at me from beneath the old man's chin, wide-eyed at such a bizarre guest.

Dinner was served. A young ram had just been slaughtered and as a special treat a plastic washing bowl of sheep parts was laid before us. Knives were handed round and we were invited to dip in and carve ourselves a few delicacies. Mongolians don't believe in wasting any of their beloved sheep. Everything was in there, floating in a sort of primeval ooze: lungs, stomach, bladder, brain, intestines, eyeballs, teeth, genitals. It was a lucky sheep dip; you were never sure what you were going to pull out. I fished carefully, not too keen on finding myself with the testicles. My first go produced an object that resembled an old purse dredged up from the bottom of a stagnant canal. It tasted of boiled rubber. I think it might have been an ear. I had better luck with the intestines which were surprisingly good, and once brought to the surface, went on for quite awhile.

Sated with sheep guts, we settled into after-dinner chat. Bold explained that I intended to ride across Mongolia to Qaraqorum, the ancient capital, then beyond to Dadal, the birthplace of Genghis

Khan. Batur looked at me for a long time without speaking. The plan was obviously too outlandish to merit comment. I felt like the eight-year-old who had announced he was going to be President. Batur saw no reason to try to dissuade me. Events would soon take care of that.

Ignoring his eloquent silence, I pressed on with my arrangements. I had decided to do the journey in stages, of four or five days each, hiring horses and local horsemen as guides. This at least met with Batur's approval. I had three months riding ahead of me and it would be too much for a single horse. Exhaustion would not be the only problem. Mongol horses, who spend much of the year roaming wild in the hills, are territorial. The further they venture from their home range the more restive they become. Batur told the story of a group of Mongol horses that had been taken to North Vietnam some years ago, and who had immediately run away from their new masters and walked back alone to their home pastures in Mongolia.

'You can travel like the messengers of Genghis Khan,' Batur said, plucking a toddler from his shoulder. 'The *orto* system.'

At the height of the empire communications over the vast distances of Asia depended on relays of horses stationed along the main routes. 'When the need arises for the Great Khan to receive immediate tidings,' wrote Marco Polo, '. . . the messengers ride 200 miles in a day, sometimes even 250 . . . They tighten their belts and swathe their heads and off they go with all the speed they can muster until they reach the next post-house twenty-five miles away. As they draw near they sound a horn . . . so that horses may be got ready for them.' Though I hoped to adopt a more leisurely pace than Genghis' racing couriers, the principle would be the same.

Over further bowls of tea Batur agreed to provide horses for our first stage, four days' ride to Hovd. He had the luxury of an inexhaustible supply of sons, and he summoned one of them now into the *ger* to inform him that he was to act as our guide. Ariunbat was a surly fellow with a baseball cap. He greeted the news of his assignment with a surly silence. A price was fixed and the deal was sealed with bowls of home-made industrial-strength vodka.

Afterwards we went outside. It was dark. Constellations, tipped to unfamiliar angles, had risen over the shoulders of the ghostly peaks of Tsast Uul. Another of the old man's sons was saddling his horse. He would ride through the night to find the family's herd of horses, believed to be about twenty miles away in higher valleys, and bring them in for the morning.

I pitched my tent on the slope above the *gers*. The journey I had idly dreamt about for years was suddenly upon me. Beneath the dark Mongolian sky a rider was galloping into the hills to summon the horses.

In the morning the horses arrived like an invading army, charging down from the hills with their long tails and unkempt manes streaming. The relationship of Mongolian horses to the wild Przhevalsky's horse of these regions has yet to be conclusively established but presumably they share the same parole officer. They looked like the outlaws of the equine world. Short stocky creatures, standing just over fourteen hands, they spend much of their career in semi-wild herds, being brought in occasionally to serve a turn as a riding horse before being released again into the hills with the others. What they lacked in stature they made up for with attitude. They were tough, wilful, unsentimental characters. They had carried the hordes of Genghis Khan to the gates of Vienna, and had given the Mongols the jump on all their enemies with their speed and remarkable endurance. Now they milled about on the slope below the *ger*, snorting and pawing the ground, a rabble looking for excitement and hostages.

It took a rodeo to bring them to heel. The men of the camp closed around the horses with *urgas*, the long poles with a lasso at the end, to try to rope three of them. The horses naturally had other ideas. They had been running free for almost eighteen months and were prepared to put up a hell of a fight to avoid going to Hovd with a weedy-looking foreigner. With their nostrils flaring and their eyes rolling, the herd charged back and forth across the plain, raising thick clouds of dust. For a time it appeared the horses had the upper hand as the lassoes repeatedly missed their targets but eventually three were roped. Once bound, they were led away from the herd with an air of resignation, like prisoners being led to court.

Departure was disappointingly sudden. It was a historic moment and I think some ceremonial part of me would have liked to have seen it marked by speeches, a fanfare, group photographs. I blame the horses. Now that they had been saddled, they were so keen to be off they almost left without us. In the scrum of horseflesh and Mongolians there were last-minute adjustments to girths and baggage packs, then Batur was suddenly thrusting the reins into my hands and I was in the saddle. There was a tricky moment when my horse reared, shying from a dog, and it looked like I was to be thrown onto my backside in front of an assembly of amused Mongolians. But I managed to keep my seat and my dignity. The old man bid us good journey. His wife emerged hurriedly from the *ger* to dab milk on the horses' forelocks, a traditional Mongolian blessing. Dogs barked, children waved, sheep scattered, and the camp horses who weren't going pulled at their tethers and whinnied piteously as we rode away down the valley, a trio of riders and a single pack horse setting sail into an enormous sweep of landscape. Ahead of us lay a thousand miles of Mongolia.

That first morning smelt of wild thyme. On the hillsides, flocks of sheep eddied across the stony ridges and pooled into grassy hollows. We splashed through water meadows where the snow-melt had spilled across the pastures. We passed *gers* standing between pyramids of dry dung fuel and sacks of fleece from the spring shearing. In the distance other horsemen were silhouetted on long horizons of grass. Above us kestrels sailed on a blue sky. The sun was already taking the chill off the pastures and birdsong whistled across the dewy grass. We crossed a stream so young it had yet to form banks. On such a morning, in such a place, the world seemed newly-born.

My horse, a tallish chestnut gelding, was obliging enough now that he was detached from the influence of his wild mates. My saddle was a joy, big and comfortable. Bold was faring well; his Mongol instincts had clearly survived life in the city. All seemed well in our travelling world.

At the end of the valley we crossed a river that came up to our stirrups then rose over a low saddle of hills to a series of desolate valleys where the boulders were patinated with red and green lichens. By midday we had gained a high plateau where we met four riders – a girl with her two younger cousins and an uncle, coming up from Hovd to visit the girl's grandmother in the Namar-jin. The girl was a cheerful forthright sort, surprised and delighted at meeting her first foreigner in this wild place. She said she was studying history at school in Hovd and wished to know what I thought of the Russian Revolution. With the fall of Communism in Mongolia this was clearly a subject that teachers were scrambling to reinterpret. I borrowed Chou-en-Lai's comment about the French Revolution, and replied that it was too early to tell. This response was clearly a disappointment and she rode away to the north with a poor impression of foreigners.

In mid-afternoon we rested in a grassy hollow, lying on our backs out of the wind with our hats over our eyes while the horses chomped contentedly round us and the guide rode up a rocky slope to find wild onions. Bold was a little stiff getting down from his horse but he was in good spirits. He was a good-natured companion, and though a long journey by horse was hardly his idea of a pleasant month in the country, he was already getting into the spirit of the thing.

Ariunbat, the guide, was less congenial. A short self-conscious man, he had taken to complaining. The four-day ride to Hovd, as a foreigner's guide, had aroused in him expectations of untold riches and early retirement. His father's quite reasonable negotiations, which had settled on a fair price for the horses and his services, had left him simmering with resentment, and he spent much of the day moaning to Bold about the distance to Hovd, the long hours on horseback, the pay that would leave him a pauper, and the dangers we faced travelling in unknown regions away from the safety of his home territory. He was not a happy camper.

We rode another four hours through empty country. These were arid regions and we needed to camp where we would find water and grazing for the horses. On the far edge of the plateau we looked down into a promising valley with a great outcrop of rock like a ruined fortress at its centre. But when we descended to its floor the grass was poor and thin, and there was no water. We rode on, climbing two passes before at last we came to a spring on the long final slope that descended from these hills to the Hovd plain. Here in a tiny parish of thorn bushes and long grasses, we made camp.

The guide hobbled the horses while Bold and I put up the two tents and made a dinner of mutton and wild onion stew. Despite this being standard Mongolian fare, the guide ate his suspiciously, and I realized he had never eaten anything before that had not been made by Mummy. To cheer him up I told him a story about once having eaten barbecued rat in Burma. It confirmed the Mongolian view about the strange dietary habits of foreigners, though rats of course were not half as peculiar as salad. Nothing horrifies Mongolians quite as much as the admission that foreigners, like animals, regularly consume raw leaves.

After dinner I lay propped up on my saddle watching the shadow of the hills stretch across the stony plain below: tomorrow's landscape, temptingly empty. The niggling anxieties about the journey, about the reception we would receive from the herdsmen, about the horses, about Bold, about the practicalities of distance and isolation, were all banished in the pleasant glow of the first day's ride. The world suddenly presented itself with a set of novel and simple priorities: a good camp, water, grazing for the horses, the promise of clear weather. Everything else fell away to insignificance.

I was awoken by birds. Their shadows, elongated by the early sun, stalked the ridge pole of my tent like prehistoric oddities. We had breakfast of dried mutton and bread, then broke camp, saddled the horses and set off.

The day had the monotony of a sea crossing. We dropped down from the hills to the dry uninhabited plain. The flies were bad and the horses, much bothered by them, were miserable. The wind had died, and the sun began to bake the plain. In the featureless expanses, my eyes became attuned to details, the minute shifts in the flora and fauna that seemed to divide the plain into distinct provinces. We began in the province of the wildflowers near the base of the hills where yellow and purple convolvulus and vetch grew among the grey shale before passing on to the province of camels where tribes of Bactrians, threadbare aristocratic figures, grazed on nothing. Beyond the camels we passed through the provinces of quail, then of lapwings, and finally of grasshoppers which whirred up from beneath the horses' hooves like mechanical toys.

Separated from the herd my horse had soon abandoned his disguise as the wild steed of the mountains. On the first morning I had been persuaded he was a bit of a goer. It did not last. The truth was that Brown Nose was a laggard, and an inveterate bottom-sniffer. He was never happier than when his nose was squarely implanted in another horse's fundament. Any diversion that involved time-out from bottom-sniffing made him fretful and restless. Parted, even momentarily, from the group he whinnied pitifully across the plain, cocking his ears for a response from another horse with a decent bottom. His attentions become focused on the guide's horse, the lone mare of our party and fifteen years his junior. Sadly Brown Nose was a gelding, so bottom-sniffing was all he could manage in the romantic line.

With my horse now in such lethargic mood the last two hours of the day were drudgery. In the late afternoon we reached a desolate line of hills that marked the far shores of the plain, and passed through a narrow gully, the kind of place where something bad always happened in cowboy films. At the end of this pass, we were ambushed by a beautiful river of clear sweet water, the Shuragiyn. After the dry plain it seemed like paradise, unreal, full of sensual delight, and wholly unexpected. In a stride we stepped from rocky ground onto soft mattresses of grass. The air was full of the sound and smell of water. Between walls of smooth-faced boulders we pitched our tents.

When Bold was eight his father departed for Russia on the Trans-Siberian Express. It was a bright day in October, one of those sparkling days that are common in the Mongolian autumn. Snow had fallen in the night. Looking down from the window of their apartment in Ulan Batur, he remembered the thin dusting of snow along the kerbs.

His parents were arguing in the kitchen as relations arrived. They went to the station in a very large black car, and he remembered the windows that went up and down by turning the handles. He thought it must have been his first time in a car, and the drive had seemed a delightful adventure.

But at the railway station the mood turned sour. On the platform his mother, his grandmother, his aunts, were in tears as his father struggled with his bag on the carriage steps. Bold stood with one of his uncles, a pillar of male restraint in the midst of the women's lachrymose distress which rose and fell in unpredictable waves. He was frightened by the sight of grown-ups crying. There seemed to be some disaster but he was not clear what it was.

He remembered the train more clearly than he remembered his father. The wheels were as tall as he was. People looked down from the windows above him through curtains of condensation, strange Russian faces with big noses and round eyes. There seemed to be a sense of merriment about the faces, a companionability about the people crowded together in the train. There were two worlds here, strangely connected, and he watched as his father passed from one to the other, from the distress and tears of the platform to the glamorous train with its cosy and promising interiors, from the sedentary confinement of home to the liberation of journeys. A man with a dark uniform marched down the platform, blowing a whistle. The train jerked and the two worlds began to separate.

It was 1964. He never saw his father again. His departure, the scene on the railway platform, was one of Bold's earliest memories.

'He went to Irkutsk,' Bold said. We were lying on the riverbank in the last of the sun. 'To an engineering course at the technical college there. Letters came from time to time. Probably he sent money to my mother. But we never knew much about his life there. After his course he stayed in Irkutsk. I think he had meant to come back to Mongolia but he never did. Maybe he had met another woman, had another life there. I don't know. He died in 1974. Of cancer apparently. He would have been forty-five, I think.'

The ease of our river camp had made Bold talkative. The tents were pitched, dinner had been taken, and we were enjoying the softness of the evening. Slate-grey boulders formed a low wall around the camp, giving us the illusion of domestic containment, a private space in the limitless steppe. The ghostly rings of *gers* which wintered here were printed on the stony bank above us. We had made a fire with some of their leftover wood. The river was our front garden. Reclining among the boulders, we talked while the horses, knee-deep in grass, grazed downstream.

Like his father, Bold had gone to Russia for his education. Mongolia had become the world's second Communist state when it declared itself a People's Republic in 1924. Throughout more than sixty-five years of Communist rule the country had been a satellite of the Soviet Union, receiving substantial subsidies and streams of technical advisors from Moscow while playing host to large numbers of Russian troops, particularly during periods of Sino-Soviet tension. One of the perks of this pervasive Russian influence was that Mongolian children learnt Russian at school, allowing them access to opportunities in Russian cities beyond the limited capabilities of Mongolia itself.

Bold had gone to Minsk to study history and philosophy. He had spent almost five years in Russia, and had travelled to East Germany, Poland and once very briefly into West Germany. His youthful odyssey in Europe had led to two rather incompatible discoveries: Love and Reason.

Mongolia was addicted to faith. Bold described it as a medieval state, a land where it was more important to believe than to enquire, where received wisdom was rarely questioned. For centuries the nomads had lived under the spell of superstition and omens, of shamanism and Tibetan Buddhism. Marxism arrived to a conveniently credulous environment; the Party demanded the kind of blind faith to which Mongolians were accustomed. By his own account, it was Bold's sojourn abroad that had liberated him from the confining need to believe. He went to Russia a Marxist and came home a freethinker. In Minsk he had become a modern man, he said. He used the term in the Voltairean sense, sceptical, enquiring, iconoclastic. For Bold the Enlightenment was a defining personal revelation.

Love had less clarity. In Minsk he had fallen in love with an East German woman. Across the space of twenty years, his voice still thickened when he spoke of her. They read Goethe together, they went on long treks through the pine forests around Zhdanovichi, they talked of marriage. But in the end he had decided to leave her, to come home, choosing his country instead. I am a Mongolian, he said plaintively, by way of explanation, as if they were a people apart, unable to survive among foreigners. The notion was to recur throughout my journey. Bold, who had rejected so much of his own tradition, was still a prisoner to the idea that only Mongolians could begin to understand other Mongolians, that some tie of blood existed between them that could not be explained to others.

But the decision to leave the East German had cast a shadow over his life. He still thinks of her, and wonders what his life might have been like had he chosen to stay with her. When he came home he married a Mongolian but the marriage had been unhappy and they had separated. Love had eluded him.

It was dark and the moon had risen above the mountains at our backs flooding the river with silver light.

'Perhaps I should have stayed away like my father,' he said. 'Perhaps he found freedom in Irkutsk.'

'An unlikely location,' I said.

'You would be surprised,' he said. 'I found it in Minsk.'

He lit a cigarette and lifted his head. 'As a child growing up, I always thought of him as lost. I imagined him homeless, migrant. I think my mother and my aunts must have spoken about him in that way.'

In the moonlight his eyes lay on the surface of his face like lozenges of dark liquid.

'I was afraid of the kind of displacement that they taught me to think he had suffered. I was afraid that away from Mongolia, I would eventually become nobody.' His eyes shifted. 'But when I think of his departure, that day at the railway station, with the train pulling away, it felt like he was escaping. The only sadness was on the platform, with those who stayed behind.'

In the morning I stripped naked and bathed in the river. The guide might have been less shocked if I had killed one of his horses and grilled it for breakfast. Then we saddled up and struck off across the iron plain towards the south-east and the valleys of the Kazakh eagle hunters.

The western *aimag* or province of Bayan Ölgii contains Mongolia's only ethnic minority, the Muslim Kazakhs. Revisionist Mongolian history likes to believe that they all arrived from China in the late 1950s and early 1960s when Beijing seemed intent upon settling the Kazakh and Kirghiz nomads in the north-western province of Xinjiang which borders Mongolia. At the time Sino-Soviet relations had taken a nose dive over the question of Communist world domination, and Tsedenbal, the Mongolian leader, was encouraged by Moscow to open his doors to the Kazakhs in China as a snub to Beijing.

The truth about the Kazakhs, who number about 130,000 in Mongolia, is more complex. Many did indeed arrive as refugees from China as an earlier generation had fled from Soviet Kazakhstan to escape Moscow's equally authoritarian policies of settlement. But most have been here for centuries, migrating through the Altay mountains, oblivious to national boundaries.

The Mongols distrust them. Bold saw them as clannish outsiders, and potential defectors whose real allegiance lies with their brethren across the border in Kazakhstan. This perception was strengthened in 1990, after the fall of Communism, when some Mongolian Kazakh leaders tried to promote Kazakh autonomy. When that idea didn't run many Kazakhs joined an exodus to the new republic of Kazakhstan, migrating across the border with their flocks. Most have quietly returned, having found in Kazakhstan a more modern world inimical to traditional nomadism.

The Mongolian Kazakhs have maintained a tradition of falconry which has a long history in the country. Genghis Khan's father was said to have been a keen falconer, and during Friar William's first audience with the Mongol khan Mongke at Qaraqorum he had inspected various falcons that were brought in to him by his attendants. Kubilai Khan, Genghis' grandson, was also a falconer; Marco Polo claimed he kept 5,000 birds. But among modern Mongolians the tradition has been lost. It survives only among the Kazakhs of Bayan Ölgii who hunt with the largest birds used by falconers, the great golden eagles of the Altay mountains. The birds are so heavy that the Kazakhs are obliged to use a wooden prop to support their arms when carrying them on horseback.

We rode all day through empty landscapes, coming late in the afternoon to a narrow lateral valley where *gers* were camped along the banks of a winding river. It was the first habitation we had seen since leaving the Namarjin valley two days before. We recognized the *gers* as Kazakh by their steeper profile.

A woman emerged from one to direct us down the valley. 'Orolobai keeps an eagle,' she said. 'You can't miss him. His *ger* has a television aerial.'

One of the most endearing features of the Mongolian countryside was that you could travel a thousand miles without coming across a television. Now, in search of eagle hunters, we rode down the valley to meet what I feared might be the only couch potato in western Mongolia.

Orolobai was a burly square-jawed fellow in a pink skullcap. Delighted at the prospect of guests, he invited us in for tea. Kazakh *gers* are generally larger than their Mongolian counterparts, and much more decorative. But even by Kazakh standards, Orolobai's *ger* was an impressive establishment: a mansion of the nomad world. Inside there was room to swing a yak. The lack of a stove made it seem even more spacious; that had been consigned to a separate kitchen tent next door. In its place, at the centre of the *ger*, was a remarkable innovation – a table and chairs.

We took our seats gingerly, like country bumpkins in the squire's parlour, trying not to gape too openly at the expensive furnishings set around the perimeter of the tent – the metal cots enclosed like four-poster beds with frilly nylon curtains, the large wall hangings with their bright geometric patterns, the laminated poster photograph of two kittens peering over a stone wall, the pile of purple cardboard suitcases. Prominently placed to one side was the talk of the district – an old Russian television set.

Orolobai fussed about us with the exuberant hospitality that is typical of Islamic cultures. Tea arrived in cups and saucers, an unheard-of pretension. Bold and the guide, accustomed to the more reserved manners of Mongolians, had a slightly stunned look. Orolobai could hardly have seemed more outlandish if he had been wearing a grass skirt and a garland of flowers.

The Kazakh proved a congenial host who became a good deal more congenial as we began to tuck into the *airag*, the fermented mare's milk. When we had demolished a few bowlfuls Orolobai invited us outside to meet the eagle. But first he had to change. Much tradition adheres to eagle handling, he explained, and he needed to be dressed for the part. I wasn't so sure. He was a vain man and I think he knew he was about to have his picture taken.

Suddenly Orolobai had the flustered air of a man preparing for a formal dinner party. One of the problems of nomadic existence was the difficulty of keeping track of things when you move house every three months. Orolobai bellowed for his wife and daughters and they began to search through the suitcases and the chests, while he stood in the middle of the *ger*, his belt undone, waving his arms ineffectually. 'They were with the blankets on the second camel,' he whined.

As the items emerged one by one, the women dressed him. With his formal black *del*, he wore a pair of leggings above his tall boots and the kind of leather cap with ear flaps last seen when Charles Lindbergh crossed the Atlantic. The hawking glove was located and an arm guard, and after some rummaging in a suitcase of voluminous white drawers, the bird's hood was discovered. Relieved, the women steered Orolobai out the door.

The eagle was perched on a boulder a short distance from the *ger* with a rather feeble-looking tether round one of its legs. The bird would have made a Dobermann look small. It stood almost three feet high. Its curved beak was the size of a carving knife. But its most striking features were its eyes, cold, black and penetrating. They were eyes made for the malevolent stare, and at the moment the eyes were staring malevolently at me. I don't think the bird had seen a foreigner before.

As Orolobai lifted the eagle gently and settled it on his arm, it never took its eyes off me. I tried to act nonchalant. I looked away; perhaps the bird didn't like anyone staring back. I gazed at some distant hills. I examined my boots. It was at this point that I realized with a start that I was wearing a sheepskin jerkin. I glanced up. The eagle was still staring at me, his head slightly cocked. It occurred to me that he had mistaken me for a stray lamb.

He stretched his wings – the wingspan was over six feet – and even Orolobai cowered. I slipped the jacket off, very slowly, and dropped it at arm's length to one side. Almost immediately the bird lunged toward it. Almost pulled off his feet, Orolobai lurched forward, and in an instant the bird was on my jacket, sinking his talons into the fleece, and savaging it with his hideous beak.

'Seems to like that jacket,' Orolobai panted, struggling to pull the great bird away.

But I was already halfway to the *ger* and moving fast.

In the evening after dinner we were invited to watch telly. Neighbours and family crowded into the *ger*, settling round the set in an expectant half circle. Orolobai had his own generator which he fired up out the back. The blue screen flickered into life. As far as one could tell it was a Variety Performance in Ulan Batur, though the reception was such that it could have been mistaken for morris dancing on the dark side of the moon. In the midst of what appeared to be a blinding snowstorm three people, or possibly six, were singing traditional Mongolian songs. Orolobai was excited with the reception, the best in weeks he declared.

Mercifully it was not to last. After a few minutes the ghostly figures disappeared into a blizzard, and then the screen went dark. Outside the tent we could hear the generator dying. Someone had obviously forgotten to pack the petrol. I tried to hide my disappointment.

Later Bold and I lay on the banks of the stream and watched the constellations falling towards the west. The stars seemed close enough to touch. Nowhere in the world is their reception as perfect as in Outer Mongolia.

Chapter Seven

THE NAADAM WRESTLERS

In the absence of other candidates, Hovd was obliged to stand in for Civilization, or at least that happy corner of it that included hot water, cold beer and a warm bed. After four days' riding the promised city came into view from a low stony ridge, shimmering far across the plain. Reflected sunlight danced in the distant windows. Jerusalem could not have seemed more golden.

I longed to rouse Brown Nose from his lethargy and gallop towards this vision. But the horses were now exhausted, and Brown Nose too worn out even for bottom-sniffing. The trudge across the hot plain seemed interminable. Its only feature was an empty army base where short stretches of trench, reminiscent of the Maginot Line, had been dug to prepare the heirs of Genghis Khan for modern warfare.

It had been my fantasy, since I first conceived the idea of crossing Mongolia by horse, to ride into remote Mongolian towns in some imitation of those scenes in countless Westerns – a trio of dusty strangers, trotting up Main Street, tying our mounts outside the saloon while the locals looked on uneasily. In the hierarchy of grand entrances, I felt that nothing could match what I had come to think of as my Gary Cooper Moment.

Our manner of arrival was only the first of Hovd's disappointments. Just before the bridge that led over the river into town, where *gers* were camped in the river meadows, the guide staged a mutiny. Annoyed that we would not pay him a week's extra wages because of the hardships of the journey, he sought revenge by announcing he would not take his horses into town. In a black sulk he took the agreed money, removed our saddles and baggage, and rode away along the river bank with the horses towards the *gers* of some relations, leaving us to catch a lift into town in a passing jeep. It deposited us ignominiously outside Hovd's only hotel. It wasn't a Gary Cooper Moment.

In the wilderness of overgrown paving stones that passed for the town square, the statue of a solitary hero on horseback, Aldanjavyn Ayush, a partisan in the early years of the twentieth century, raised his arm against Chinese oppression. Sadly the gesture only got as far as his elbow. The rest of the arm was missing, a casualty of the dereliction that infected every structure in Hovd. The broken windows of the town hall were adorned with laundry, the bank had abandoned finance for tanning, and the hotel had neither hot water nor cold beer. Civilization had proved an illusion.

On the pavements of Hovd the middle classes were distinguished by sunglasses and umbrellas. In the streets traffic was light – a few horsemen, the occasional jeep. On our first afternoon a donkey cart toured the town aimlessly with two men slumped in the back, presumably drunk, possibly dead. The handful of small shops, which occupied the front rooms of sagging Russian buildings, lacked any outward sign to announce their presence. You pushed open the heavy street doors to find a makeshift counter, a gloomy shopkeeper in gum boots, and an eclectic array of goods – candles, bricks of tea, bars of soap, confectionery from Latvia, boots from Russia, brassieres from China. Alternatively, if you chose the wrong door, you found a family eating soup.

But after Bayan Ölgii, Hovd seemed a happening place, and I dived into a round of cultural activities. On the first morning I went to visit the museum, an old Russian dacha in a side street. In the lobby I found the ticket seller asleep by the window. When I woke him, he shrugged and shook his head, then took me by the hand to show me the problem. The electricity was off, as it was most days. Hand in hand we peered into the dark windowless rooms of the past and agreed it was hopeless.

Undeterred I went round to the theatre whose pink neo-classical façade is Hovd's only brush with glamour. A grand doorway was flanked by Corinthian columns. The building rather dwarfed Hovd's theatrical tradition; treading the boards was not generally part of nomadic life. But facilities for art and culture, like medical care and universal education, were part of the socialist blueprint for a brave new world that had arrived from Russia almost eighty years ago with earnest young Bolsheviks, and every *aimag* centre was equipped with a theatre to host the annual visit of the national touring company.

Peering in through the grimy windows I could see that attendances had withered when the Russian subsidies had dried up in the late 1980s. The place looked abandoned. Potted geraniums had grown wild on the window ledges. The vaulted entrance hall was given over to dust. A grand stairway leading into further gloom had been stripped of its carpet. In the cloakroom, hooks meant for the herdsmen's fur hats and horsewhips were adorned with cobwebs.

Round at the rear of the building I found the stage door open. Inside was a lobby dominated by a huge gilt-framed mirror where actors of a previous era could admire their entrances into the real world. A piano was playing somewhere. Then it broke off. I heard footsteps, and a moment later an elderly phantom appeared, carrying a mop. He drew up short as he found a foreigner standing in the lobby.

The caretaker might have been Albert Einstein's bohemian brother. He was an old man with wild hair, bushy eyebrows, a cardigan, a pair of wire-framed spectacles, and a startled but intelligent face. Recovering from his initial shock, he raised his hands with delight. 'Come,' he said immediately. 'Let me show you'.

Einstein turned out to be a one-man theatre. In a series of enthusiastic and animated performances, he took on all the roles of the establishment. In the dressing rooms he mimed the actor's making up in front of the cracked mirrors, and modelled a moth-eaten velvet dressing gown apparently left behind by some touring

production of Chekov. In the gloom of backstage, among dilapidated scenery, he showed me how to operate the fly ropes, making
a considerable success of the two roles of a beefy fly-man and the
scenery descending from the heavens like a dancer floating to
earth.

Round in the front lobby he sold me a make-believe ticket, and
in lieu of a programme, showed me over the framed black and
white photographs of old productions which were displayed around
the walls. Though the actors were Mongolian, the plays appeared
to be Russian, a succession of drawing room scenes. Einstein was
delighted when I suggested that one was a scene from *The Three
Sisters*. *'Teem, teem,'* he nodded excitedly, *'Tri Sestry. Tri Sestry'*.
It appeared to be one of the scenes in which Andrei was complaining
of his despair about life in the countryside among illiterate and
uncultured peasantry. In the depths of Outer Mongolia, a thousand
miles from anything resembling a city, this complaint by a man
living only a couple of hours' train journey from Moscow must
have seemed a trifle melodramatic. Einstein nudged me in the ribs.
His eyebrows danced mischievously. I looked again at Andrei. It
was the caretaker, forty years ago.

Then he ushered me into the auditorium. It smelt of dust and
old velvet. I glimpsed ancient chandeliers and walls armoured with
enormous radiators as the caretaker took my hand and led me down
the aisle. In the front row he settled me in a seat, then hobbled
up the steps onto the stage where he proceeded to re-enact Andrei's
monologue in Act Four. I knew the scene well for I too had
been Andrei in a student production. It was a wonderful part for
a sixteen-year-old, angry, whingeing, thwarted by the unfairness of
the world, and complaining that no one understood him.

I joined him on the stage and we did a bilingual version, emoting
splendidly to the empty stalls. Then we laughed and shook hands.
Russia had united us.

On the edge of the town, where the single paved street begins to
founder in the encroaching steppe, I came upon an older ghost,
the walled enclosure of a Manchu city, one of China's colonial

outposts during the two centuries that they had ruled Mongolia.

China and Mongolia had never got on. 'We hate the Chinese,' Bold would say when I touched upon this ancient antipathy. 'It is in our blood. And the Chinese hate us right back.' The fitting symbol of their relations is the Great Wall, the spectacular but ill-fated attempt by the Chinese to keep the rowdy Mongolians at bay. To the Chinese, the Mongols are the neighbours from hell, barbarous, noisy, chaotic and given to irrational outbursts. To the Mongolians, the Chinese are cynical, duplicitous and horrifyingly numerous. Their contempt for one another reflects the temperamental differences between settled and nomadic peoples. Even today, in the homogeneous stew of the modern age, the ninety-minute flight between Ulan Batur and Beijing presents one of the great culture shocks of modern travel. No two cities, no two countries, no two peoples could be more different than these two neighbours whom geography has tied unhappily together.

Plagued since the earliest periods of recorded history by nomadic incursions from Central Asia, the Chinese tended to see the Mongols as a natural catastrophe like flood or famine, some displeasure of the gods that had simply to be endured. Eventually they would go home, their saddle-bags bulging with rice and porcelain. But the climax of these nomadic invasions, Genghis Khan's conquest of China in the thirteenth century, had brought a new horror. The idea of empire had entered the Mongol consciousness; the barbarians had decided they wanted to stay and rule the most ancient and sophisticated civilization in the world.

Yeh-lu Ch'u-ts'ai, the Khitan advisor who had reminded the Mongols that the dead don't pay taxes, also managed to persuade them of the truth of the old Chinese saying, that they could conquer an empire on horseback, but they could not rule it from the saddle. Kubilai Khan, Genghis' grandson, ruled China by recasting himself as a Chinese emperor. When Friar William arrived in Qaraqorum he was received by Kubilai's brother, Mongke, in a palatial tent. When Marco Polo turned up in China, twenty years later, he found Kubilai installed in a palace in Beijing, the forerunner of the Forbidden City. Mongolian traditionalists never forgave him of course, but the dynasty that Kubilai founded, the Yuan, governed China for almost a hundred years.

Kubilai's acceptance of the Chinese world of cities and agriculture marked the beginning of the end for nomadic culture. Over the coming centuries the balance of power would tip in favour of sedentary societies. Fuelled by the technological advances of Europe, they were no longer prey to nomads with their ancient advantages of endurance and horsemanship. For a time nomadic incursions would continue to trouble the Chinese borderlands, but they were a force in decline. When in the fifteenth century the Oirat Mongols managed to capture the Ming emperor, it is symptomatic of their disarray that they settled for a cash ransom rather than the reins of power. It was China's turn to dominate Mongolia.

The Chinese first arrived in Mongolia in the seventeenth century, initially in response to a request for assistance from the Khalkh Mongols fighting to resist the advances of the Oirats. The muskets and cannons, which the Chinese had recently acquired from European traders, proved decisive. Unsurprisingly the Mongols found that the price their new partners demanded for their assistance was subservience. Mongolia became a tributary state of Manchu China before being gradually subsumed into the Chinese Empire. It was not until 1911, when republican pressures emerged inside China, that the Mongolians were able to reassert their independence.

Of Sangiin Herem, the old Chinese settlement on the edge of Hovd, only the weathered city walls remain, the same four-square construction with which the Chinese enclosed every city, from Manchuria to Canton. The buildings have vanished and the inhabitants of Hovd now use the fertile soil of Chinese defeat for vegetable plots. These allotments may be the only echo of the Chinese presence here. However much the Mongolian government tries to encourage the planting and eating of vegetables, it is an uphill struggle. I wondered if the gardeners of Hovd, stooped over cabbages, had Chinese blood.

The ruins were a quiet reflective place, and on empty afternoons I gravitated towards them. From the old walls I looked down on the ghosts of avenues, aligned to the points of the compass. I pictured bell towers with vermilion gates, temples with upturned eaves, houses with courtyards and lattice screens and rock gardens: an enclosure of Chinese order planted in this wild land. I imagined the Chinese here clinging to familiar rituals, like English colonists, their manners exaggerated by a foreign land. I saw them at endless games of mah-jong, hunched over bowls of noodles and pak choy, filling the vacant corners of their gardens with azaleas, trooping off to the ancestral graves with joss sticks and picnics of dumplings, while outside the city waited the empty vastness of Mongolia, unwalled, unplanted, untended, unsettled. Perhaps the Chinese buried their anxieties beneath philosophical meditation, contemplating the polarities of life, yin and yang, as they peered over the walls at horsemen galloping through untamed landscapes.

Perhaps the reason I found the abandoned ruins of Sangiin Herem so compelling was that I recognized my own ambivalence here. However much I indulged my unruly desire for movement, I understood the longing that these shattered walls seemed to express for permanence in an impermanent world. I too wanted to contain that which I loved.

Hovd saw the beginning and the end of my dentistry career. Among my supplies was a emergency dental kit, and in an act of foolish generosity, I had offered to have a look at the teeth of one of the hotel attendants who was miserable with toothache. Mrs Tsolom arrived early for her appointment and found me in my underwear. Mongolians never knock on doors – it is considered impolite to knock on the door of a *ger* – but her faith in my professional abilities was happily undiminished by the sight of me smoking a cigar in my boxer shorts.

I showed the patient to a chair by the window. Bold acted as nurse, shining a torch into the dark cavern of Mrs Tsolom's mouth. I got to work with the little dental mirror, inspecting the teeth one by one for signs of decay. I had no idea how I was going to identify decay, or what I might do when I found it, but I endeavoured to maintain a confident and professional air. Fortunately Mrs Tsolom's problem was easy to identify. She had lost a filling.

'Have you been having pain for long, Mrs Tsolom?' I asked in my best dentist's voice.

'Bhummfghskooorfgh,' she said.

'What does she say, Bold?'

'I don't know,' Bold said. 'I think you need to take your hand out of her mouth.'

'Ah yes.'

As chance would have it, a lost filling was the only dental problem I was able to treat. With the little leaflet that came with the dental kit propped open on the window sill, just beyond Mrs Tsolom's line of sight, I cleared and rinsed the cavity as per the instructions. In the sad shops of Hovd vodka had been the only available disinfectant but Mrs Tsolom didn't seem to mind.

'Do you want to spit that out Mrs Tsolom?' I said.

Mrs Tsolom looked at me quizzically then swallowed.

I proceeded to install a temporary filling consisting of a mysterious pink paste, squeezing it into place in layers with a nifty filling device rather like a miniature garden hoe. When the operation was complete, I rubbed clove gel around the area.

'If you would just like to rinse your mouth out, Mrs Tsolom,' I said, turning aside to check the instructions while Bold handed her the vodka bottle.

'Now then,' I said in a stern medical voice. 'We don't want to eat anything hard for twenty-four hours. Don't eat anything at all for at least five hours and then only soft matter on the other side of your mouth. And remember. The filling is only temporary. You must go to a real dentist as soon as you can for a permanent one. Is that understood?'

Mrs Tsolom took another swig of vodka and nodded.

'That's probably enough rinsing for now Mrs Tsolom,' I said taking the bottle from her steely grip. 'Let me know if you have any further problems.'

When she had gone Bold reminded me that there were no dentists in Hovd. She would be unlikely to get any further treatment unless she went to Ulan Batur. In the countryside dental treatment generally consisted of removing the offending tooth with a pair of pliers. Vodka was both a disinfectant and the only anaesthetic.

As an alternative to this barbarity, my practise was soon the talk of the town, particularly when news got out that patients did not have to forgo the vodka. The following morning when I came downstairs I found five patients waiting in the hotel lobby reading old Mongolian magazines. This glut of work forced my early retirement. I decided it was probably better that the citizens of Hovd pulled their own teeth when decay was in the early stages rather than delay the inevitable with my temporary fillings. It seemed a good idea to close up shop before Mrs Tsolom returned for root canal work. Besides I was worried about the liquor bill.

Mongolia is only pretending to be a huge country. There are days when it feels like a small rural parish, its inhabitants sharing gossip, relations, and anxieties about foot and mouth disease across vast distances. Even in the remotest *aimag* the chances of running into someone you know are remarkably high. In the streets of Hovd, Bold ran into Ganbold. They had been at teachers' college together in Ulan Batur twenty years before.

Ganbold was a history teacher in the secondary school in Hovd, an institution with a catchment area the size of Scotland. He had a round flat face and a constipated grin that involved clenched teeth and bulging eyes. He was agreeable, malleable and eager to please, traits ideally suited to the shifting sands of the Mongolian history curriculum. Twenty years of teaching fourteen-year-olds about the glories of the Communist Revolution had honed his conversation to laborious banalities. Ganbold was a connoisseur of the obvious, never happier than when explaining something you already knew.

He was also a man of enthusiasms, and he now took up the cause of our journey with a speed and eagerness that was startling in this lethargic town. It was the summer break and he was going to the countryside to visit his mother. He could arrange horses for us, he said, and he would act as our guide south-east through the Altay Mountains. We spread maps across the floor of our hotel room and discussed routes and distances. He knew everyone in that direction, he said. He could accompany us as far as the *ger* of one of his students whose family was camped near Mönkh Khairkhan. The student could then take us the next stage of the journey to Möst.

I was eager to be off. The sybaritic lustre of Hovd had worn off.

'After the Naadam,' Ganbold announced. 'Life begins again after the Naadam.'

The origins of the annual Naadam Festival lie in the *quriltai*, the great clan meetings that were the social events of the medieval Mongol season. In the days of Genghis Khan, tribesmen gathered from the furthest corners of the land to settle matters of leadership and pasturage, of war and peace, as well as that most contentious of issues – who had the fastest horses. In 1242 when the Mongols vanished suddenly from the suburbs of Vienna, Europe was saved by one of the greatest *quriltai* of the age. Galloping back across the long reaches of Asia, after the death of Ogedei, the clan leaders were anxious to get home to see if they could back a winner in the succession race. The ordinary clansmen would have been just as excited by the prospect of the Derbies. No one wanted to waste time sacking the cities of Christendom when there was a race meeting to attend.

In the modern age politics are largely absent from the Naadam allowing Mongolians to concentrate on the more important issues of sport and socializing. The great Naadam at Ulan Batur is a combination of Wimbledon, the Cup Final, a gypsy fair, and Newcastle on a Saturday night. But all over the nation there are provincial Naadams in the little stadiums that stand on the edge of every *aimag* centre. They are celebrations of Mongolian culture as expressed in four national sports: horse racing, wrestling, archery, and drinking. When Mongolians party, says a Chinese proverb, the rest of Asia locks its doors.

The stadium in Hovd might have been home to a Fourth Division football club whose groundsman had passed away some years before. Between open stands and two small pavilions the pitch was overgrown with wild flowers. At its centre, where the Red Flag used to fly, was a group of nine poles topped with yaks' tails, the standard of Genghis Khan. The tails were white, which was just as well. Black meant war.

Crowds milled about in their best silk and velvet *dels*. Everyone was in a good mood and a hat. Men and women alike were partial to rather handsome fedoras and trilbys. A few of the more august figures wore bowlers. Naadam was a great occasion for medals. To keep the long-suffering herdsmen sweet, the former Communist government had doled out gongs with abandon. The result was medal inflation. Medals that were once great honours quickly became worthless and new ones had constantly to be minted. There was the Order of the Red Banner, the Order of Sukhbatur Medal, the National Hero of the Mongolian Revolutionary Party, the Order of the Pole Star Medal, and the Best Worker in the Fifth Five Year Plan. Men got medals for acts of courage and patriotic devotion like party membership and high livestock yields. Women got them for bearing children. One old woman proudly showed me 'The Order of Glorious Motherhood, First Grade', the Victoria Cross of motherhood. Pinned to her formidable bosom, it celebrated the fact that she had had more than ten children.

The loudspeakers were droning with speeches by local dignitaries. No one seemed to listen, not even the band who struck up a catchy tune in the middle of the governor's peroration on civic duty. When the band was joined by a singer with a voice that would have been the envy of Jessye Norman, the governor retreated to the reviewing stand. Mongolian politicians, generally ex-Communists forging new careers, somewhat shakily, as democrats, are struggling to get used to that most fundamental ingredient of democracy: the right to ignore politicians. They sat darkly in a row, beneath their bowler hats, muttering about the good old days.

A frisson went through the crowd as the wrestlers were introduced according to their status: Falcon, Elephant, Lion, and Giant, last year's champion. Most of the participants were of the Sumo tendency – huge fellows who looked like they got through half a yak at breakfast. Among the big stomachs were a scattering of slim men, looking understandably nervous. The wrestlers' costumes appeared to have been designed for a dance troupe: boots with elfin toes, pointed hats, short sparkly jackets, and pretty embroidered Y-fronts. One by one the big men trotted out into mid-field where they performed the Eagle Dance, flapping their arms in slow motion and bowing before the standard of Genghis Khan. Each was accompanied by his second, generally an elderly fellow whose main job it was to hold the wrestlers' hats when the bouts got underway. A hat in Mongolia is the repository of a man's dignity; while the wrestlers struggled to trample one another underfoot, no one wanted to step on the hats.

I asked an old fellow next to me the reason for the curious design of the jackets – long sleeves but an open front that left the chest bare.

'Keeps the women out,' he muttered. In Outer Mongolia women wrestlers are much feared; anyone who has had dealings with the stewardesses of Mongol Air will understand why. The annals of Mongolian wrestling are full of stories in which devious viragos disguised their sex, entered the wrestling competition and destroyed all the best heavyweights. Marco Polo related a tale of a Mongol princess who decided she could only marry a man who could throw her. Despite a succession of muscle-bound suitors, she remained a spinster. The idea of the open-fronted jacket is that it allows the more alert judges to spot a woman straight away and hustle her out of the competition before she causes any damage.

As the wrestling got underway it was quickly evident that the slim fellows were warm-up material to the guys with the big bellies. The early bouts were full of action as large men threw small men with satisfying thumps. But as the small men were gradually weeded out in the round robin tournament, the competition became stiffer and the contests duller. Locked together like stalled bulldozers the big men could go fifteen rounds without moving. The only action came between rounds when the seconds straightened the wrestlers' Y-fronts and patted their bottoms. The end invariably came with a whimper: a brief flurry of pushing and shoving, and one of the big men was inexplicably on the ground.

The horse races were better value and the following morning we set off in a hired jeep, bouncing across the empty steppe, to where a large crowd had assembled at a finish line in the middle of nowhere. Naadam races are run cross-country over marathon distances, twenty miles in the case of the Hovd races. People milled about in their hats, greeting one another with elaborate salutations. Many of the men had arrived in the same straw fedora whose hatbands bore the bewitching legend: Strength Through Milk.

The approach of the three-year-old field was announced by a distant cloud of dust. The crowds pushed forward towards the finish line where three policemen, rather the worse for drink, threw stones at them to try to hold them back. Dodging a couple of rocks I got out into the middle where the stewards, a distinguished forum of older men, squatted in a line, peering through their binoculars. As the horses began to emerge from the dust, the chief steward ran forward waving an enormous red flag to guide the riders to the finish line. A crescendo of whoops and whistles rose from the crowd. Young men hollered, women shrieked, old men stamped their feet, and babies, waving fat arms, burst into tears.

The jockeys were children, both boys and girls, few of them older than eight, who had completed the course bareback and barefoot. In their paper race hats they looked as if they were returning from a rather jolly children's party, dazed with too much cake. As the first finishers crossed the line, the crowds broke ranks, overrunning the inebriated policemen and engulfing the lathered horses. Fathers caught hold of the bridles, sisters started frantically wiping the sweat from the horses' flanks with special paddles, and mothers revived their child jockeys with mare's milk.

One horse collapsed a few yards from the finishing line. Its rider, a young girl of about seven, picked herself up and began to kick the horse in the chest, apparently the Mongolian equivalent of an equine kiss of life, meant to revive the poor creature. The owner had a more traditional remedy. He ran out from the crowd, produced a bottle of vodka from the folds of his *del* and poured the contents down the horse's throat. The effect was immediate. The animal leapt to its feet and hared off back towards Hovd, riderless, without bothering to cross the finishing line. A stewards' enquiry presumably disqualified the beast: 'retired, drunk'.

Back at the stadium in the afternoon, the wrestling final was underway, when a great party of horsemen arrived – the Naadam winners, their owners, their trainers, and their pals. To the roar of the crowd they cantered round the arena beneath the terraces in a couple of laps of honour burying the wrestlers in veils of dust.

For the presentation the riders gathered beneath the equivalent of the royal box where the politicians were seated. Professional praise singers sang the praises of the horses, the races and riders in thrilling nasal arias. The governor, pleased at last to be the centre of attention, handed out the prizes – Chinese carpets and bricks of Russian tea – as if he had bought them himself. The grand prize was a Russian motorcycle. Actually it was a promissory note for a motorcycle. Though ordered some months ago, the governor explained, the machine had yet to arrive. The winning trainer gazed at the note with the sceptical look of a man familiar with politicians' promises.

Then amidst further whoops the horsemen galloped out of the stadium and we rediscovered the wrestling final. Not a lot had happened in the interval. The two colossi were as we had left them, like mating dogs that had got stuck. They might have been posing for a statue.

We were rescued by a spectacular storm. Thunder rolled in from the mountains, lightning split the black skies, rain swept round the terraces and the crowds fled. Within minutes the stadium was empty save for the two wrestlers, their seconds forlornly holding their hats in the downpour and a panel of judges sheltering beneath a leaky canopy.

Hunched against the rain, the Mongolians ran to their horses, tethered in long rows in the horse park. Cantering away across the wet plain, standing slightly in their saddles, they laughed and called to one another. Long after the sound of their voices and the horses' hooves had died away we could still see them, wreathing like smoke across the glistening steppe, towards distant *gers*.

Culture had not completely abandoned the theatre in Hovd. Now that the state theatrical companies of the Communist era were bankrupt and no longer toured the provinces, *aimag* centres like Hovd were visited by small private troupes who hired the theatres hoping to turn a profit with their entertainments. Bold and I met one of these itinerant bands, an unhappy company of alcoholics, nursing hangovers in the caretaker's *ger*. They had taken the theatre for three nights during Naadam, and invited us to their Hovd première that evening.

Einstein had fired up the generator which lived in a shed in the back yard next to his *ger* and we arrived to find the auditorium dimly lit by ancient chandeliers suspended from the vaulted ceiling. We took our place in the front row. Behind us five small boys were busy firing missiles at their friends and sticking chewing gum on the empty seats.

After a long wait the curtain rose rather shakily to reveal two musicians, one with a bass guitar and the other playing a keyboard synthesizer, who might have been auditioning for a spoof of the 1970s. They were attired in white frilly shirts, white flares, white boots, long gold lamé coats and Rod Stewart haircuts.

They accompanied a series of singers. The first was a small man with a large voice and an even larger suit. He fought valiantly with the latter, tripping over the cuffs and wrestling to free his hands from the sleeves while rattling the chandeliers with huge soaring notes. He was followed by a man who did impressions. As most Mongolians do not have television, there are no familiar national figures to impersonate. The mimic concentrated instead on characters with which all Mongolians were familiar: animals. He did a yak that had become separated from the herd, a cow stranded on the wrong side of a river, four different dog personalities, a new-born kid, a two-year-old goat, a four-year-old goat, an old goat, and a dying goat. He rounded off his routine with a camel that didn't want to stand up and three sheep trying to negotiate a stream without getting their feet wet. The Mongolians were in stitches. For an encore he did a mare on heat.

Next up was an elderly ballet dancer. He was a slightly bowlegged figure with tall pomaded hair. He had trained in Irkutsk, Bold whispered. I assumed this was a recommendation. He performed a series of stirring numbers in which classical training had been wedded to traditional Mongolian folk themes, producing an unlikely hybrid.

Two women singers were the salvation of the evening. The older woman sang a series of very beautiful Mongolian folk songs. Bold translated some of the words for me, *sotto voce*. Songs in Mongolia have only four subjects, Bold explained: Landscape, Horses, Love, and Mother. The older woman concentrated on Landscape and Mother. The younger woman, a shy performer with a wonderful voice and an enchanting smile, took care of Love and Horses.

Afterwards, on impulse, I went round to the stage door and invited her to dinner.

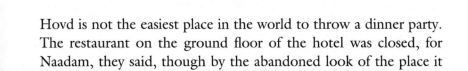

Hovd is not the easiest place in the world to throw a dinner party. The restaurant on the ground floor of the hotel was closed, for Naadam, they said, though by the abandoned look of the place it might have been the Naadam of 1957. But as Mrs Tsolom's filling had not yet fallen out, I was able to persuade her to open it to allow us to use its facilities for our soirée. In the shops, among the batteries and saddles and women's underwear, I managed to find a selection of exotic ingredients: potatoes, onions, and Latvian chocolate bars called Spunk. Our guests arrived at eight; the young singer was escorted by her father, the ballet dancer. Ganbold joined the party with a friend, an enormous wrestler who must have been twenty-five stone. Like many Mongolian men troubled by chapped lips in this dry climate, he wore lipstick, in his case the same fetching shade of pink favoured by the young singer who looked ravishing in a sleeveless blouse. I had prepared an elaborate menu – onion soup, sautéed potatoes and grilled mutton supplied by my friend the caretaker – and mixed passable cocktails from the unpromising ingredients of lemon squash, out of date cola and a Mongolian vodka called Genghis Khan.

The ballet dancer, whose name was Batbold, revealed himself to be an astrologer. Tall and gaunt, he looked like the Kazakh eagle with a fifties quiff. The austere effect of his piercing eyes was much softened by a wonderful smile and a gay Hawaiian shirt worn beneath a three-piece polyester suit. He arrived with a mysterious black attaché case.

It transpired that Batbold had lived in Hovd as a young man, and that he and Ganbold had been comrades in the local branch of Young Communist League in the mid-1960s. The YCL was rather like the Young Conservatives – a social club with traditions of political extremism and excessive drinking. Young men nodded through resolutions calling for the imprisonment of Buddhist monks in order to meet girls at the dances after the meeting. In the sixties membership of the YCL, like that of the Party itself, was the only way to prosper in Mongolia. Bold had been obliged to join in order to ensure he proceeded beyond the tenth grade.

The three reminisced about a misspent youth criticizing one another's bourgeois tendencies and printing government leaflets urging the herdsmen to increase their livestock yields. None of them would confess to believing any of the rhetoric they had once been charged with promulgating. It was merely the prevailing orthodoxy of the time, no more unusual apparently than a passion for flares and big-collared shirts. I struggled to remind myself that those with an attachment to less fashionable ideas like independent thought had ended up in labour camps. Among the victims of political correctness was Batbold's own father, also an astrologer.

To the Party, astrology, shamanism and Buddhism were all part of the backward beliefs that hindered Mongolia's progress. Various measures were taken against them. The lamas were sent to labour camps while the astrologers went underground. But belief in star charts, in messages from the spirit world and in prophetic cracks in the shoulder bones of butchered sheep are tenacious in Mongolia, and among those who sought the clandestine advice of shamans and astrologers and even lamas, through the worst years of their repression, were many high-ranking government and Party officials. One such was the Communist mayor of Ulan Batur, in difficulties with both his health and his mistress, who regularly consulted Batbold's father, after the family had moved to the capital. When the mayor found a new astrologer whose predictions he preferred, he dispensed with Batbold's father's services by having him arrested. Batbold, who had joined the YCL at his father's urging in order to advance himself, was obliged to join in the denunciation.

Now that religious freedom has returned to Mongolia, Batbold has unearthed his father's hidden charts and materials and taken up the old profession. After dinner he opened the black attaché case and brought out old Tibetan manuscripts wrapped in cloth, faded charts which unrolled like ancient maps, a *feng shui* compass, wooden blocks carved with the symbolic figures of Tibetan Buddhism, and a box of artefacts including Tibetan coins and a small silver whistle. Batbold laid them all very carefully and very precisely on the table before him as if each had a specific place in our midst. The materials clearly fascinated him, and for a moment he had the look of one of those obsessive characters, more interested in equipment than what it might do.

With a moist stick dipped in ash, he inscribed my birth details on a square of rice paper then delved into his texts to discover my fate. His face darkened. I had good conjunctions for a writer, he said, but I would be better off financially going into the business side – publishing or printing – advice that hardly needed a mystic.

I would have a long life, and numerous love affairs. He predicted six wives. He noted I was a dragon and warned me against women who were dogs. As for health, I would have problems with my heart, my kidneys, my stomach, and my lungs, which didn't seem to leave much in the way of working organs. He concluded by announcing that it was a bad year for travelling.

Over dessert – out-of-date Spunk bars – Bold and I chatted to the young singer. The circumstances of the dinner – the candlelight, her father's reflections on the past, the strange manuscripts and charts, perhaps even my potent cocktails – had released some knot of feeling. She was full of Chekovian longing. She longed to be back home in Ulan Batur with her mother and her friends. She longed to learn English. She longed to be a great singer. She longed to write poetry. She longed to find her own place. Bold hesitated over the translation as she had hesitated over the sentence. She meant her place in the world, he explained, her own voice, some ellusive understanding of herself.

Her confession silenced us. She seemed to believe that so much was possible.

Chapter Eight

THE SHAMAN'S JOURNEY

The shaman's tent lay in the high Altay on the edge of another world. All morning we rode through narrowing valleys, each higher and bleaker than the one before. Boulders protruded from the grass, glazed with lichens the colour of dried blood. We passed a dead yak. Grass grew through the eye sockets and the desiccated hide peeled like parchment from the white bones. At a lonely watershed where the north wind howled down from further heights, we came to a single *ger* standing on the skyline in a stone-coloured light. The name of this place, Ganbold said, was Balkhuun. A conclave of ravens circled noisily over the abyss beyond the *ger*. I peered over the edge. Wreathed in cloud the earth fell away into fathomless depths.

We tied our horses and went into the *ger* where we found the shaman's wife. She had a brutish face, flattened, masculine, amber-yellow. Strips of sable fur and dried mutton fat hung from the roof poles. A surly boy sat on one of the cots stitching a saddle. The fire had gone out and the *ger* was cold.

The shaman was not in, the wife said, but she was expecting him shortly. We settled down to wait in the place of the guests while the woman busied herself lighting the fire. We struggled to make conversation then fell into a self-conscious silence. The shaman had been a school friend of Ganbold's thirty years ago in Dutt. But even his cheerful anticipation had been subdued by the poor *ger*, the sour wife, the cold wind, the bleak remoteness of this place.

The old spirits have a tenacious hold over the Mongolian imagination. Even as the country became predominately Buddhist in the
sixteenth century the herdsmen continued to find solace in the
reassuring rituals of shamanism. Some of the practices found their
way surreptitiously into Buddhist rituals, while the rites of the lamas
began to inform the chants and methods of the surviving shamans
who saw no conflict between Buddhist beliefs and a shaman's calling. They seemed to have divided the religious world between them.
Shamans dealt with the material needs of the present. Buddhism
concentrated on the future and the afterlife. Yet when all religion
became illegal under the Communists, the shamans often survived
under the cover of their neighbours' silence when even the Buddhist
lamas had disappeared. Their roots ran deeper.

Shamans are travellers among the dark secrets of the spirit world.
In trances induced by ecstatic chanting and the heartbeat of the
tambour drum, they embark on journeys through the shadow lands
of a parallel universe ruled by the great sky-god, Tengri, and the
earth goddess, Itugen. Relying on the hospitality of friendly wraiths,
avoiding the attentions of hostile demons, they seek cures for the
complaints of the living among those of the ninety-nine spirits
whose patronage they enjoy. Dressed like the vagrants of the underworld in a layered confusion of tassels and feathers and headdresses
of rags, they root out the dark forces who are consuming the souls
of their petitioners with divinations and exorcisms. They seek to
turn the course of ill fortune, to prophesy the future and to accrue
blessings for herds, for pastures and for children. White shamans
seek the assistance of good spirits while black shamans deflect the
baleful influence of the evil spirits. The mysterious forces with which
they deal, and the dark world they inhabit, are unpredictable and
dangerous. The shaman's journeys are fraught with difficulties, and
they return to our own world exhausted and depleted.

'There is my boyfriend,' Ganbold whispered in one of his rare
ventures into English. Through the open door of the *ger* we could
see a man coming across the slopes on foot. In the folds of his *del*
he was carrying a new-born lamb.

I had expected a compelling and charismatic character, but the man who stepped through the door was a shambling bashful figure. Ganbold's boyfriend had a drained face and a limp handshake. When he took his place at the head of the *ger* his daughter crawled into his lap like a kitten.

He answered our enquiries about shamanism in a faltering voice, sounding like an artist, uneasy about discussing his work, as if any commitment to explanation might undermine the mystery of the thing. His wife was more forthcoming, and interrupted to illuminate his mumbled responses. She had clearly assumed the role of his manager, mediating between the shaman and his clients in the same way that the shaman mediated between the physical and spiritual worlds.

Shamanism was a family tradition; he had inherited his powers through his mother's line. He was the ninth generation to fulfil this mystical destiny. Though he always knew he would be a shaman, the powers did not manifest themselves until he was thirty-seven, perhaps not coincidentally when government regulations about religious activities were first relaxed. His powers announced their arrival with a fit like epilepsy. He became dizzy, and had fainting spells, shortness of breath, and convulsions as the spirits began to whisper their entreaties. He was in bed for a fortnight, troubled by bizarre dreams and a raging fever. When he came round he knew the spirits had captured him, and his life as a shaman had begun. He spoke of it as a hardship, a cross he was obliged to bear.

'It is a bitter calling,' he said. Beneath a thatch of dark hair, his rheumy eyes examined the earthen floor. 'I am often afraid. The way to the spirits is littered with the souls of fallen shamans.'

On his journeys our shaman called upon eight or nine different spirits who lived between the land and the sky and who had been familiars of his mother. He discussed the difficulty of getting in touch with them. Apparently they adhered to quite a strict schedule of auspicious days and hours, and did not like to be disturbed out of office hours.

At this point his wife and manager intervened. The spirits could be contacted on other days, she insisted. The schedule wasn't prohibitive. She clearly didn't like the idea of minor technical details standing in the way of such prosperous-looking clients.

Treading delicately around the matter of the spirits' schedule, we arranged for the shaman to perform 'a beckoning', not so much a shaman journey as a brief house call. Such rituals are usually nocturnal, but practices vary from place to place and our shaman, under considerable pressure from his wife, accepted the engagement provided it was before midday. This gave us an hour. The wife took charge of negotiating his fee. Then she asked us to step outside while the shaman made his preparations.

Outside the tent we stood about uneasily, like truants awaiting a tricky interview with the headmaster. Ganbold was intrigued to learn that my father was a vicar, and enquired if I had inherited his powers. I said I had not.

'Sometimes the powers are latent,' Ganbold reassured me. 'You must wait. They will manifest themselves.'

Back inside the *ger* we found the shaman standing with his back to us facing the small dresser on which the ancestral photographs were displayed. Sticks of incense had been lit in small copper pots between the mug shots of his shaman mother and grandmother. The shaman had changed into a tattered blue silk *del* adorned with layers of bric-a-brac – bronze mirrors, small bells, circles of coloured tin, the feathers and bones of birds. His headdress, known as the *umsgol*, was a similar clutter. Strips of coloured rag hung down in front of his face like a veil. The idea was to protect the shaman's eyes from our gaze, and to allow him to concentrate his own sight on the spirit world.

We were settled and waiting for the rituals to commence when there was a last-minute hitch. We had not brought any vodka. To help induce a trance, shamans have traditionally employed a range of aids from hallucinogenic plants to smoke inhalation, fasting, sleep deprivation, and prolonged drumming. These days vodka often acts as the shaman's send-off and a contribution from the petitioners is part of the fee. The shaman's wife, who communicated the request, now had a whispered consultation with the shaman's back and it was decided to proceed, vodka-less. A couple of large bowls of *airaq* were substituted. The shaman tossed them back, and an expectant hush fell over the *ger*, like that moment in a theatre when the house lights dim and the curtain begins to rise.

Taking a bowl of fermented mare's milk, the shaman threw a

pinch into the air, then another to the hearth fire, before finally baptizing his own forehead. His wife began to beat the hand-held tambour drum and the shaman started to sway. This went on for some time before the shaman introduced another instrument, a small Jew's harp with a whining banshee tone. Between refrains he rocked on his feet, breathing deeply. There was more Jew's harp interspersed with a low throaty singing. He was calling the spirits. Clouds passed overhead, and the circle of sun on the *ger* floor disappeared. The shaman chanted and swayed, his voice and his movements increasing their tempo until suddenly he went rigid and fell backwards into the arms of his wife and son. They propped him against the dresser. He shook himself, rattling the bells of his *del*. A spirit was among us. It was Dayanderkh, the wife whispered, a spirit of the sky.

In a deep strangulated voice, like a tape playing at half speed, the shaman offered the greetings of the spirit. 'How are you, my children?' Dayanderkh drawled. He sounded uncannily like Marlon Brando. The shaman's wife replied on our behalf, saying we were very well thank you. The shaman crooned and swayed some more. His limbs were trembling and he seemed to be gasping for breath. Another message was coming from the spirit.

'If you have any questions,' the spirit intoned through the shaman, 'ask them now.'

I had no idea there was going to be a question and answer session, and I felt stumped. What does one ask the spirit of the sky? I looked to Bold for assistance but he didn't seem to have any pressing queries for Dayanderkh either. I knew the moment our session was over a flood of pertinent and intelligent questions would arise, and I would curse myself for missing the opportunity to get a few tips on global warming and the meaning of life. But in the shaman's tent with the great spirit among us, waiting on my enquiry, my mind was a blank. I had gone for years without a single question for the spirit of the sky, and I was damned if I could think of one now.

The shaman had begun to groan alarmingly. Flecks of spittle dribbled from his lips. He was frothing at the mouth while Dayanderkh waited for my enquiry.

I asked about my journey. Did the spirit know if my travels would be successful?

The shaman's limbs convulsed as if an electric current had passed through his body. He rocked his head, and the rags of his headdress trailed across his wet mouth. Perhaps Dayanderkh didn't like the question.

'Difficulties,' the spirit of the sky growled through the shamam's twisted lips. 'There will be difficulties.'

There was a pause. I wondered if the spirit was going to expand on our difficulties when the voice came again.

'Beware of the horse with the man's name.'

No sooner had this declaration been made than the shaman begun to cry out. The spirit was departing, skipping out of the shaman's body with a stabbing pain and a polite farewell. 'Good luck to all my children,' he said, the voice rising to a high-pitched whine.

The spell ended as it had begun: swaying, heavy breathing, convulsions, and finally the limp collapse into the waiting arms of his wife and his son who lowered him gently to the ground. The shaman sat for a moment slumped forward on his knees then conveyed a request for a post-trance cigarette to his wife who cadged a Marlboro from Bold.

The shaman seemed stiff and exhausted. He was yawning and stretching the muscles of his neck, as if he had awoken from sleeping in a strange position. When he had steadied his nerves sufficiently, we asked gently about the trance and the words of the spirit. But he knew nothing. The spirits spoke through him, he said. He was their medium but when he emerged from a trance he could not remember very clearly what they had said. It was like a dream, he said. The explanation accorded with the odd vacuity of his personality. If the spirits had chosen him, it was because he was an empty vessel which they could fill.

Millennia of religious thought stood between us. The shaman adhered to the most ancient religious belief, the stubborn idea that everything from the elements of nature to inanimate objects had a spirit with which it was necessary to establish a good relationship. He was untroubled by questions of how or why. The spirits did this and did that, the shaman said. They brought the rain, they withered the pastures, they made the winds blow and the cows abort. No enquiry, no scientific discovery, was allowed to disturb these reassuring simplicities. Bold, I could see, viewed the whole business with disdain. But one cannot judge the value of religion by its truth. That verdict was in the hands of the gods. For us religion could only be a question of effect, whether it made people happy or virtuous.

Compared to the shaman's powerful spirits, the Christian God of our own era was a strangely diminished figure. It took an effort to remember that he had once been omnipotent. These days he was no longer required for the big practical matters. Gasses had created the world, evolution had created Man, and we had prosaic explanations for everything in between from the weather to the unemployment figures. Our God had been stripped of all the best turns, leaving him with black holes and the mysteries of the quark, and the best minds of our age did not expect him to hang on to those for long. He had been reduced to an avuncular figure, ready to listen to our problems but with little he could do, other than change the way we thought about them. It was little wonder that so many people had given up on him.

Ganbold had provided me with one of the most evil-tempered horses in western Mongolia. We had collected the horses at his family *ger* in the windswept valleys beyond Dutt. From a rowdy crew a black gelding had been led out for me. He was a mutinous creature with wild eyes, a shaggy winter coat, a fat belly and a spattering of rather sinister white markings across his head. No one had ridden him in over a year and when I approached him he skittered away, his ears laid back and nostrils flaring. I decided to call him Ivan the Terrible. It took four of us to saddle him. It would have been easier to sell him double glazing.

From the shaman's *ger* the horses were restless and eager to be away. They fled down the length of the grey valley with quickening pace. Ivan broke into a rough canter, and his nervous energy infected the others who jostled forward at full gallop. Squalls of cold rain and short bursts of sun scudded across the landscape on north-westerly winds. Cloud tails hung from the mountain heights like dark tattered banners.

The steep ground at the far end of the valley slowed the horses. We climbed for an hour through rocks and tussocks of grass, emerging on a high windswept ridge. Below us on the far side of the pass lay a vast canyon, stretching away towards the south-east between towering escarpments of purple-veined rock. A few feet away, an eagle was perched on a boulder on the canyon's lip. It examined us for a moment like a surly border guard. Then with a disdainful twitch, the bird turned its head, spread its enormous wings and stepped out into the vaults of blue air high above the canyon, sailing majestically upwards on a thermal.

We found a shelving trail, and picked our way slowly down to the grassy floor of the canyon, almost a mile wide, where we followed a trickling stream eastward. Ramparts of fissured rock reared against the sky. In this vast silent place, I felt dwarfed and insignificant. High above, the eagle turned on invisible currents. I tried to imagine how we looked from those aerial heights, a quartet of horses, tiny as prey, inching our way across an autumn-coloured infinity.

At the eastern end of the canyon we crossed another pass into a series of narrow valleys where a stream tumbled among a chaos of water-smoothed boulders. Escarpments surged above us, banded with colour – malachite, auburn, cobalt, aureate, slate grey and coralline. Beyond, the Altay summits loomed in a brooding assembly.

After a couple of hours in these narrow defiles we turned up a long slow pass, climbing between two bare mountains. Rain had come down to meet us from the leaden skies above and we rode hunkered into our waterproofs, strung out on the rocky slope almost half a mile apart. On the steep ground my saddle kept slipping and Ivan threatened to mutiny each time I stopped to adjust the girths. He was in a vicious mood, looking for any chance to bolt, and I tiptoed around him. When I dropped a strap on his right side – Mongolian horses hate to be approached from the right, the side from which wolves are said to attack – it was the excuse he wanted. He reared up and threw the saddle and the bags in a bucking tantrum. I hung on to the lead rope for dear life. Had I lost it, he would have been halfway to Hovd before I had wiped the rain out of my eyes. With soothing and duplicitous words I managed to re-saddle him on the steep ground, and we started again. Rain dripped from the brim of my hat, and a mountain wind moaned among the boulders. It occurred to me that Ivan and I had something in common. We both hated one another. I took comfort from the fact that the other horses, a sensible crew, were on my side. They hated Ivan too, and tried to bite him whenever he came within range.

In this dark mood we climbed through descending clouds. I hadn't seen the others for an hour or so; Bold was somewhere below, Ganbold above. Near the top of the pass I passed a black lake and then an ancient graveyard with mounds of wet stones. Suddenly I broke through the weather and emerged above the clouds on a long ridge under a blue sky and a pale sun, a new and innocent land beyond the reach of the rain and the sombre graves and claustrophobic valleys. Ganbold was already there, grinning like a smug angel in an anteroom of Heaven. Round us the bald summits, spotlit by the afternoon sun, had the pristine unnatural look of stage scenery. On all sides the wide saddle of the pass tipped into the insubstantial arms of clouds.

'Very high,' Ganbold said. He was a reassuring fellow; you could always rely on him to state the obvious.

After about a quarter of an hour Bold materialized, a wraithlike figure slightly bent in the saddle, riding forth from the swirling cloudscape like an ascendant soul.

Then we dropped down the other side of the pass through the clouds and the rain to another valley where a *ger* stood in wet pastures atop a dark mound of sheep and cattle dung. Hobbling our horses by a stream-bed of white boulders, we picked our way gingerly across the wet dung to the door of the *ger*.

Inside we found Ganbold's aunt and uncle. Auntie was a robust figure with a formidable bosom; uncle was a thin stick with big ears. A trio of daughters went in and out with milk buckets. They were country people, shy, modest, taciturn, with thick accents and ruddy faces and big cracked hands and cow-shit on their trousers. They did everything slowly and deliberately as if hurry had never been part of their lives.

They had been here for twenty days, they said, though the deep yard of dung that surrounded the *ger* might have suggested twenty years. I broached the subject of the dung as gently as I could. I didn't wish to imply criticism by pointing out that their doorstep was a shit heap but it seemed odd that they had chosen to pitch their *ger* in the middle of the animal toilet.

Apparently the wolves were to blame. In Mongolia flocks are often kept near the camp through the night to deter wolf attacks. In these mountains the wolves were so audacious that the family were obliged to keep the animals tight round the *ger*: I should probably have been grateful that the sheep weren't inside with us. Thus it was that one stepped straight from the kitchen to the barnyard. I learned to make excursions outside with elaborate care. The vast sloping slick of wet dung that had to be crossed before you reached terra firma was as slippery as an ice rink. Bold was unlucky and returned from a brief excursion to relieve himself smelling like a drain.

We dined on sheep bones, sitting in a circle round the stove, gnawing contentedly. Afterwards there were bowls of a very delicious meat broth. Later tea was served in the same bowls, so that it would mix nicely with the remnants of the greasy broth. In the candlelight our lips glistened with mutton fat.

In the night I heard the wolves howling in the pass above us, and the daughters of the *ger* calling the straying sheep. A lamb was born during the night, and in the morning one of the girls brought it inside where it stood on trembling legs by the door, a soft mass of curls, bleating piteously. In Mongolia only unusual animals are given names. As the last of the lambing season, this one was deemed to be special. They called it Stalin in my honour.

Our route took us across the grain of the Altay Mountains. In spite of the fact that the mountain ridges ran roughly in the direction of our journey, south-east, we never seemed to linger long in the inviting flatness of the intervening valleys but were forever climbing dizzy passes from one to the next. It was only later, when I tried to plot our route on maps, that I realized how circuitous our passage through the mountains had been. It was dictated entirely by the situation of the *gers* of our guide's relations. No pass was considered too formidable if one of Ganbold's aunties lived on the far side.

In the next valley to the Camp of the Dung Heap we stopped for lunch at the *ger* of Ganbold's cousin, a woman in her thirties married to an impulsive fellow who was the dismay of the family. His most recent outrage was to blow 70,000 Tögrögs, about £55, on a fancy handmade saddle that sat conspicuously outside the *ger* like a new sports car. His children seemed to share this strong-willed self-indulgence. The daughter, a child of six, had proved impossible to wean and spent most of lunch beneath her exhausted mother's sweater sucking noisily. The yaks had a similar problem. In the pastures above, mother yaks were being cornered by huge hairy brutes with horns and attitude, who suckled them with the rough enthusiasm of hooligans downing pints of lager.

An enormous flat-topped mountain loomed above us. Inevitably the *ger* of one of Ganbold's aunts lay on the other side. The mountain's brow was streaked with snow, and skeins of silver streams unravelled across the high slopes. We climbed into a waterlogged world of blue pools and shallow boulevards of snow-melt running through steep meadows. Near the top, shields of ice armoured the lee side of the rocks.

At the summit of the pass we came to an *ovoo*, one of the tall cairns of stones that mark significant points in the Mongolian landscape. *Ovoos* are an ancient tradition, shrines erected by local travellers to the spirits of the place to ensure good fortune for their journeys. They reminded me of coral formations, growing organically and outlandishly over long years. Each person who passes adds a stone to the cairn; those who hope for specific assistance or protection from the spirits often add an offering as well, some memento of themselves. With time the *ovoos* become strange spiritual junk heaps piled with the debris of Mongolian life – coloured bits of cloth torn from clothing, small banknotes and coins, empty vodka bottles, shotgun cartridges, animal skulls, old bridles, a boot, a roof pole from a *ger* – a rickety construction of anxieties and hopes.

On this wide saddle the *ovoo* was almost twenty feet high. We dismounted and walked our horses around it three times in a clockwise direction as tradition dictated, adding a few rocks to the cairn as we went. Ganbold lit a small pile of incense on one of the stones then plucked a strand of hair from his horse's mane and tied it to the broken barrel of a gun that someone had placed there years ago perhaps in the hope of better hunting.

'For good luck,' he called, looking up at me. 'For our journey.' His smile seemed unconvincing. In the strong winds the incense glowed briefly then went out, and the tiny cone of grey ash blew away across the grass. I sat my horse. With its absurd bric-a-brac, the *ovoo* seemed to mock the very aspirations and fears it was meant to allay.

For myself I seemed to have forgotten whatever aspirations and fears I may have had. In the immense solitude of these places, with the great bare summits all about us breasting distant reaches of sky, I felt completely liberated from my own desires. I was content with the physical sensation of the present, the feeling of this pass between two deep valleys, the scent of snow, the endless waves of grass, the magnificent sweep of landscape below, the horses jerking their heads, eager to push on. This present, as insistent as the winds tugging at our clothes, was so wonderful to me that I could think of nothing else.

Friar William's guides through these mountains could think only of demons. A host of malevolent spirits was said to inhabit such vertiginous regions and to carry off travellers mysteriously. Sometimes they seized the horse, leaving the rider behind to the mercy of the weather. Other times they would pull out a man's innards, leaving a corpse on the horse. The guides, who took William for a European shaman, pleaded with him for some spell to ward off these evil spirits. The friar, rather unnerved himself by the loneliness of the place with its 'dreadful crags', took to chanting Credo in Unum Deum in a loud voice. Impressed by the effectiveness of William's magic, the guides asked for charms. William provided them with the Creed and the Lord's Prayer written out on small squares of paper which the guides solemnly stuck to their foreheads.

It seemed to work. They managed to slip through the Altay without being disembowelled. So did we. Ganbold's pile of incense was as deserving as the Lord's Prayer.

We rode on through the afternoon, following a milky river down the other side of the pass to the *ger* of another of Ganbold's aunts, a very erect regal-looking woman who invited us in for tea and biscuits, served with bowls of creamy butter. The aunt was married to the brother of last night's host. I was beginning to appreciate the intricate and rather claustrophobic family relationships of these mountains. To me the Altay were an infinite landscape where the nearest neighbour was four hours' ride away. To its inhabitants, the mountains were like a small village where gossip was the chief staple of conversation. Ganbold reported on the shaman and his bossy wife, on the family of the Camp of the Dung Heap with their three daughters still unmarried, and on the unsuitable husband of our lunch *ger* who, not content with his saddle extravagance, had been boasting about buying a motorcycle. Our hosts nodded knowingly, their prejudices confirmed.

In the late afternoon light we crossed a vast marshy plain towards the east, the horses paddling in the sodden grass, their leggy shadows stretching ahead of us. Plovers were calling across these wetlands. When we breasted a low ridge we found ourselves looking down on a round lake whose surface held the pristine reflection of a single *ger* pitched picturesquely on the far shore.

When we rode up we found two young girls milking a herd of shaggy ginger-haired yaks. Yak milking is a tough job requiring nerves of steel, a domineering manner, and a weightlifter's build. The consensus in Mongolia is that it is best left to the womenfolk. The girls were bullying the big beasts with resounding slaps on their hindquarters while their three older brothers, weedy boys conspiring in adolescent silence, were inside the *ger* where Mummy was serving them bowls of warm yak milk.

Our host, the younger brother of Ganbold's grandfather, was something of a yak himself – a huge grizzly fellow with a long obstinate face and mournful eyes beneath a shaggy wool cap. He rode up on a fine paint horse, scattering his sons who took refuge in Granny's *ger* next door. He took his place without speaking, and accepted a bowl of tea from his silent wife. Then he farted thunderously, and asked what news I had brought.

'News?' I said. 'No news.' I sympathized with his sons. With his head lowered the Yak was eyeing me over the rim of his bowl as if he was debating whether he should charge or just piss on my leg.

'NO NEWS!' Badam bellowed. 'You come from Hovd, and you have no news! You ride through the Altay and you have no news!'

I made with the news. 'Pastures are poor between here and Hovd,' I burbled. 'It has been such a dry spring. But it rained all day yesterday towards Dutt. The family of your niece have a new lamb, last of the season it seems. Name of Stalin. Ochir has bought a new saddle, very expensive apparently. Couple of horses died in the three-year-old races at the Naadam at Hovd. Wrestling matches were jolly exciting . . .'

Unimpressed by such stale news, Badam didn't wait for the full translation. His wife produced some lamb bones and we sat about gnawing them for a time. Then Badam fetched the milk vodka out of the bag hanging behind him. Mongolian *gers* are regular liquor stores. As well as the inevitable *airag*, the alcoholic mare's milk fermented in goatskins, most Mongolian households also produce *arkhi*, a clear spirit distilled from milk. *Arkhi* is an unpredictable tipple, a sort of liquid land mine.

Pouring it from a plastic jerrycan, Badam handed it to each of us in turn in a small china bowl. We performed the requisite rituals, tossing a pinch of liquid to the sky, to the hearth of the *ger* and then to our own foreheads before drinking. Badam seemed to soften slightly when he saw I knew the form. I sipped, then held tight while the *arkhi* detonated somewhere behind my eyeballs.

Now dinner was complete, Badam settled back like a saloon bar raconteur and embarked upon a long story about a monster who lived in the lake – a huge black bird that comes out only at night. He has seen it three times. Its wing spread is wider than a *ger*, he said, and it makes a soft humming noise. He believed it to be the product of a union between an eagle and a yak. He was impressed when I told him about the Loch Ness monster which seemed to leave his bird a poor second in the monster stakes. But Ganbold rather undermined the hardy allure of Scotland by informing him that it was a country where the men wore skirts.

Later when I made my way back to my tent, pitched on a ledge above the lake just out of sight of the *ger*, I discovered I had been burgled. My cameras and my priceless saddle, the envy of Mongolia, had been left untouched. The thief, who must have crept into the tent while we were at dinner, had sought out more precious items: a small mirror, a pair of nail clippers, a packet of Bold's Marlboros, and our entire supply of chocolate digestive biscuits. The thief had been so excited by the biscuits that he had eaten them all at the scene of the crime, leaving only the empty box and a litter of crumbs behind.

In the morning the camp was in upheaval as the three sons prepared to set off for the Naadam in Mönkh Khairkhan. In the *ger* the eldest, a bit of a dandy, was going through the chests round the perimeter of the tent, trying on various combinations of clothes. He settled finally on a pair of rather queer jodhpurs and a frilly white shirt. Had any of his sisters been to hand, they might have helpfully pointed out that the shirt was actually a girl's blouse. 'I am looking for a wife,' he confided, as he struggled with the silk-covered buttons. He looked to me expectantly as if I might be able to offer a few tips. I decided the best thing was to lend him some lip salve for his cracked lips so he wouldn't be tempted by his sister's lipstick.

After breakfast I mentioned the Great Biscuit Caper to Badam. He was visibly upset that guests under his protection had suffered such an indignity. He said he would make enquiries about any suspicious individuals in the neighbourhood and I gave him a description of the suspect: well-manicured, smoking Western ciga-rettes, a known associate of chocolate biscuits. But when we rode away towards Mönkh Khairkhan I stopped on a low ridge and got out my binoculars. In front of the *ger* I could see Badam horsewhipping his eldest son, the boy in the girl's blouse. I sus-pected he had the right man.

The wind pushed all day at our backs. The snow-capped summit of Mönkh Khairkhan, the second highest peak in Mongolia, loomed ahead of us, trailing long scarves of cloud. In mid-morning we crossed a swollen river. The water was up to the horses' bellies, and they stumbled as they searched for footing on the loose stones of the river bed.

Later we dropped down into a long stony valley where a white river pooled into a series of lakes. An hour's ride up the valley we came to the *ger* of Ganbold's cousin's wife's stepbrother. Dinner was the inevitable bowl of sheep parts. Our host fetched out the ovaries and presented them to me as a special treat.

The weather was turning again. All night a howling wind rattled the tent.

We spent the following day at the Mönkh Khairkhan Naadam. A couple of hundred racegoers had gathered in a small plain between low hills when the heavens opened suddenly in an apocalyptic deluge. In the shelterless plain the whole assembly hunched their shoulders, turned their backs to the driving rain, and watched the water run from the brim of their hats for the next four hours. It was bitterly cold, and entirely miserable.

When the clouds eventually lifted, everyone was keen to make up for lost time. Vodka and *arkhi* bottles were produced from the folds of *dels*, groundsheets were laid on the wet grass, and boisterous drinking parties got underway. Within minutes the most enthusiastic were roaring drunk.

Sadly I wasn't in the mood for binge drinking on a windswept hillside. The rain seemed to have crept into my soul. I climbed into the back of a lorry to stretch out and read a book. My solitude was shattered by the sudden arrival of an elderly gentleman in a sodden scarlet *del* and a battered trilby. Toppling from the sides of the truck into my lap, he seemed to arrive from the newly-blue heaven.

He had come to tell me he loved me. He peered into my eyes then took one of my hands between his and pressed it to his cheek. He seemed on the verge of tears. He was breathing heavily and the vodka fumes were beginning to make me dizzy. Once or twice he was about to speak but emotion got the better of him.

After a time he recovered himself. 'Stalin,' he sighed, 'we will

Choosing a horse, Namarjin Valley

The author and the indomitable Fred, Khentii

Summer pastures,
Mönkh Khairkhan

Yak milking, Altay
Mountains

Lunch is served, a Kazakh ger, Bayan Ölgii

Packing for departure

A Mongol archer, the Naadam
Festival, Hovd

A couple of lightweights, the
Naadam Festival

The eagle hunter, Bayan Ölgii

The guide and her daughter, Dadal

Before the battle, the newly-weds, Arhangay

Migration, Altay Mountains

Preparations for goat stew, Zag

The three musketeers, Arhangay

The old lama, Ikh Tamir, Tsetserleg

The site of ancient Qaraqorum,
capital of the Mongol Empire and
centre of the thirteenth century
world.

always be together.' He was fighting the lump in his throat. 'We cannot survive if we are parted. You know that, don't you.'

My inamorato was sixty years old with yellow teeth, a whiskered face and breath that made him a fire hazard. He had hold of my hand as if he never intended to let it go. He made a sucking noise through his lips like some facsimile of sobbing. In his drunken state seventy years of propaganda about Mongolian-Russian friendship had curdled into sentimentality.

'Together in 1921,' he said. 'Together again in 1945 against the Japanese militarists. We are comrades. We cannot be parted. Russians and Mongolians have been comrades for seventy years.' He pressed me with a mighty bear-hug into the bosom of his *del* which, after the morning rain, had the consistency of day-old trifle. I mumbled something reassuring into the wet wool. It seemed churlish at this point to try to inform my new comrade that I wasn't Russian.

Then he asked if he could kiss me. Without waiting for a reply he seized my face in his two enormous hands and planted a sloppy kiss on each cheek. 'Comrades,' he cried. 'We must exchange hats.' His hat was in character with the rest of his outfit. It looked as if his horse had slept on it.

I was rescued by the races. High-pitched cheering arose on all sides announcing the approach of the leading horses. Momentarily distracted the old man released his hold on me and I was able to escape over the side of the lorry without further tears.

We were entering a landscape of elemental simplicity. The complexities of the mountains, the escarpments, the steep passes, the abrupt valleys, were unravelling into a country of languorous horizontals. Treeless, smooth as felt, and thick with wild flowers, long vistas of grass were draped between soft hills. With miles of nothing between them, the domes of the *gers* echoed the gentle curves of the country. On distant hillsides, herds of horses galloped in slow motion.

In Mönkh Khairkhan, Ganbold had handed us on to one of his students whose family we found camped at the top of a slope of wild primulas, anemones, and musk orchids. Ajii was a strapping lad of nineteen with the manners of a shy schoolgirl. I was the first foreigner he had met, and for the first day he never took his eyes off me in case he missed something. Among the horses he brought for us was a handsome paint gelding which I was delighted to take. Spirited and intelligent, he had a high-arched neck and a long narrow face like a medieval saint.

We rode away through a series of narrow defiles full of blue delphiniums and purple rock. When we emerged, the landscape unrolled before us, pristine expanses of grass adrift among cloud shadows. We passed *gers* ensconced in waves of sheep, and riders returning from Mönkh Khairkhan with their Naadam horses caparisoned with ribbons. A strong westerly wind was blowing and skylarks wheeled over the grass.

We rode for four days towards the south-east through a dry and largely uninhabited country. On the first evening we climbed to a rocky ridge where, in another land, in another age, a feudal baron would have built a castle with a commanding views into two valleys. Instead there was only a poor-looking *ger* in the thickening twilight guarded by a dozen sentinel camels. Inside we found a sullen group of men slumped around the stove in the chiaroscuro of a pair of guttering candles. A huge woman with a broken nose offered us bowls of thin gruel from a pot on the stove. When she had finished hers she tossed the dregs out the door to the dogs, rolled away into the shadows, belching milkily, and began to snore. The men grunted monosyllabically to our greetings. They were all drunk. They handed round a tin pail of *arkhi*, staring at us and our things over its rim, as if assessing the best moment to strike. When they fell to quarrelling among themselves we slipped outside, unhobbled our horses and rode away in the moonlight to another empty ridge where we pitched our camp.

On the second day we descended a long stony valley where yaks were gambolling under the command of a long-haired bull. A river appeared, twisting through rose-coloured rock. At the bottom of the valley it flowed through a small canyon at whose far end, on shelves of lavender and soft grass, we made a fine camp. In the evening we bathed in the deep clear pools of the river, washed our clothes and dried them by the fire.

On the third day we crossed the plain of Möst where wild herbs grew among the stones. In the still hot air the mingling odours of rosemary, lavender and chives rose from beneath our horses' hooves. We camped that night where a frail river petered to a mysterious conclusion in shoals of gravel and sand.

In the morning I was awoken by a stranger who poked his head into my tent to ask if I had seen his camels. When I emerged some minutes later the man had vanished, as if he had dropped off the edge of the world in the wake of his animals. The sky was tall and white. Far away in the east a salt lake floated in empty air. To the north a range of camel-coloured mountains climbed to snow peaks.

We rode all day down the monotonous length of the plain among the chives and the lizards and the small flies that fretted the horses. In the vastness of the place our progress seemed so slow we might have been standing still. The plain shimmered. To the east of us the lost camels had appeared, paddling in fantasies of water. When we reached the foot of the mountains we were met by a new wind, cool and fresh and smelling of stones. We climbed for over an hour, the horses stumbling among loose rocks. On the escarpments above mountain goats peered down at us from vertical rock faces.

At day's end on the far side of the mountains we looked down on a large encampment of *gers* scattered across a grassy valley. The sweet sounds of nomadic domesticity drifted up to us – children's voices, dogs barking, the bleating of sheep, neighbours calling to one another across the golden pastures.

Tuvud was a literary man with a flowery sash, a young wife, and a vodka habit. He had a rumpled face like an unmade bed with grey whiskers, broken yellow teeth and a wide flattened nose bearing a delta of red veins. He reminded me of a down-at-heel Edwardian gentleman, wedded to the manners, the ideas and the accessories of another age. In his case the latter included a decorated horsewhip, a bowler hat, a knife in an elaborate scabbard tucked into the back of his sash, and a traditional long-stemmed pipe and tobacco pouch on a heavy silver chain, the trappings of a Mongolian swell in 1910.

His *ger* was a fabulous clutter. Red and gold painted chests with elaborate locks were piled around the walls. Oil paintings of him and his wife stood on a dresser among a display of medals and a souvenir clock in the shape of the Leaning Tower of Pisa. Silver bridles hung from roof poles, and a collection of silver bowls was arrayed across a low table. Tuvud came from an old and illustrious family; his great-uncle was Aldanjavyn Ayush, the partisan whose rather forlorn statue stands in the square in Hovd, but his family could trace their ancestry, he said solemnly, to Genghis Khan. Tuvud himself had been to Europe and America, touring with a Mongolian cultural group in the mid-1960s, reading extracts from his interminable verses.

He was a shepherd, he said, of images and stories. His books were stored in saddle-bags, tied with string inside grey oily cloths. There were volumes of poetry, biographies, humorous histories, an account of legendary Mongolian heroes, a book about fantastical animals including the yeti who is said to inhabit the mountain range we had crossed the day before. Thin softback editions, unravelling at the seams, the books were as light as birds. They threatened to disintegrate in our hands, as if books in a nomadic society were as vulnerable as timber in a world of termites or leather in the dank humidity of jungles.

Tuvud's wife served us tea from an old-fashioned copper kettle while he sang a song about a horse. Mongolians have as many ways of describing horses as the Inuit have words for snow, and the song went on for a bit. But Tuvud's real passion was carving. He drew a great tangle of keys from the depths of his *del* and began to unlock the ornate chests. They were a treasure trove. One by one he lifted out carvings swaddled in rags. Miniature horses and ibex, mountains goats and yaks gathered round his feet. There were twisting snakes, a mother breast-feeding an infant, a Tsaatan riding a reindeer, men wrestling with wolves, men on horseback. Each one was a legend. He threw back the lids of more and more chests, the museum of his life, and the herds of carved figures spilled across the floor of the *ger*.

In the bottom of one chest he found a carving of himself wrestling a wolf. It was one of his favourites. Tuvud was in the Hemingway mould, pitting his own life against those of his characters. Killing a wolf is the defining moment in the life of any Mongolian hero, and the carving celebrated the fact that he had killed six.

'One of them has also carved me,' he joked. He held up his fore-finger which was missing its tip.

I asked what he had thought of the West, if it had been as he had expected. He said the biggest surprise was the lack of crimi-nality. What limited material he had been able to study before his departure – films chiefly – had led him to expect a good deal of gunfire in the streets. For the first few days the wolf wrestler had not dared leave his hotel for fear of being caught in the crossfire. A descendant of Genghis Khan, arriving from the steppes of Central Asia, his anxiety about London, Paris and New York had been of barbarian lawlessness. He was quite right of course. Compared to any city in the West, Outer Mongolia was a model of law-abiding order.

There was one book he still hoped to write, he said. It would be about the way people have adapted to the market system after almost seventy years of Communism, the way a nation overnight had abandoned its belief in collective endeavour for the new mantra of market forces.

'A tragedy?' I suggested.

'No, no,' he said. 'A farce.'

Chapter Nine

ON THE EDGE OF THE GOBI

On the maps pale shades of desert now crowded our route. We were emerging from the foothills of the Altay, framed in reassuring cartographic browns and greens, and entering reaches denoted by bleached tones. A rather sinister-looking white spread eastwards, streaked with the blue of salt pans. This was the Shargyn Gobi, a northern colony of the greater Gobi which lay to the south along the Chinese border. The new colours threatened a parched void of dead rivers and spiralling temperatures. For the past week route discussions over the boiled mutton in *gers* along our way had focused on the impossibility of crossing these desert wastes. No one would be willing to accompany us on this stage, and no one would subject their horses to conditions where there would be neither grazing nor water.

There were always camels of course, but I had long since forsworn them as a means of transport. In my experience camels are evil-tempered beasts with an attitude problem, appalling personal hygiene and an irritating habit of spitting at you when the going gets tough. My only pleasurable encounter with a camel was when I once ate one in northern Sudan, and even that experience was spoiled by sand, an alarming quantity of which had blown into the pot. Barring camels, the only option was to take a jeep to the *aimag* centre of Gobi-Altay across 150 miles of the worst of the desert. From there we could continue our journey by horse. Over lunch in someone's *ger* we met the director of a local coal mine who offered us a lift in his jeep to Dariv, some twenty miles away, where we could look for a jeep to Gobi-Altay.

The director had a suit jacket and a pot-belly, both a rarity in Mongolia. His mines were threatened with closure and I tried to cheer him up by telling him about the collapse of the British coal industry. Tuvud travelled with us. He had some bureaucratic problem that seemed to turn on the Mongolian equivalent of his National Insurance stamps, and he hoped to be able to sort the matter out with the help of the mayor of Dariv. He fetched his bowler hat, his long-stemmed pipe, and his best Lytton Strachey manner, and climbed into the back of the jeep. The director of mines treated him with the respect due to an older man, but he eyed him warily. He was unaccustomed to artistic types, and seemed to feel it was only a matter of time before Tuvud started with the rhyming couplets.

We toiled through low hills, stripped of grass. In a pass we stopped at an *ovoo* for a drink. As well as being locations of spiritual resonance, *ovoos* play the part of pubs in the Mongolian countryside. When travellers stop at them to pay their respects, one of the more popular rituals is to anoint them with a tot of vodka. Having opened the bottle the custom is to settle down with your travelling companions and finish it off. In this way jeep rides often disintegrate into *ovoo* crawls. Finding ourselves without a glass, the driver ingeniously unscrewed the taillight cover, rinsed it carefully with water from his jug and poured the Genghis Khan vodka. Like its namesake, it packed quite a punch.

After this refreshment we came down from the hills, and sped across a plain as big as Texas. We were entering the fringes of the desert. A line of telegraph poles moored the sky to a landscape of bleak horizontals. Dariv was a smudge in the empty distance, the only town for a hundred miles.

It proved to be a ghost town. The entire population had packed up and gone to summer pastures in the mountains leaving the mayor as the sole inhabitant. Like the captain of a sinking ship, he seemed determined to go down with the town. We found him on his doorstep, a solitary windswept figure, squinting through thick spectacles at the vision of our jeep emerging from a white wilderness.

The mayor's house was arranged like a tent. There was no furniture, only carpets. Against the back wall was the same pile of chests and cheap suitcases that feature in any *ger*. We sat on the floor on the mayor's right while he served us black Russian tea from a Chinese Thermos decorated with a postcard of the lobby of the Mandarin Oriental hotel in Hong Kong. His wife had departed as well, he explained, taking the children to her parents near Hovd for the summer.

The mayor was part of the new breed of politicians in Mongolia, unconnected to the Communist Party and the old regime. Like all nomads, Mongolians are politically conservative. Given the opportunity to vote for the first time in 1990, they promptly re-elected the Communist Party that had ruled for almost seventy years without bothering with elections. But the idea of change eventually percolated from Ulan Batur into the countryside, and the later elections of 1996 had brought the Social Democratic Party to power, mainly men in their thirties with a lot of progressive ideas and no experience of government. Young people were excited by the prospect of a new broom; older people feared they had elected a bunch of undergraduates.

The mayor was the SDP figurehead in these parts. He wanted me to understand he was very much a modern man. He had lived most of his life in Ulan Batur, and had been to university. He also wore shorts, in Mongolia a sure sign of urban sophistication. He commiserated with me about the hardships of the countryside and the difficulties I must have experienced with the herdsmen.

'They are very ignorant people, unused to foreigners,' he said.

I said I had found them very hospitable.

'They drink too much,' the mayor sighed. 'Alcoholism is the bane of this country.'

'Everyone has been very pleasant,' I reassured him.

'Drink, drink, drink.' The mayor was pounding his bare knee. 'How can we modernize in a country where half the male population is drunk all day.'

I hoped our little tipple from the taillight was not too evident, and turned the subject to the next stage of our journey. The mayor was keen to assist. He was sure he could find us a lift with a passing vehicle.

I asked how many jeeps came this way heading east.

'Four or five,' the mayor said.

'A day?'

'Four or five a month,' the mayor said. The paucity of traffic might have discouraged others but the mayor, new to executive power, was sanguine.

'I will inform the petrol station,' he said. 'Everyone needs to stop here for petrol. I will give instructions vehicles are not to be given petrol until they have spoken to me.'

It was the hitchhiker's dream. No driver was to be allowed to leave town without us before he had been interrogated by the mayor. Pumped up with the authority of his office, he smiled reassuringly at us.

Tuvud saw this as his moment to broach the pension problem. To get things off on the right foot he withdrew a bottle of Genghis Khan from his *del*. This seemed rather rash in view of the mayor's views about drinking but old habits die hard. A bowl was produced and handed round. The mayor made a face as he drank.

Thus fortified Tuvud embarked upon the labyrinthine tale of his pension. I saw him suddenly, with his bowler hat and his pipe, as Vladimir in *Waiting for Godot*. With a sad and defeated air, he was Waiting For His Pension. Apparently he had been waiting for his pension for years, and the waiting had become part of his persona. He led the mayor slowly through the bureaucratic thicket that was his social security history. Pensions in Mongolia were linked to the number of years a person had worked in his *negdel*, the herding collectives of the Communist era. A writer, with books rather than sheep, was difficult to fit into the system. The mayor listened patiently, and made a few notes. The exchange had the air of a ritual that was performed to keep faith with Tuvud's years of waiting, rather than in the hope of any immediate outcome. The vodka played a useful role here. After a few rounds of Genghis Khan, the pension began to seem insignificant, even to Tuvud.

With the pension question satisfactorily disposed of, the mayor announced he would open the hotel for us. He searched in one of the chests for the keys and we set off through the empty town. The buildings looked forlorn and ruinous. We passed boarded up kiosks and abandoned houses whose loose boards flapped in the wind. Litter blew through the deserted streets. The whole party had become involved in our fate – the mayor, the director of mines, Tuvud, the jeep driver. They all seemed delighted to have something to do. Boredom wafted through the streets on the sultry desert winds.

The hotel was one of Dariv's more substantial edifices with proper windows and doors. The mayor led the way upstairs, and we all trooped after him, our riding boots resounding on the bare plank floors. Fumbling with the keys at the end of a bleak corridor he opened the best room. Inside it was like a furniture store. Huge dark bureaux filled the small room. Once we had all crowded inside there was barely space to turn around. The jeep driver punched one of the mattresses to check for buoyancy. Tuvud looked out the window to inspect the view, a vista of bleak plains studded with thorn bushes. The director of mines opened and closed the drawers of a dresser, nodding sagely.

'Romania,' the mayor said proudly. He knocked loudly on the side of a wardrobe in which you could have stabled horses. 'Solid mahogany. All the furniture was sent from Romania as part of a development package some years ago.'

I imagined Ceaucescu's state reception rooms had been full of this kind of stuff – heavy, monumental, highly polished, rather sinister. Deployed across the vast spaces of one of his kitsch palaces, they must have been appropriately intimidating. Here in the twelve by twelve foot square of a Mongolian hotel room, they lost a little of their splendour.

Once Bold and I had been ensconced in the Romanian suite, the whole party retired to a room next door which, being unencumbered with Romanian aid, had space to sit down. It was now the turn of the director of mines to produce a bottle of Genghis Khan from his inside pocket. Mongolians on a day out, I was beginning to realize, were like a travelling bar. The driver was despatched to fetch bowls from the hotel kitchen in lieu of a taillight.

The mayor grimaced elaborately each time the bowl came round to him. He shook his head after he had supped as if trying to keep his mind clear.

'Nepotism,' he said suddenly. 'That is the problem of Mongolia. Nepotism, corruption, lethargy and greed.' I could not help but notice that vodka had fallen off the list. 'We are a new generation,' the mayor said. 'It is our responsibility to free Mongolia of its bad habits.'

Sadly the other members of our party were not fully up to speed with the new regime, and were keen to play court to the mayor as if he was a Stalinist with a drink problem. When they had finished the director's bottle, the mayor threw it out the window and the driver was despatched to the jeep to fetch another. The mayor sat back on one of the beds, grinning foolishly, his face flushed.

'Irresponsibility,' he mused. He seemed now to be talking to himself. 'The herdsman only thinks of this year, this season. They cannot plan for the future.' He raised his arms then let them fall again to his sides in a gesture of defeat.

Bold and I, seeing our chance, made our excuses and retired, squeezing into our room among the Romanian mammoths. Bold stood by the window looking out on the empty town.

'Before 1990 there would have been people here, even in the summer,' he said. 'Now everyone has become a herdsman again.'

All over the Communist world the collapse of the old regimes brought inevitable hardships. In Mongolia the transition to a market economy was exacerbated by the withdrawal of Russian subsidies. The Soviet Union's strategic interests in Mongolia had led to a level of financial subsidy that had allowed the country to live far beyond its means. For a poorly developed nomadic society with a subsistence economy and little hard currency, Mongolia enjoyed remarkable social services with education, health and pension systems that few Third World countries could aspire to. The Russian support that artificially maintained these systems amounted to as much as $800 million US dollars a year, about $400 for each Mongolian, a figure higher than the per capita GDP. By 1990, when the Russians went home, Mongolia's cumulative debt to the USSR was said to be six billion US dollars.

Within months of the end of the Russian subsidies Mongolia was broke. Inflation, devaluation, shortages, rationing all followed quickly on one another. Most state industries, centred around Ulan Batur, were crippled, and in the countryside everything from local power stations to medical clinics closed down. Their employees, most of them first and second generation townsfolk, returned to their family pastures. Mongolia became one of the only places in the world where the drift to cities, common in underdeveloped countries, was reversed. In their hour of need urban Mongolians were rescued by the self-sufficiency of the nomadic life to which the rest of their countrymen had clung tenaciously for millennia. The lesson was not lost on traditionalists.

Few people spoke of the dark years of 1991 and 92. Mongolians are an intensely proud people, and their reduction to a state of penury was not a topic for discussion with foreigners. When I had broached the subject with Bold he had restricted his comments to generalities. Now this ghost town had brought it all back.

'Things were very bad in Ulan Batur,' Bold sighed. 'The food shops were empty. Some of the stores were even selling off their shelving. Sometimes I queued for hours for bread.'

We had stretched out on the two Romanian beds, happy to have a moment of peace. Dariv might have been an empty town but our vodka-drinking companions and the feverish mayor had a way of making it seem crowded.

'Things were desperate,' Bold said. 'I knew people who went hungry. How could that be possible in Mongolia, where there are more sheep than people?'

'Ten times more sheep,' I reminded him.

He was silent for a time, drawing on his cigarette, sending long channels of blue smoke towards the ceiling.

'I'm not a Marxist,' he said. 'I didn't support the Communist Party. In fact our KGB had a file on me. I was part of the pro-democracy movement. But now I am not so confident about the free market. Perhaps it is not suited to a country like Mongolia. How can a herdsman, a thousand miles from a market, be a part of a market economy in a country without roads or trains?'

'Sometimes I feel guilty,' he went on. 'When the Communists were in power, we thought only of the corruption, the oppression, the lack of democracy. We wanted capitalism because we wanted choices. We wanted to vote, to read the truth in the newspapers, to travel abroad, to buy Western goods. But these were our concerns, the concerns of people with salaries in Ulan Batur. To the herdsman in the countryside what did they matter?'

He gestured to the empty window. 'Here in Dariv the medical

centre is closed. There used to be doctors here who went out to the countryside, to the most remote *gers* if they were needed. Now that is gone. There was a school here that was free for everyone. Now the herdsmen have to pay to send their children to school, and many of them cannot afford it.' He twisted his face into an expression of distaste. 'So now they get to vote every five years. Now they have a mayor of their choosing. So what? It doesn't bring the doctors back.'

'Change was inevitable,' I said.

'Of course,' he said. He turned his hands upward in some admission of reality. 'It is easy to forget how insane the old system had become. It was rotten. No one told the truth any more, about anything. We were living in a fantasy of lies. But the changes . . .' he drew a hand across his forehead. 'Everything happened too quickly. Everything seemed to collapse overnight and now we have to begin again. Everything that had become . . .' he searched for a word '. . . civilized – education, health – was lost and people here have gone back to an earlier time, fending only for themselves.'

We could hear the drone of voices from the men next door, rising slightly in vodka-induced certainties. 'When we were at school we were taught the history of Marxism,' Bold said. His own voice had dropped to a confessional murmur. 'That it was a system based on economic principles. But it wasn't, at least not here. You have seen the towns. In every one a theatre, a school, a clinic. This was not economics. It was idealism.'

From the window came the sound of the wind keening around the corners of the abandoned town. 'In this new world of the market there is no room for such idealism,' Bold said. 'Now we have economics. If we have doctors it is only because we can pay for them. Not because they are right or necessary. This is what is difficult to accept.' He looked across at me. His face was a troubled mask. 'The end of idealism. It feels like a kind of barbarism.'

Later that evening we were awoken by a knock at the door. It was dark, and in the confusion of furniture and interrupted sleep, I walked into two wardrobes before finding the door.

The jeep driver stood outside in the corridor holding a candle. '*Machine bain*,' he whispered. A vehicle had arrived.

Bold and I followed him through the empty town. Night had brought a desert chill. Above us the Gobi sky was packed with constellations. I examined my watch in their faint light. It was only 11 o'clock.

We came around the corner of a building to find a huge articulated lorry parked outside the mayor's house. A spacecraft could hardly have been more surprising. The nearest paved road was five hundred miles away, in Russia. Suddenly here was the kind of vehicle I was used to seeing thundering down the middle lane of the M25.

An interior light, the only light in this dark town, illuminated the cab. Inside, pressed against the windows, was a row of strange faces.

One of the doors swung open and Bold and I were hauled up into a squirming mass of people crammed into the cab. There appeared to be at least six strange men inside, who presumably had come with the truck, as well as our friends from the afternoon. The director of mines was pinned against the far door while Tuvud was pressed onto the dashboard like a flattened ornament, his bowler hat pushed down over his ears. Everyone was roaring drunk.

I glimpsed the mayor beneath three other people on the passenger's side. His face, the colour of beetroot, was fixed in terrible smiling grimace as if in this melée of limbs he had just realized he had been parted from a leg.

'Foreigner,' he giggled. His voice had risen several octaves. 'There are no horses. There are no horses anywhere.' He was struggling to free himself from the pile of bodies. 'Comrade foreigner,' he gasped for breath. 'We have found a truck.'

Under the pressure of bodies a door sprang open again, and two men tumbled out. Other men struggled to pull them back like drowning sailors being hauled aboard a dangerously overcrowded life raft.

We were parked on the edge of the Gobi, in a country so vast you could go for days without seeing anyone. For some deranged reason, everyone in this empty town had decided to crowd into a confined space the size of a w.c.

My presence seemed to bring them to their senses. Trying to shoehorn the tall sober foreigner into this crush suddenly alerted them to the absurdity of the whole enterprise. A consensus mysteriously emerged that the cab was a trifle crowded and we should transfer to the mayor's house. One by one everyone was pulled outside. There were a few dissenters and thus plenty of opportunity to do some counter-pulling. It was all frightfully merry.

The mayor was legless. He made his way inside his own house by clinging to my neck. Somewhere in the course of the evening's adventures he had torn his shirt and scraped his knees. Blood was oozing down his shins. With his shorts and his skinned knees and his glasses askew he was like the good schoolboy led hopelessly astray by the boys from the back of the class.

We got him inside without further mishap, and deposited him on the floor. The modern face of Mongolia was not an encouraging sight, slumped drunkenly against the wall, chewing the tails of his shirt, mumbling inanities.

In the beginning the desert wore a transparent veil of grass that revealed the flesh-coloured soil beneath. Adrift in the hot expanses were small rounded hills riding like whales in silver mirages of water. Occasionally we passed herds of camels trotting stiff-legged away from the track. There was no sign of people. As the morning dragged on, the grasses thinned until the landscape was reduced to dust blowing away beneath the eighteen wheels of the big truck.

The truck had come from Russia. Its cargo was two enormous steel plates, 4" thick, and probably fifteen foot across. Under their incalculable weight, the truck laboured through its gears, barely able to reach a top speed of thirty miles an hour. The plates were bound for a construction site in Ulan Batur. Presumably they were too wide for the freight cars of the Trans-Siberian, and the brave decision had been taken to load them onto the flatbed of this lorry and try to drive them across the wild tracks of Mongolia.

If the journey was like a sea crossing, the truck was a ship of fools. The captain, a short impish Mongolian driver in a baseball cap, had set sail almost six weeks ago in this behemoth from Barnaul in the Russian province of Gorny-Altay. At the Mongolian border the asphalt had run out. From Bayan Ölgii he had struck south-east, as we had done. Fortunately he had not been obliged to visit any of Ganbold's relations, and so had avoided the more mountainous stretches. Among the meandering tracks, he had pulled up at remote *gers*, frightening the horses and scattering the sheep, to ask directions. When there were no *gers* he had navigated by the sun and the stars.

In ports along the way he had collected a crew of fellow travellers who had found places in steerage – the open deck of the flatbed atop the steel plates, cushioned on a great mound of sacks that the captain had taken aboard as private freight. In Bayan Ölgii a pair of silent twins had joined the truck, tall gaunt men with *dels* that came down to their ankles. They were travelling to Dornod in the north-east of the country for reasons that no one was able to fathom. Somewhere in Kazakh country a man and his young daughter had walked out of the hills to flag them down. He was a coarse figure with a harelip and gabled eyebrows. A driver himself, he had slid into the role of first mate, occasionally taking the wheel when drink or exhaustion overcame the captain. He was a wayward tempestuous character and his daughter, a very serious girl of seven, struggled to keep him in line with a maternal authority.

In Hovd the driver's girlfriend had joined the truck with sacks of vegetables, presumably grown among the dust of the old Chinese city, that she hoped to sell in Ulan Batur. Attentive and selfless, she was his nursemaid, always by his side, mopping his brow, massaging his neck muscles, pouring him draughts of water from a plastic jug at her feet. A couple and their young son had also signed on in Hovd. She was a peevish disapproving figure. She rode in the cab wearing a white face mask against the dust, cradling the boy in her lap. The husband, who had clearly done much to inspire her career of disapproval, was a key figure in the drinking escapades that were such a feature of the voyage. He rode in the back wrapped in a tarpaulin with a weightlifter travelling to Ulan Batur to visit his mother whom he had not seen since the age of eight. A gang of young rowdies formed the bulk of the ratings, a piratical crew perched at the very back of the flatbed where the dust and the ride were the roughest. The least of their number was the cabin boy, a

Dickensian vagabond of no fixed address, travelling the length of Mongolia because he had nowhere else to go. His trousers, torn and patched, were held up with string. His toes protruded through the ends of broken shoes. He was covered with a dark film of engine oil, and whenever we stopped he clambered over the truck cleaning the windscreen, checking the oil, the water levels, the tyre pressures. He was the only reliable person on board.

The ride to Altay, some 120 miles, took eighteen hours. It felt like a week. It ranks as the worst day of my entire journey. Imprisoned in this wretched truck, I thought longingly of camels. With gears grinding we lumbered in and out of deep ruts, swaying and pitching like a galleon in high seas. I rode in the cabin which had the suspension of a child's tricycle. It was noisy and cramped, but as nothing compared to the open deck of the flatbed where the misery of the others was cloaked in choking clouds of dust. Eighteen wheels meant that we travelled inside our own dense sandstorm.

We had no food. No one appeared to have eaten in twenty-four hours. We stopped only for grog. Bottles of Genghis Khan seemed to be secreted in every nook and cranny of this ship, and captain and crew were in need of continual refuelling. By midday everyone was drunk again. Sometime in the afternoon we had a puncture and while the vagabond boy repaired it the senior members of the crew demolished another three bottles.

The disapproving woman took me aside and said she hoped I would not think that all Mongolians were like this. Her husband, standing on the front bumper, swathed in dust and bits of tarpaulin, was roaring drunkenly at the sun. A fight had broken out between one of the twins and the first mate, and the captain was throwing up over the front wheels.

'Of course not,' I said.

At day's end a yellow gale began to blow. Provinces of dust rose into the air and swept back and forth across the desert, thickening our own sandstorm into a preternatural gloom. The deck crew swaddled their heads in cloths like Bedouin. Through this swirling maelstrom, the spectacular sunset might have been announcing the end of the world.

We arrived in Gobi-Altay at 2 am. The truck deposited us in a dark street outside a dark hotel then disappeared again into the night, its tail-lights bouncing away like errant stars, bound for Ulan Batur. We pounded on the door until a sleepy woman appeared. By candlelight she ushered us upstairs. We left a trail of Gobi sand along the bare corridors.

This arrival wasn't exactly a Gary Cooper Moment either.

Altay marked the end of Bold's contract. He was returning to Ulan Batur, and a new translator was coming out from the capital to join me. He had been a loyal friend, and I was sad to see him go though I felt he needed a break. He was a fastidious fellow and two days labouring under a trickling cold water tap in the hotel in Altay, trying to wash the dust of the Gobi from every fabric of his being and his belongings, seemed to have subdued even his good nature. He worried how I would cope without him. At the airport he was paternal, fussing over my arrangements for the next stage of the journey, warning me about the horsemen's charges and cautioning me to get fuel for the stove before I left Altay. I feared in a moment he was going to remind to wash behind my ears. We shook hands and the Gobi winds blew him across the dust runway to an ageing twin-propellered Russian Antonov.

The next day Mandah arrived. She had just graduated from the Foreign Languages Institute at the State University, and had come to me through contacts in Ulan Batur. Though she was a city girl, she arrived full of enthusiasm for the trip. She had a moon-round face, and the uncomplicated optimism and ambition of youth.

We left the same day for the countryside, with a driver I met in the hotel. He had a brother-in-law near Guulin to the north-east of Altay whom he thought would be able to act as our guide for the next stage of the journey. We crossed a vast plain tufted with white grass and arrived at a stony valley where four *gers* were camped in the falling twilight.

Sambuu, our prospective guide, had a tragic clown's face with a bulbous red nose and a large rubbery mouth turned down at the corners. He wore a pointed Mongol hat pushed back on the bald dome of his head, revealing a forehead creased with the lines of perpetual anxiety. He smoked a long thin-stemmed Mongolian pipe and had the air of a man expecting the worst.

For Sambuu our arrival was the worst he could expect. When we floated the idea that he might accompany us for four or five days towards Zag his face froze in an expression of theatrical horror. Sambuu was a man of habit, and he let it be known that he was not in the habit of setting off across the open plains with unknown foreigners. His wife however was of a more active persuasion. She saw the ride as a nice little earner and put the heat on him until he relented. He finally agreed only if he was allowed to bring his eldest son as his minder.

In an atmosphere of candlelight and pipe smoke, we discussed terms. Previously I had tried to keep things simple by working on the basis of an all-inclusive daily sum for horses and guides. But the wife was of a more complex turn of mind. Figures were proposed for our horses, other figures suggested for the guides' horses, and a third figure for the guides themselves, Sambuu and his son. The outbound journey was to be reckoned on one scale while their return journey back to Guulin was calculated at another rate. Any reconciliation of the opposing positions on one part of the deal immediately produced a larger discrepancy elsewhere. I felt it would have been easier to negotiate a stock-market flotation.

These protracted dealings were made more complicated by my frequent and very sudden absences. I was suffering from a severe bout of dysentery, and spent much of the evening hurriedly searching for new boulders in the moonlit landscape. The wife inevitably saw these absences as a negotiating ploy and whenever I returned to the *ger* her position had hardened, unlike my bowels. Eventually we hammered out a ramshackle deal that satisfied no one. The following morning, the wife began to renegotiate before we had had our first bowl of tea.

'When democracy came,' Sambuu said, 'I wasn't ready. I wasn't used to thinking for myself.'

Night had fallen, and the sky bristled with stars. In the middle of a vast plain, at the end of our first day's ride, we sat propped up against a low windbreak of saddles and horse blankets. Conversation had turned to politics.

'It took time to adjust to the new ways.' Sambuu shrugged. His clown's face crumpled into a dark frown. 'I lost my job. I dithered when it was the time for action.'

Sambuu had been a jeep driver like his brother-in-law in Gobi-Altay, part of a collective which owned the vehicles and paid the drivers a salary. The collective had been privatized in the early 1990s in the usual messy way, with a confusion of employee vouchers and management buyouts. Some of the drivers, like Sambuu's brother-in-law, had managed to buy their own jeeps from the collective. Unused to the notion of personal risk and unwilling to bet his savings against a future he could not read, Sambuu had returned to traditional Mongolia.

'I went back to the countryside,' he said. 'I didn't know what would happen, with all these new ideas. We weren't used to taking risks.' With a fat thumb he pressed tobacco into the tiny bowl of his pipe. 'It was a whole new way of thinking, to take responsibility like that. The government had always given us direction. Now we were on our own. I was not a young man. It was difficult to adjust.' He shook his head. 'I should have tried to buy a jeep like some of the others. Now they are doing very well. But I was afraid. In the old system, everyone worked together. Now they say we must do everything on our own. If we fail, we fail alone. This is a new world to us. It made me feel old.'

Bold's translation of this would have been halting, as much from his sense of historical burden as from the quality of his English. Mandah translated sympathetically but efficiently. A twenty-year-old, she was free from culpability.

I wasn't. Whatever my own ambivalence about market forces, Sambuu, like most Mongolians, tended to view me as a representative of this New Economic Order. We had won the Cold War, Communism had collapsed, and now the dogma of the free market, which had made the nations of the West so extravagantly rich, which allowed me to travel in distant lands, was to be imported into fragile Mongolia. The collectives were swept away and even the herdsmen, like the jeep drivers of Gobi-Altay, were encouraged to think of themselves as individuals and not as a group.

'What were the difficulties that the transition to democracy caused in your country?' Sambuu asked pulling on his pipe.

'Not so many,' I said. 'In our country it was more gradual.'

'How long did it take?'

'Three or four centuries.'

'You took your time,' Sambuu said. 'We did it in twelve months.'

A star fell down the tremendous sky. Somewhere far off, at a distant *ger*, a dog was barking. Sambuu was watching me over the bowl of his pipe. He had never had any dealings with a foreigner before. He had been taught a distrust of foreigners, particularly Westerners, since childhood, and he was bemused to find himself now escorting one across the steppe.

'Six years ago I would have reported you to the police in Gobi-Altay as a spy,' he said, momentarily cheered by the memory of simpler times. 'Now here we are discussing politics.' He sighed. 'They say you can get used to anything. But I am too old to get used to these changes. It is not the world I understood.' A wave of nostalgia overcame him as he sucked on his pipe. 'Life used to be simpler. I was a member of the collective, the government told us what to do, we didn't bother with all this voting nonsense, and you were an enemy alien. Those were good old days. Before our misfortunes. Before Freedom.'

In the morning we woke to the sound of seagulls crying above a saline lake that lay below our camp. Sea birds are one of Mongolia's mysteries. No one knows why they are here; few places could be further from the sea. Yet gulls, who have travelled thousands of miles along the complicated rivers of Asia, haunt the lakes of Mongolia. Their instinct for movement, for migration, had overwhelmed their sense of direction. A navigational error in some distant inlet had turned them inland, the wrong way. In the mornings and the evenings in this landlocked country, their plaintive calls along the shores of small lakes were like the sound of keening, a sharp-tongued mourning for the sea, a melancholy unease about journeys and destinations.

We broke camp and rode away towards the north-east across dry carpets of grass. The morning was bright and freshened by winds blowing from the hills to the north. Sambuu's son, a carefree lad with a wrestler's build and an angel's face, sang as we rode. They were traditional Mongolian songs known as *urtyn-duur* or long songs, so called because of their innumerable verses and drawn-out tones.

He sang for hours without pause, and on his melancholy notes we were borne across long yellow landscapes.

Chapter Ten

RIDING TO ZAG

I had expected riding across Outer Mongolia to be a more solitary pursuit. I imagined landscapes melodramatically empty, long on physical splendours but short on social opportunities. I wondered, in all that space, how I would meet Mongolians.

I need not have worried. In Outer Mongolia my social calendar was packed. Lunch invitations, drinks parties and dinner engagements came thick and fast. There were times when crossing the Mongolian steppe felt like a royal tour of which I was the unlikely focus. There were always hands to be shaken, babies to be patted, gers to be visited, herds to be inspected, bowls of airag to be accepted, toasts to be made, photo opportunities to be endured. I developed a formidable small talk about pastures and sheep and the remarkable record of the great Batardene in capturing the national wrestling championship for a record tenth year.

There was also splendid isolation, long days in which we saw no one, and pristine country with no trace of human passage. But in Mongolia people materialize as mysteriously as clouds. On our first night with Sambuu, chatting in the lee of our saddles, the only inhabitants of the immense plain appeared to be a herd of horses led by a fine chestnut stallion galloping restlessly from slope to slope. Yet we had three groups of visitors in the course of the evening, all of whom pressed dinner invitations upon us should we find ourselves in their neck of the steppes.

The first were a couple of horsemen out looking for their camels. The second was a family in a jeep who were heading for Gobi-Altay and wanted news of the height of a river we had crossed. The third was a posse of adolescent boys, riding young horses as spirited and gangly as themselves, who paused to squat on the grass, smoke cigarettes and make the usual enquiries of how far we had come, where we were going, and how the pastures had looked along the way. When they departed, the darkening country swallowed them so quickly and so completely it was as if we had imagined them.

The next day, twenty miles to the north-east, we stopped for lunch at a *ger* by a chalky river. Our hostess was a friend of Sambuu, a formidable figure who doled out the *airag* in quantities that were to make the afternoon drowsy. Her husband and children were away, driving 500 head of cattle to Ulan Batur. It was forty days' ride and most herdsmen, accustomed to a barter subsistence economy, would not have contemplated such a bold and risky incursion into the cash market of the capital. Sambuu kept shaking his head, astonished that the world had come to this. Lunch was mutton and noodle stew.

Four hours later we were making camp on a steep knoll above a *ger* surrounded by a battalion of shaggy yaks. While we were pitching our tents the owner of the *ger* paid a call. He was a disreputable individual with a reputation for drink and social outrage, known locally as Vodka Bottle. His shoulder was heavily bandaged and his cheekbone was swollen from a recent fall from his horse; his was a lifestyle that carried a high risk of injury. Inevitably he invited us to dinner – dried marmot meat which had the consistency of old tyres. The evening was a trifle tense as our host and his wife were not on speaking terms, and any communication between them had to come through us.

The following day we lunched with a pair of newlyweds. The unimpeded views in Mongolian landscapes and the widespread use of East German binoculars often meant that our hosts knew about our impending engagements before we did. A nephew was sent out to intercept us with an invitation, and we arrived to find the couple dressed to receive us in their wedding *dels*. Their marriage had taken place the previous day.

Everything in their life was brand new as custom demanded –

the *ger* and its furnishings, the plates and bowls, the iron stove and the gleaming pots, the felt rugs and their own marital happiness. In their shiny wedding *dels* – gold for her, royal blue for him – the couple themselves looked as highly polished and as indivisible as a new pair of boots.

Surrounded by the hospitality trays of yesterday's reception – vast plates on which layers of cheese and biscuits and mutton fat alternated to precarious heights – we felt like guests who had turned up disastrously late. But far from being put out by our arrival on a day that might have been more usefully committed to hangovers and clearing-up, the newlyweds seemed relieved to see us. The wedding party might have gone home but the bridal couple, still basking in the glow of the Big Day, were reluctant to bring the celebrations to an end. Real life awaited them and they were in no hurry to get back to that.

We were served cheese and cream and freshly baked biscuits and tea made on the new stove. Beneath her wedding make-up, layers of white pancake and scarlet lipstick, the bride was austerely beauti- ful. She fussed anxiously over us, keen to make a success of these early rituals of hospitality in her new home. Inevitably hers would be the more difficult adjustment. She had married a family, not just a man. She had left her own family home, some sixty miles away, to begin a new life here at the camp of his parents and his brothers and their wives. Their acceptance of her, and her ability to fit into the established patterns of their relationships, would prove crucial to the happiness of her marriage.

The groom, who was rather less easy on the eye, was rumoured to have plenty of sheep. We were joined after a time by his brother, a meaty fellow with broad forearms, a square head and a squaddie's haircut. He had just finished his stint in the army; all Mongolian men were conscripted for a year's service. It was hell, he said happily. He missed it. The discipline was frightful. When the officers weren't beat- ing the recruits, the recruits were diligently beating one another. The beatings had made for a great sense of camaraderie, he said.

Beatings aside, the army had been a revelation. He had seen things in Ulan Batur that previously he had only read about – streetlights, buses, girls in short skirts, a cinema. He made the capital sound like Paris or New York, a gilded romantic city where life had a breathless unpredictable quality. I asked if he was content to return to the life of a herdsman.

'Oh no,' he said. 'I plan to join a temple.' Apparently the ascetic regimented life, the idyll of male companionship and the severe haircuts had convinced him that he should be a monk. While it was relatively easy to imagine him happily thumping his fellow squaddies, it was more difficult to see him in saffron robes whispering sutras. I hoped he was not going to be disappointed by brotherly love.

There were six *gers* camped at this place, all members of the groom's extended family. We went next door to call on his mother, a strong-willed woman who immediately served us a second lunch of mutton stew, as if anything we had received in her new daughter-in-law's *ger* could hardly have satisfied us. The groom's two ugly sisters-in-law turned up with mewling infants under their arms. They were big bovine women, their blouses stained with regurgitated milk. They settled themselves prominently on the cot opposite, undid the straining buttons and pushed enormous black-nippled breasts into the mouths of their babies. The children, both boys, were badges of their status and their acceptance.

The new bride, slim, ethereal, intimidated, sat politely and silently inside the door. No one spoke to her. Suddenly among these rough people her beauty seemed a kind of vulnerability. Her wedding *del*, her white make-up and her scarlet lipstick looked like the trappings of pantomime, the fairy-tale garb of someone who had yet to address the real issues of life.

Later I took the post-wedding photographs. The bride organized the poses. She arranged a portrait of her and her husband, their heads tilted sweetly together. Then she wanted one of her alone. While I positioned her with her face upturned into a shaft of light from the chimney hole of her *ger*, we could hear the ugly sisters-in-law outside crudely teasing the groom about his new wife. In the aqueous channel of light, she had closed her eyes, adrift in some reverie of her own. She was very serious about the photographs, as if she felt the need for some kind of record of these first happy days, as if she had already understood that none of it was meant to last.

Afterwards she pleaded with us to stay for dinner, and to spend the night. She did not want us to go; we were the unlikely last guests at her wedding, and our departure and the drawing in of that evening would mark the end of the festivities. After us came the deluge, the disapproving mother-in-law, the coarse sisters-in-law. When we were departing she slipped a letter into my hand. It was to her mother who lived in Zag, a place we would pass along our way. She made me promise to see that she got it.

We rode away across a yellow plain beneath galleon clouds in full sail. The soft flanks of hills draped themselves around the horizons. The sky grew huge and the *gers* fell away. Beyond a low pass we entered a vast vacant world where provinces of sunlight and cloud shadow chased one another across the tawny grass.

We rode another ten miles, camping on the far shores of this yellow sea. There were no *gers* here and I was happy for a respite from dinner parties. We found wood, made a fire, and lazed about our camp relieved of the necessity of conversation. The sun slipped beyond the horizon and moments later, behind our backs, a bloated full moon rose into an ivory-coloured twilight. Night came suddenly. The horses, grazing on dry grass, trailed cold moon shadows towards a low ridge. A wolf howled somewhere, then fell silent. Two whooper swans passed across the sky. For a moment the crack of the fire and the whispered beat of wings were the only sounds in this empty world. I laid my bedroll in the open, on a mattress of grass. Under the caress of moonlight my saddle was my pillow.

The world was unfolding long languorous limbs. The following day we rode for seven hours through a succession of lateral valleys, their sensuous curves open to acres of sky. Each was an echo of the one that had gone before, vast, treeless, uncomplicated. They might have been sculpted by winds, smoothed to primeval simplicity. Detail and elaboration had been blown away leaving only stark essentials and two colours: the yellow of the grasses and the hot troubled blue of the sky.

In these enormous reaches the winds were the sole agents of change, carrying weather back and forth. All morning pillars of rain menaced the horizons. At midday a storm engulfed us. The sky darkened, the winds rose to gale force and a moment later freezing sleet lashed across the slopes. We dismounted, and turned our backs to this sudden violence. The temperature plummeted, and for half an hour the world was reduced to a whirling cell of hailstones. It was like a Biblical visitation, a moment of God's wrath. Then it vanished as mysteriously as it had appeared, leaving only curling snakes of mist on the baking grasslands. The valleys stretched out again as the sun spread across their flanks. It was as if nothing had happened. We mounted and rode on through the innocent afternoon.

Mandah was the kind of Mongolian that Friar William dreamed about: a Christian convert. William had fared poorly as the Billy Graham of the steppes. In the two years of his Mongolian mission, which by his own account had a purely evangelical purpose, he records only six converts. Not all of those would have stayed the course; Mongols found Christianity's insistence on the renunciation of other religions something of a barrier, and backsliding was endemic.

Aside from poor translators, which was William's own excuse for his lack of converts, part of his problem was the political and military insignificance of Christian Europe when viewed from the centre of a new world empire. Mongols, a practical people, found it difficult to take very seriously the religious ideas of a man from such distant and paltry nations. In our own age Christian missionaries in Mongolia have had rather more success. They have the advantage, unlike William, of coming from a world power.

One of the effects of the recent religious freedom in Mongolia has been the arrival of considerable numbers of William's successors, Christian missionaries, almost exclusively from America. Not only do they offer young Mongolians an opportunity to improve their English, the language of advancement, but they have the additional incentive of scholarships to American Biblical colleges. With the carrot of travel and residence in the United States, young Mongolians have been particularly keen to hear the message of Our Lord Jesus. If nineteenth-century China was full of 'rice Christians', more enthusiastic about the missionaries' kilo of charitable rice than the gospels, modern Mongolia has seen the rise of 'green-card Christians'.

Mandah's Christianity was rather more sincere. For her the religion was part of a more general alienation from her own culture. As a young Westernized woman, she was fed up with Mongolia. When I tried to speak about the virtues of a traditional society, she replied impatiently that she saw no reason to keep traditions for their own sake, and that in Mongolia most 'traditions' were simply an impediment to progress. She despaired of Mongolians and their backwardness. The best were corrupt, and the worst were lazy, ignorant, unambitious and unreliable.

Most of her friends in Ulan Batur were expatriates, she said. She found their company congenial. They knew how to have a good time without resort to coarse drunkenness, and they knew how to work. She admired the professionalism of foreign firms. Mongolian companies were chaotic and fraught with petty personal jealousies, full of time-servers and the owners' relations. Religion suffered from similar comparisons. To Mandah, Buddhism was a backward faith, full of superstition and darkness. With its emphasis on salvation and personal responsibility, she found Christianity enlightened and progressive. William would have adored her. I found her harsh verdict on her own country depressing.

Having taken us as far as Zag, Sambuu and his son left for home. Departure made the old man tearful. His clown's face became an exaggeration of sentimental concern. He wanted me to know that he had meant no harm with his talk about my former status as an enemy alien. I must excuse him, he said. He was old and he was nostalgic for the sweet days of his youth when life had been simpler. He took my hand and pumped it feverishly. I was a good foreigner, he said, and he was glad we could now be friends. It was some compensation in a world that was otherwise going to the dogs. He rode away sniffling. From the ridge above Zag they turned to wave, then dropped from sight into yesterday's landscapes.

At Zag we spent five days camped among a scattering of *gers* on the river bank. Passing horsemen stopped to chat, dinner invitations were frequent, and we were soon part of the neighbourhood. We came to know the richest and the poorest people on the plain.

Prevdorj was a frequent visitor. He was the big man of the district. He rode about the plain like a medieval lord inspecting his domain, fat, flushed and suffering from gout. He had a reputation as a braggart and a bully. No one liked him, the gossips said, not even his own family who courted him only for his inheritance. He spent his afternoons at drinking parties on the other side of the river and rode home unsteadily each evening lurching slightly in the saddle. Outside our tent he conversed with us without dismounting. Every day he grandly promised horses and a guide, but none was ever forthcoming. One morning, when we went to visit him to ask about the horses while he was still sober, we found him shirtless, reclining in a palatial *ger* stroking his great belly, attended by a quartet of daughters like a sultan in his private quarters. He claimed he had sent for a horseman and horses who should be arriving any day, but on the way out one of his long-suffering daughters warned us it might be as well to make other plans.

Our immediate neighbours were a very poor couple with four children. Their resources were limited and their hospitality boundless. She came to call every morning bearing pails of yak's milk and yoghurt, chatting incessantly, delighted to have someone new to talk to. Her husband had worked in the small power plant in Zag but the sudden rise in the cost of coal had prompted its closure. They were the only family I met in Mongolia who did not own a horse.

'We are not part of the market economy here,' the man had declared proudly one evening when we were visiting with a group of other neighbours. He recounted a story that he had heard about the train station in Sainshand on the Trans-Siberian line. Apparently women sold cups of tea and *airag* on the platform to the train passengers. He paused to let this sink in, lifting his hands to us in a beseeching gesture. Tea and *airag* are the first things to be offered to any visitor to a Mongolian *ger*. 'Imagine,' he whispered. '*Selling* tea and *airag* to people.' His incredulous neighbours shook their heads at this barbarity. I tried to look suitably shocked, unwilling to let on that the sale of tea was commonplace in my own barbarous land. Mandah too was silent; in this poor *ger* the traditions of the countryside were revealing themselves with considerable honour.

We located the bride's mother after a few enquiries, and sent a message to her that we had a letter from her daughter. She arrived within the hour, immediately recognizable with the same clear brow and fine almond eyes. She was delighted that we had been guests at the new *ger*; she seemed to feel a foreign guest was a good omen for her daughter's married life. We made reassuring noises about how happy she had seemed, and how well she was settling in, and the mother accepted these gratefully without entirely believing them. She took the letter and folded it away inside her *del*. 'We have never been parted in twenty years,' she confided to Mandah. 'I pray for her happiness, but to me her marriage feels more like a death. I am ashamed of my feelings.'

Between visits to the neighbours, while we waited for horses, we played cards, walked on the river bank, and read. I was reading Chekov. Mandah's only book was the Bible. The missionaries had given her a copy of an edition in New American English which fortunately she had lost. On a street stall in Ulan Batur she had found a St James Version to replace it. She disliked its archaic language but I reassured her that this was the edition that God himself read. She decided that God's English must be better than hers.

In the evenings she read me psalms. The language and the images seem to spring from the landscapes about us.

The horseman that we eventually enlisted for the next stage was a country innocent, a goofy young man with a porkpie hat and a crooked smile of horsey teeth. His own innate decency made the rest of the world seem rather worse than it was. He did not know the country through which we would pass, and in the fertile ground of ignorance anxieties blossomed. His chief concern was horse thieves. He was convinced the valleys were heaving with rustlers. Every night he hobbled and staked the horses with elaborate care before laying his bedroll in the open among them. He slept only fitfully. During the day he was apt to doze off in the saddle, waking with a start as if some sneaky thief was about to steal the horse from beneath him.

He was accompanied by his ten-year-old nephew, a grave boy who rode atop the baggage like a child emperor. In the evenings the two played cards with Mandah. She taught them an American card game called Cheat, based on elaborate bluffing. The ten-year-old was a shrewd competitor with a poker face. His uncle never got the hang of the necessary duplicity.

On the second day we crossed the Hangay massif into Arhangay *aimag*. At the top of the pass two black dogs crossed our path, like omens, slinking away towards the south. When we dismounted and circled the *ovoo*, adding a few stones as we went, I noticed that one of the votive offerings was a wooden chest. It had split open and I could see it was stuffed with small banknotes which would be as safe here as in the vaults of the Bank of Mongolia.

On the far side we dropped down to the Chulutt river, a fast stream riding over copper-coloured boulders. It curled beneath a rocky cliff inhabited by ravens whose calls fell like stones about us. Beyond, the valley widened into meadows of *gers* and horses. On the far slopes were forests of larch trees, the first real forests I had seen in Mongolia. The bare simplicities of the grasslands were being invaded by more complex terrain; Arhangay has a reputation as one of the more sylvan provinces of Mongolia, softened with wide rivers and trees. After so much open space the forests looked intimate and seductively inviting.

Accounts of riding in Mongolia invariably contain a whine of complaint. The enormous distances, the continual diet of mutton, the uncomfortable gait of the short Mongolian horses, the extremities of the weather, the bleakness of the country, have troubled travellers from William to the great Przhevalsky in the nineteenth century. I cannot add to this literature of discomfort. In Mongolia I wondered if it was possible to be happier. When the horses were good, and the weather fine, I felt I was in paradise. In the movement of journeys there is a wonderful stillness. For four months I was untroubled by arrival.

On the morning of the fourth day we rode hard across a stony plain, chased by squalls of rain, reaching the town of Chulutt as the clouds broke and the sun struck the sad buildings.

It was a Gary Cooper Moment with overtones of Agatha Christie.

Chapter Eleven

FISHING WITH THE LIBRARIAN

Galloping into the town of Chulutt, with our horses snorting and rain-lashed, we found the leading citizens assembled like suspects at the dénouement of a murder mystery: the mayor, the policeman, the shopkeeper, the librarian, the hotelkeeper, and the postmaster. They sat about on broken benches in the front garden of the town hall as if chance had brought them together. But their binoculars were the telling clue. They had seen us coming, miles off, a quartet of riders with a baggage horse and a foreigner – at a distance my height invariably gave me away – and they had gravitated towards the town hall so as not to miss out on the excitement.

They proved a shy reception committee, a little bewildered by my arrival. The librarian did most of the talking. He was a highly-strung young man, a trifle starved of intellectual stimulation. Hearing I was a writer, he wanted my opinion about the influence of Shakespeare on Russian literature before I was out of the saddle. While I tied up the horses, and unstrapped our baggage, he hovered at my elbow dissecting character development in the *Brothers Karamazov*. My Gary Cooper Moment was being hijacked by Literary Criticism.

The librarian, the policeman and the mayor shouldered our bags and saddles and we all trooped inside the town hall where two rooms on the ground floor served as a 'hotel' for visitors. There was a short delay when the keys to the rooms could not be found.

171

The hotelkeeper, a glamorous woman who had turned out in lipstick and a gold *del* for her first official engagement in months, remembered giving the key to the policeman. The policeman felt sure he had given it to the mayor, the mayor thought he had deposited it with the postmaster, the postmaster remembered handing it on to the policeman. The hotelkeeper's assistant, a burly woman with the face of a wrestler, and the only one unconnected to the odyssey of the key, eventually produced a large axe. While the men stood back she tore the lock from its moorings with a single blow. Beyond lay our temporary home – two bare rooms with metal cots.

Chulutt was a case study of now familiar dereliction. It consisted of about twenty buildings in various states of collapse. The newer they were the more dramatic their disintegration. At the school, built in the late 1970s, the battle to maintain the gymnasium had been abandoned and swifts now flew through the gaping windows to nest among the bleachers and the basketball hoops. The town hall, which might have represented fifty years of neglect, was only fifteen years old. Only a handful of Russian cottages, far older than the municipal buildings, maintained their architectural dignity. They sagged charmingly behind picket fences; dilapidation suited them.

The disintegration of the town hall had a rather sinister character. It was being consumed by a mutant fungus. Feeding on the timber floors, a dry rot of monstrous and aberrant proportions was gradually moving through the building. When a room succumbed it was simply abandoned, and the doors nailed shut. After a few months an ominous tendril would be spotted curling up the skirting board in the next room. Soon there would be the familiar outbreak of triffid-like growth, and the fungus would claim another victim. The smell permeated the building, sour and cloying as cabbage. To visiting herdsmen, in town to collect the post or to pick up a kilo of sugar, it was the smell of sedentary life.

No one referred to the fungus in Chulutt, locked away behind the nailed doors. When I was alone in the building I peered through cracks at the lost rooms. In the dim shuttered light, I could see the black growth sprouting hideously over the floor and climbing the walls. Rumours about the closed rooms and their sinister plant life spread almost as quickly as the fungus itself. The further one travelled from Chulutt the more grotesque its proportions became. On the next stage of my journey, in distant *gers* on the borders of this district, I would meet herdsmen who believed the rot infected people who visited the town hall, appearing as a black blight across their faces. The consensus everywhere was that the fungus was proof of the superiority of tents, and the unsoundness of buildings. This is what comes, I would hear old men say, of the virus of towns.

'It is a question of personal jealousies,' the librarian whispered. 'Every time I try to publish my poetry someone puts a stop to it.'

His hands were the first thing you noticed about him. They hovered nervously in front of him, the long fingers twitching like antennae. His eyes were dark and intense but evasive. When he listened, the eyes peered at the speaker furtively. When he spoke they darted away, so that it was the outstretched hands, anguished and beseeching, that became the point of contact. He was a frustrated poet. Dark forces had prevented his recognition. Chulutt was full of conspiracies against him.

'I don't know why they hate me,' he said, the fingers momentarily jammed together.

The librarian was yet another Chekovian figure – the intellectual, the aspiring writer, the hopeless romantic, trapped in the countryside where no one understood him. He saw our arrival as portentous. In his world nothing happened by chance. Throughout our time in Chulutt the librarian seemed to believe, bizarrely, that we might be able to rescue him. I would know how to arrange for the publication of his work, so cruelly ignored. I would appreciate his talents, and my acknowledgement would allow his neighbours to see him in a new light. Mandah, for her part, might provide an outlet for the unrequited love central to romantic suffering.

Like most of the townsfolk, Mandah gently ridiculed him behind his back. His face had a kind of dark beauty but his body was graceless. 'Look at his legs,' she would cry, struggling with a fit of the giggles, as he passed outside. 'Look, look.' I couldn't see the leg problem myself, but Mandah seemed to find them hysterical.

The librarian lived with his wife and innumerable children in considerable poverty in one of the old Russian cottages next to the town hall. The hotelkeeper and her assistant, who came to make tea and meals for us in the small kitchen next to our room, shared the gossip about them. The librarian's mother had been a rather notorious local figure with a tumultuous romantic career. As a young woman she had been very much in love with an unsuitable man – there were rumours he had a wife in Ulan Batur – until her family had separated them. She had then married someone sensible, a teacher here in town. They had two children, the librarian and his twin sister who had died in her first year. The mother had been deranged by grief, and the grandmother had brought up the boy.

The librarian carried on the family tradition by feeding the gossip mill of the district. People swapped stories about him.

'He forgets his children,' said the burly woman who broke the lock.

I thought she meant he neglected them.

'No, no. He actually loses them. Once in Ulan Batur he left their first child behind in a restaurant, and when he went back to find him the police had taken charge of the boy. He had a great deal of difficulty persuading them it was his child. They could not believe he had just forgotten him.'

Their gossip was not malicious. The townsfolk were sympathetic to the librarian's difficulties. His poverty, his lack of animals, the paltry government salary that rarely arrived was a concern to everyone, and the family survived on small acts of quiet generosity.

But from the windows of the library their charity looked like another kind of conspiracy. The librarian saw his life as blighted by refusals, rejections and obstructions. The inability to find a publisher was only the last in a long line of thwarted ambitions. The library, a modest establishment, was housed in a single room in a low building on the other side of the town hall. It smelt of pine and old books. The librarian sat by the window reading Dostoevsky and three-month-old newspapers. When we passed he looked up and his narrow anguished face floated darkly behind the thick pane of glass like an exhibit: Man at the End of His Tether.

'His wife was a beauty once,' the hotel woman sighed. 'But their life has been very difficult.'

Mandah wanted to telephone Ulan Batur to inform her parents that she was still alive. The Chulutt telephone exchange was a small hut with a large modern satellite dish outside. Sadly the dish had been never connected. Someone said it had come as part of an aid scheme, but the instructions were in French and no one knew how it worked. The exchange ran on traditional methods. Behind a high counter, the telephonist cranked a handle and shouted into an antique mouthpiece. The delays in establishing a connection were considerable, and callers were few.

On a bench in the waiting room we found Rudy, a young German backpacker. He was without his backpack on this occasion but it was a simple matter to identify him by his clothes. He wore the loose tie-dyed trousers fashionable among rice workers in the paddies of the Upper Mekong and *de rigueur* for young backpackers in Asia. An army surplus jacket, once the pride of the Viet Cong, was his concession to the Mongolian climate. The ensemble was completed by a batik handbag and a embroidered pillbox hat. The latter looked rather splendid on the Himalayan tribesmen of the Upper Hunza valley for whom they were designed but faintly ridiculous on Rudy. He had a long potato face, lank orange hair, and the kind of big European nose that gave Mongolian children nightmares.

One of the many pleasures of Mongolia is that it is far from the beaten tracks to which young backpackers generally adhere. At moments of difficulty I was always able to revive my spirits by reminding myself that I was thousands of miles from cafés with banana pancakes, threadbare *Lonely Planet* guides and notice boards full of people looking for other people they had met two months ago in India. My heart sank when I saw Rudy. His face lit up when he saw me, and I felt guilty about my lack of charity.

'Are you going to Ulan Batur?' he asked eagerly.

I said we were.

'Do you have room in your jeep?'

I explained we were travelling by horse, and that we would not reach Ulan Batur for at least another month. Rudy was crestfallen. 'By horse,' he muttered, making it sound like a personal affront.

Beyond the counter the telephonist was shouting into the mouthpiece. *'Bano, bano, banooooo.' Bano* is less a greeting than an enquiry, meaning 'Is anybody there?', and its use when answering the telephone says much about the reliability of the Mongolian network. In this remote place, trying to establish contact with the outside world, the phrase had a certain poignancy.

'BANooo, BANoooo, BANOOOOOoooo,' the telephonist chanted, rocking in his seat. Repetition had made it a song.

I asked Rudy how long he had been waiting for a connection.

'Two days,' he said.

'How did you come here?' I asked.

'I was going to China on the Trans-Siberian,' Rudy said. 'I stopped for a couple of days in Ulan Batur. I wanted to get in touch with real nomads. I met a man in the railway station who said he could arrange for me to come to the countryside.'

Apparently Rudy had paid the man three hundred dollars, three months' wages for the average resident of Ulan Batur, to drive him to Chulutt and deposit him with some of his relatives. Rudy had been in Chulutt for a week getting in touch with real nomads and he was now trying desperately to get back in touch with Ulan Batur. Unfortunately there were no vehicles for hire in Chulutt and he hoped that a contact in the capital might be able to send a rescue jeep.

Rudy was a mystery to the people of Chulutt. He spoke no Mongolian, and no one was entirely sure where he had come from or why he was there. He was staying in a *ger* on the edge of the village. He paid the family twenty-five dollars a day for three meals, a mat on the floor, and the privilege of watching their sheep. The family kept having to pinch themselves at their remarkable fortune. The men of the *ger* invested Rudy's money in store-bought Genghis Khan and spent the week in an alcoholic haze while Rudy sat on a hillside counting their livestock. The rest of Chulutt shook their heads at the bizarre nature of foreigners. One or two older people thought he might be a spy but most were content to believe he was simply bonkers. His clothes and his hair seemed to lend some weight to the latter theory.

Rudy believed pastoralism was Man's natural state. According to Rudy the migrations of nomads reflected our innate restlessness.

'We need to move,' he said in a Teutonic monotone. 'Man's character is restless. Our pain comes from standing still.'

In his eclectic garb, Rudy had the displaced air of a refugee. In his case he was fleeing the suburbs of Hamburg, an understandable compulsion.

'Streets are a prison, man,' he said. 'In the city I feel trapped. I need space to be free.'

'Is anybody theeeeere?' the telephonist sang. 'Is anybody theeeeere?'

To Rudy, the Arcadia of Mongolia was spoiled only by the presence of Mongolians. He had expected better of a people free of office jobs and mortgages. In Chulutt he had come to feel besieged. Everyone seemed too keen on money, particularly his money.

'They have been corrupted,' he explained. 'The nomads are not free any more. They want the things of the West.'

I commiserated with him about this outbreak of consumer desire.

'And the food.' He made a face. 'They don't eat vegetables. Think of what they could grow here.'

'It is difficult to grow vegetables and move at the same time,' I said.

'BanOOO,' the telephonist's chant suddenly had a different tone. There was someone out there. 'Ulan Batur, Ulan Batur,' he cried. 'This is Chulutt, Chulutt. Come in Ulan Batur.'

He held the handpiece up for Rudy who bolted to the counter, upending his handbag on the way and spewing the contents across the floor.

'Jack?' Rudy whispered. It was as if he was trying to wake someone in a dark house without disturbing the other inhabitants. 'Jack? Are you there?'

He listened for a moment. 'Jack, can you hear me?' Rudy's voice rose. 'Jack. Help me.' Rudy gripped the telephone like a lifeline. 'Jaaack. Jaaack,' he screamed. 'I need a jeep. Jaaack, can you hear me? A jeep, send a jeeeeeep.'

But the line had gone dead. Rudy slumped his head onto the

counter and the telephonist prised the telephone from his whitened grasp.

Chulutt was an opportunity to extend my fly-fishing career. In spite of some very fine fishing rivers, Mongolian herdsmen are generally horrified by the idea of eating fish, leaving the way clear for demented foreigners like myself.

One afternoon I went to the river to try my luck. The librarian acted as my guide. For the librarian and his family fish were a necessity. They had no animals, and very little money. Occasionally people helped them out with a spare sheep but most days the librarian fished for their supper.

At the river he was another man, composed, quiet and reflective. We talked about landscape. The librarian was a great natural historian with a detailed knowledge of the birds and plants along the riverbank. He pointed out the different rock formations that the river had laid bare – dolomites and limestones and pelites. To the librarian the ice age was recent history, almost current affairs. But most of the time we did not talk at all. Silent, the librarian was remarkably good company.

Like riding, I had taken up fly-fishing only the previous year when I had found myself in Idaho on the Henry's Fork, one of the great fly-fishing rivers of the American west. Between catches I had read Norman Maclean's splendid book *A River Runs Through It* with its wonderful opening line – 'In our family, there was no clear line between religion and fly-fishing.' I was entranced with the idea that fly-fishing was angling for philosophers, and the whole thing had rather gone to my head. With the passion and innocence of the new convert I was apt to rattle on embarrassingly about the artistry of casting, the mysteries of rivers and the meaning of life.

In London I had visited a tackle shop in Pall Mall where a very helpful chap, thrilled with the idea that I was going to Outer Mongolia, apparently a paradise for the fly-fisherman, had sold me a lot of surprisingly expensive tackle. So far my journey had offered few fishing rivers but now that I was in the lush well-watered landscapes of Arhangay I was looking forward to a variation in the monotonous Mongolian diet.

The Chulutt river was wide and shallow, rattling over a bed of pale grey stones, what my fly-fishing manual described as a riffle run. Under the bemused gaze of the librarian, I jointed my rod, fitted the reel and chose one of the mysterious flies from my box. I went for the largest, a black furry thing called a Woolly Bugger, that I thought might suit the decidedly butch Mongolian fish. I did not know a great deal about my quarry, other than their names – Mongolian rivers are home to the lenok and the taimen – but a photograph that I had seen in the shop in Pall Mall showed an angler wrestling with a Mongolian taimen the size of a small alligator.

The librarian's equipment was more modest. He fished with a length of string wrapped around a stick. His bait was a piece of dried mutton. I was going to commiserate with him and see if I might lend him something from Pall Mall but we were interrupted when he began to haul in a big lenok. I pushed upstream a bit and had cast for an hour or so without result when the librarian, who by now had caught two more lenok, offered me a piece of mutton. I could see that he hadn't really understood fly-fishing. I tried to explain about the artistry of casting, the mysteries of rivers and the meaning of life, but he was distracted by yet another bite on his line. The hunger of Mongolian fish for dried mutton was a thing to behold.

I had better luck when the librarian and his mutton went home. I stayed on the river into the early evening and managed to catch four small trout. They were nothing compared to the librarian's fish, but they might make a decent supper. I trailed home across the pastures with the yak carts bearing barrels of water from the river, happy with the day's catch.

Not wishing to alarm the hotelkeepers with four dead fish, I gave them the night off. The mayor came to dinner. He had been introduced to the idea of eating fish during a short stay in Irkutsk and he was almost as excited as I was by a break from mutton. He joined me in the kitchen where I was preparing a fish risotto. The mayor's enthusiasm was shaken somewhat when I began to add pepper and garlic that I had found in the market in Altay. Mongolian cuisine is a dour business that makes even English cooking appear exotic and highly flavoured.

The fish was almost ready when there was a knock on the door. Four men were outside; they had arrived in a jeep with a blue light on top. The mayor introduced them as spies by which I believe he meant security men, an advance party checking on the arrangements for the local Member of Parliament, who would be touring the area next week. Their leader was a former Mongolian KGB agent, a square character, with a bullet head.

Playing host, the mayor and I ushered them into my room where they took seats on the cots in the candlelight. I had been the guest in enough *gers* to know the rules of Mongolian hospitality. Pretending we had already eaten ourselves we handed round bowls of risotto to our guests, with apologies for the fish. The three sidekicks nibbled at theirs politely but tentatively. The KGB man however was like a man possessed.

'Delicious,' he grunted between mouthfuls. 'Fresh fish. And plenty of garlic.' He spooned the risotto into his mouth as if he had not eaten in days.

In a land of fish-haters, I seemed to have had the misfortune of landing the one guy who liked trout. The KGB man had trained in East Germany during the Communist era. Along with the Stasi torture methods, he had acquired a taste for European food. He looked up eagerly from his empty bowl, and in the sudden silence I heard myself offering him seconds.

He devoured four bowlfuls in the end, polishing off our entire dinner. Sitting back on my cot, belching quietly, he asked to see my passport, then ran through a few routine questions to check if I was a foreign assassin, before departing into the night without further ceremony. When they had gone the mayor and I consoled ourselves with bread and a bottle of Bulgarian wine that I had hidden surreptitiously beneath my pillow.

Bolstered by my fish dinner the KGB agent had gone straight round to investigate Rudy who he discovered had left his passport in Ulan Batur. Initially this looked like a stroke of good fortune for them both. The KGB agent fined him and pocketed the money, while Rudy looked forward to escaping Chulutt. But when he learnt he was not to be arrested and transported to the capital as an illegal alien, he broke down in tears. The Mongolian steppes were proving a good deal harder to escape than the Hamburg suburbs.

The librarian invited us to his home one day for tea. There was much to discuss, he said ominously. He was anxious to discover my 'autobiography'. It sounded grim.

In a previous incarnation, the room that the librarian inhabited with his family had been a carpentry workshop, part of a defunct collective, and domesticity had something of a struggle against the atmosphere of the workbench. It was a spartan space with an iron stove in one corner, and a vast wood pile in another. The only furniture was a table in the window and four cots arranged around the walls. A variety of small children clung to the legs of the cots, struck dumb by the frightful apparition of the tall foreigner. The librarian's wife, a harassed-looking woman with rounded shoulders, greeted us with a silent ambiguous nod. The room stank of fish and charred wood.

We sat at the table. Flies buzzed against the window. The librarian was in an agitated state, his fingers wound into a tight knot on the table in front of him. Before we got started on my autobiography he wanted to tell me his own, he said. He had cast his whole anguished life into verse. He embarked upon this epic in a dirge-like monotone, breaking off from the main text frequently with annotations, notes and explanations which Mandah painstakingly translated. A child's book lay open on the table, a collection of fairy tales among the fish bones. The fingers had descended on a pen, and as he recited he doodled on the flyleaf, weaving dense contorted patterns around a pale line drawing of what looked like a Russian *Red Riding Hood*.

The Life of the Librarian would have made *Paradise Lost* seem both upbeat and concise. It was an everyday tale of tragedy, misfortune and betrayal. He had married too young, and his responsibilities had meant he was unable to take advantage of his early opportunities. His silent wife, who was grimly chopping wood, had the tired look of a woman who had heard this verse a few times before. He had trained as a geologist and had sought a post in Tsetserleg, the *aimag* centre, but it had been given to a relative of a local politician in a blatant act of nepotism. When he had finally secured a stint as a geologist in Dornod it had been cut short when his hair began to fall out and his teeth went bad. Less inflamed imaginations might have accepted this as the normal ageing process but the librarian knew a full-blown medical crisis when he saw one. Balding and suffering from toothache, he had fled to Chulutt, his homeland, where things went from bad to worse. He had been one of the founders of the Chulutt Social Democratic Party but when the candidates were chosen, political conspiracies had removed his name from the list. The newspaper he founded went belly-up, due to personal jealousies. He had lost his local govern-ment job as environmental inspector, when the former mayor had conspired against him, and had been given the librarian post to keep him quiet. The shopkeeper began to refuse him credit, his uncle left all his sheep to a second cousin, and they had only a short-term lease on the workshop.

Here the autobiography began to degenerate into the bathos of a leaking roof and children stealing from his wood pile. This was the problem with life. It lacked the narrative construction of art. It might have been better to have leave political chicanery to later and move the roof problems up with the hair loss but life tends to climax at inconvenient moments. Exhausted by his own misfortune, he ran out of steam and the epic petered out in unfinished stanzas and explanation.

Deep inky ruts had been worn around the ankles of Red Riding Hood. His narrow eyes darted back and forth over the table top as if he was looking for something – hope, perhaps – among the flies and the fish bones and the crumbs of dried cheese. A bitter smell came off him: halitosis and sour milk.

With his own life out of the way, the librarian turned to mine. I felt a rather prosaic soul not having set the thing to verse. But it emerged that the librarian didn't want to hear about my life from me; he preferred to tell me about it himself. He was a palmist. Relieved of the burden of autobiography, I offered him my hand.

I hoped my own comparatively bland life might lighten the atmosphere a little. I was wrong.

The calligraphy of my palm seemed to confuse him, as if its
configuration was something he had not encountered before. He
trailed his index finger along the lines towards my wrist then back-
tracked again towards the fingers, like a man searching for a place
name on a map. Finally he spoke.

'You were a very sickly child,' he said. He tilted my hand further
into the light from the window.

'You will continue to have severe health problems,' he said. 'Not
a long life but you might reach your fifties.'

On previous readings the news from my palm had been casually
upbeat – long life, few financial difficulties, happy love affairs. But
with his finger pressing hesitantly on the yielding lines the librarian
was discovering a hitherto unsuspected subtext.

'You will marry,' he said. I hoped for a moment the tides were
turning. Domestic bliss seemed to beckon.

'But your wife will not reciprocate your love and will be unfaith-
ful,' he said.

I felt myself unconsciously pulling at my own hand, trying to
get it back. But the librarian hung on tight.

'There will be financial difficulties. You will become bankrupt.
You will be forced to sell your home,' he tilted his head and pursed
his lips. 'Sometime in the next five years, perhaps sooner, there will
be a death of someone very close to you.'

His wife spoke to him sharply from across the room.

'Your own death will come in one of three ways,' he continued
matter-of-factly. 'Heart attack, accident, or murder.'

At the grim moment of my death his wife intervened with bowls
of tea. She shot him a dark look. He let the hand drop, my future
in tatters, and we drank our tea in silence.

Later Mandah explained that his wife had reprimanded him about
his predictions. Apparently he had read someone's palm a few years
ago. A similar tale of misfortune, it had all come to pass, including
a premature death. The family had blamed the librarian, implying
his predictions had been a curse. No one in Chulutt now braved
the librarian's palm readings. His own tragedies were seen to be a
virus capable of infecting others.

On our last night in Chulutt there was a staccato rapping on our door, two long and two short knocks, like a mysterious code. Outside in the dark hall was the librarian. It was gone midnight. After my palm reading I had been rather avoiding him. Now he had appeared at my door like the dark god of misfortune.

'The museum,' he whispered.

We had kept promising to visit the small museum attached to the library, and had kept putting it off. Now on our last night he had come to fetch us. His paranoia made refusal impossible.

The great arch of the Milky Way spanned the sleeping town. A yak, wandering aimlessly towards the telephone exchange, stopped in front of the library to gaze stupidly at us. The librarian fumbled with a batch of antique keys, then led us inside past dark rows of books. He struck a match and managed to light a candle stub. We pressed forward into the dank rooms. The flickering shadows, the smell of dust, and the cobwebbed cases in the gloom made me feel like Howard Carter.

A collection of stuffed animals, including a wolf with moth-eaten ears, lurked in the shadows by the door. Above us a huge piratical vulture spread its wings. It had lost an eye and part of its left leg to curatorial neglect.

'They used to eat the bodies,' the librarian said. 'In the old days we left our dead exposed to the sky, like the Tibetans. These birds devoured them.' The librarian gazed respectfully at the bedraggled creature as if it might contain some essence of his ancestors.

Holding the candle aloft, we pressed forward like a trio of explorers. I found myself tiptoeing. We peered into glass cases past our own ghoulish reflections. Most of the antique artefacts – saddles, stoves, halters, *dels* – were indistinguishable, bar a few layers of dust, from items found in a *ger* today. I was reminded again of how static nomadic life could be, of how innovation was viewed with suspicion.

The only historical development that the museum documented concerned the one feature of the district that was not nomadic – the town of Chulutt itself. A series of black and white photographs showed the school, the hospital and the kindergarten, all looking bright and well-maintained. There was a picture of the opening of the small power plant with its promise of local electricity. There were photographs of harvest time in the hay and wheat fields of a collective farm on the edge of the town and of pigs and chickens that were introduced to give variety to the Mongolian diet. They might have been illustrations for some happy future. But this was Chulutt in the 1960s. Since then every one of these optimistic ideas about agriculture, electricity and education had foundered.

The librarian lifted his candle to a wall of local maps and charts, to drawings of plants, and to cases containing old Tibetan sutras from a long-vanished monastery. He began to unburden himself of a stumbling torrent of geographical and historical information about the district. His knowledge was encyclopaedic. He expounded on local rivers and mountains, on standing stones and tectonic plates, on the medicinal qualities of plants and the migration patterns of the demoiselle cranes. By the guttering light of his candle he was like a supplicant, petitioning us with his education, muttering the endless mantras of knowledge, as if they might rescue him from a cynical world and the hopeless position he occupied in it. But the longer he spoke the more agitated he became, as he realized that all this information was not taking us anywhere, that some opportunity was slipping away from him.

We listened patiently, waiting for a chance to escape. Somewhere in the course of the geology of the Upper Chulutt river I managed to draw the lesson to a close. It was late, I said. We had a long day tomorrow. The librarian turned his head into the candlelight, momentarily confused by this intervention. His gaze settled fleetingly on my face. He seemed to wince with a vague and unhappy recognition as he saw before him not a sponsor but a stranger, a foreigner, a man departing.

'*Teem, teem*,' he mumbled in agreement. His long fingers coiled around the keys. The absurdity of his own hopes clouded his brow. He ran his hand over his face and turned towards the door.

In the morning the same assembly of leading citizens gathered to say goodbye and shake our hands. The mayor, the policeman, the two hotel ladies, the postman stood in a group among the dead saplings in front of the town hall, waving as we rode across the plain.

But the librarian was not among them.

Chapter Twelve

THE COMPANY OF OLD MEN

The weather was turning. As we forded the Chulutt river, the horses high-stepping in the shallows, a new wind was blowing from the east, against the current, whitening the surface of the water. The morning was cold, the sky was stone-grey, and people talked of snow. It was late August, and already the summer was closing behind us.

After five days in Chulutt I was delighted to be back in the saddle. In the ramshackle towns between stages, the journey seemed to have stalled. I grew restless and fretful. I felt a fool lugging my saddle in and out of cheap hotel rooms like an out-of-work cow-poke. The arrival of fresh horses, pawing the ground, eager to be away, was the moment of liberation.

Horses and a guide had been difficult to secure in Chulutt. At this season families were busy moving to the autumn pastures. A criminal-looking character had presented himself at the town hall as a prospective horseman but I had decided against him on the grounds of a severe case of builder's bum. We posted a notice on the door of the telephone exchange, the local equivalent of the small ads, but I had already learnt that the best way of achieving the widest publicity for anything was to mention it casually to the hotelkeeper. The whole district already knew about my shaving rituals, my fondness for afternoon siestas, and my colourful boxer shorts.

The hotelkeeper eventually enlisted one of her uncles. He was an august gentleman, over seventy years of age, with flocks that were the envy of the whole district. He reminded me of my own Irish uncles with his ruddy face and his bowlegged gait, his thick country accent and his hat which belonged to another era. His was a battered trilby with an upturned brim as if he hoped to catch the rain. He had eyes the colour of tea, pale tufts of hair on his upper cheeks, four teeth, traditional Mongolian boots with curved elfin toes, and a Tibetan name – Balginnyam.

Beyond the river we rode up a rising valley between pine woods then swung north-east into pastures of tawny grasses. Among the bare hills we met a family on the move, heading north for the autumn pastures around Öndör Ulan. Everyone, from grandparents to toddlers, was mounted on fresh horses. The wide wave of their sheep rippled across the grassy slopes above, herded by two adolescent girls in red *dels* and headscarves. An elderly granny, astride a lively paint mare, led a string of three laden camels, bearing their *ger* and all its contents. Her son rode shotgun, out on the flanks of their tiny caravan, hoping to bag a marmot for dinner with his antique Russian rifle. Two boys of eight and ten riding black ponies stopped to chat. The move had put them in high spirits, and they were disappointed that we were heading in the opposite direction.

We waved them away over a long ridge of wind-blown grass then stopped in for tea with some friends of the old man. It was the best kind of *ger* with freshly baked biscuits and three beautiful daughters. Fortified by both, we pressed on beneath descending skies. The horses were good. I had a fine strong red, with long rabbit ears. The old man rode an old white horse so potbellied it made his legs stick out.

As we rode, Balginnyam talked of his grandson. The boy had come to Chulutt from his parents in Ulan Batur three years ago as a sickly and rather difficult sixteen-year-old. It was thought that the countryside would do him good. Balginnyam had nursed the boy with various traditional remedies including the powerful tonic of human urine. Once he had recovered his health, the boy had taken to life in the countryside with enthusiasm. He learnt to milk the yaks, to ration the calves' suckling and to shear sheep. He learnt how to make rawhide from cow's skin and how to distil *arkhi* from mare's milk. He rode well and took care not to overtax his horse. Within six months he was a transformed character, the old man said, hardworking and disciplined.

The boy had become the centre of the old man's world. He loved him, he said simply. He loved the sincerity with which he approached everything, he loved his enthusiasm and his energy. He loved rediscovering his own world through the boy's eyes. It was a love that had come late in his life, and it seemed to surprise him. He had the serenity of a man who had found meaning.

He asked about my own family, and was startled to learn I had no children. Assuming that only misfortune could have produced such a result, he hesitated to enquire further. But curiosity got the better of him. When I mumbled something about not having met anyone with whom I wanted to have children, he found the answer so inadequate that he dropped the subject to avoid further embarrassment.

By late afternoon we had reached a long autumnal valley where small groups of *gers*, set half a mile or so apart, trailed vertical lines of smoke into an ash-coloured sky. We camped next to a narrow stream beneath a slope of pine trees, made a fire and cooked the mutton we had brought from Chulutt. A fulvescent sunset seeped into the hills we had just crossed. The hollow notes of cuckoos tumbled out of the deepening gloom of the woods above us.

Over dinner Balginnyam talked gently about the infirmities of age, his weakening eyesight, his stiff knees, his cold feet at night. He even admitted that he had become anxious about horses and the danger of being thrown, an extraordinary confession for a Mongolian. But they were not complaints, merely observations. 'I am loosening my hold,' he said, smiling slightly and unclenching his hand in a gesture of release. 'I will leave everything to the boy,' he said. 'I do not worry about dying.' Finding meaning in the world, he was now ready to abandon it.

Night was falling and the features of the old man's face retreated in the firelight. In the thickening dark he looked insubstantial, almost spectral. A wolf was howling intermittently from the far side of the valley and the cuckoos had been succeeded by owls hooting in the woods, like watchmen marking the passage of the night.

'There is a liberation in age,' he said. 'I look at the world as if I am no longer a part of it. I have become a spectator.' He looked at me across the fire. His eyes were pools of shadow. 'Like you,' he said.

'Like me?'

Mongolians were far too polite to offer any opinion about the bizarre nature of my travels. In any case most would have accepted my journey as inexplicable rather like the weather or market forces. I was a traveller. I had come from London. I had ridden across Mongolia from Bayan Ölgii. People were impressed by this feat of horsemanship, by my adoption of Mongolian ways, by my ability to survive the hardships of the country. But beyond that I was essentially a mystery. No one understood why I should want to come here, or what point there was to my journey. Once they had dispensed with the possibility that I might be a spy, my motives were too enigmatic to merit enquiry.

But the old man had been contemplating me. 'You are the *bada-chir*,' he said, using a word that meant a lone itinerant. 'You have no home, no family, no commitments. You are the outsider. That's why you have come to Mongolia. To be an outsider in your own land is more difficult.'

I had been drawn to Mongolia by my fascination with nomads and by what I took to be their restlessness, their mobility, their preference for fresh geography over stale history. But the reality of Mongolia had proved more complicated. The mobility of this world was restricted to the physical sensation of the landscape and the quest for pasturage; otherwise nomadic life was moored to conventions as strict as those in the narrow streets of any city. Camped in this high valley of tents and horses, the old man could see that I was the only figure adrift.

We woke to a thick frost, the first of the season, crackling in the folds of the tents. In a neighbouring *ger* we had a breakfast of *tsamba*, a floury paste like porridge eaten mainly in winter, washed down by a bowl of milk vodka, 'to warm our hearts,' Balginnyam said. Our host, an old friend of Balginnyam's, consulted an astrological almanac and declared that the previous day, the beginning of this stage, had been the day of the dragon, an auspicious date.

We rode north-east keeping to the winding line of the stream. Straggling flocks revolved in slow orbit round the *gers*. Cloud shadows raced away in front of us, dipping in and out of the contours of the valley ahead. In the clear air scraps of sound drifted on the wind – the lilting song of children's voices, the bass chorus of yaks growling, the rhythms of galloping hooves, the drawn-out notes of neighbours calling to one another across the grasses. The horses had caught the infectious mood of the morning, shouldering past one another as we trotted over a low saddle into a wilderness of empty valleys, autumnal grasses, and pristine blue skies.

Sometime after midday we came upon a road accident. A yak-cart had lost a wheel. The passengers were three damsels in distress – an old woman with a stick and her two daughters, accompanied by a collection of children. They stood gazing at the stricken cart in a state of mild shock while the yak, free of its traces and oblivious to the crisis, was getting on with lunch in the long grass beyond the track. They gave dramatic and conflicting accounts of the accident. One rather hysterical version had the youngest boy falling beneath the cart where the good wheel had run over his chest. The casualty seemed to have recovered surprisingly well. When we arrived he was chasing his sister through a meadow below the road.

Friar William had travelled by cart in the early stages of his journey when his minders thought he was too fat for any of their horses, and Genghis Khan's enormous royal *ger* was famously transported by cart drawn by a team of oxen. But this was the first cart I had seen in Mongolia, and it struck me as a newfangled contraption that predictably had gone badly wrong.

Chivalry beckoned and we spent an hour repairing the damage, fashioning a new wheel pin from a piece of wood with a long knife that Balginnyam drew out of one of his boots. While we worked the women unearthed milk tins from the medieval sacks that filled the well of the cart and kept us supplied with *airag*. When the wheel was slotted onto the axle and the new pin hammered home, granny was reinstalled on top of the sacks, the bemused yak was backed into position, and the whole cumbersome contrivance jerked into motion. Turning on its axle, the wooden wheel emitted

a thin high-pitched whine, the first primitive complaint of mechan-
ization.

We doffed our hats and rode away up the valley. The pause had
made the horses restless. They tossed their heads and broke into a
fitful gallop, as if they needed to show their superiority over this
historic rival: the wheel. We spurred them over the rising ground
at the southern end of the valley where they danced between the
boulders, sure-footed on the broken ground. At the top of the
pass, where an *ovoo* was streaming blue rags across the skyline, I
turned to look back. It took me a moment to locate the cart,
creeping almost imperceptibly along the valley bottom. It was
already a mile behind us. I pitied them, and their ponderous progress. In that moment I inhabited a distant world, still convinced
of the superiority of the saddle, where the wheel seemed a foolish
project, unlikely to stand the test of time.

Then I turned my horse and galloped after the others, swooping
down a long slope between stands of pine trees to a narrow valley
where a yak stood knee-deep in brackish water, gazing tragically at
his own reflection, as if unable to believe that God could have given
him such a face. The bad water was a disappointment; we had
hoped to fill our flasks there. When we finally emerged in a wider
valley, where two *gers* stood on the banks of a feeble stream, Balginnyam suggested we camp. He was concerned it might be the only
good water we would find. But it was still early and I did not like
this bleak place. I longed for trees and soft grass. This was the lush
district of Arhangay, and I wanted to enjoy its benefits. Through
the binoculars I could see a distant line of hills to the east, and I
decided to risk riding on. I felt sure there would be water at the
base of the hills. Balginnyam was sceptical but he decided to trust
my judgement. He could have offered me no greater compliment.

It took three hours to cross the empty plain. The ghosts of *gers*,
camped here during the summer, haunted the grass: pale circular
shadows among the litter of old animal bones. Magpies bounced
about looking for scraps, and I spotted a fox retreating up a hillside,
heading for more promising terrain. Through the tired hours of
late afternoon, we seemed becalmed in this vast place. Every slight
rise opened further unexpected expanses of sun-washed grass. The
promising hills never seemed to come any nearer, as if they were

an illusion of light, forever retreating in front of us. My two companions, now convinced we had been mistaken not to stop earlier, fell into a weary and ill-tempered silence. Even the horses began to flag.

But in the last sweet hour of daylight a band of trees finally appeared along the base of the hills. Scenting water and fresh pasture, the horses lifted their heads. Twenty minutes later we were splashing across a fine wide river into a grassy parkland of broad-leaf poplars. After the thin larches of the previous days they looked gracious and stately and as ripe as late fruit. The first colours of autumn were upon them and a dusting of yellow leaves lay across the swathes of grass between the fat trunks. It was a sylvan paradise.

After supper I sat with my back to a rough trunk, watching the light fading across the plain we had just crossed, while our horses chomped happily on thick grass. The bare steppes of Mongolia had made me rather desperate for such trees. In their scented shade, I was overcome with nostalgia. The dappled and shifting light was sweetly familiar. I remembered excursions into the woods of childhood, the dry odour of fallen leaves powdering beneath our feet on the way to school in the early autumn, stormy winter evenings when the trees about the house had pitched and rolled like ships, and the beckoning fingertips of the longest branches had tapped the window panes. I sat in the company of the trees until the dark came and stars appeared in bunches between the boughs.

In the morning I fished unsuccessfully in the river. Then we rode hard all day through busy valleys of flocks and *gers*, reaching the *aimag* centre of Tsetserleg in the late afternoon.

Balginnyam did not want to linger in the town, which he viewed with some distaste. He had decided to spend the night with friends on the other side of the pass before riding home to Chulutt. He had been a remarkable companion, dignified, wise and entertaining. Mandah had adored and respected him, and I could see that he had tempered her cynicism about her own countrymen. We accompanied him to the edge of town where he dismounted to say goodbye. As a farewell he drew my face to his with his two hands and touched his lips to one of my cheeks inhaling deeply. It was a Mongolian gesture, breathing a person's scent as you pressed your lips to their head.

'When you return,' he said, 'you can have the kiss on the other cheek.'

It was a pretty notion but we both knew we would never meet again.

Tsetserleg was more like a proper town than any place I had seen since Kazakhstan, almost three months before. Its buildings were aligned along real streets; most had windows, many had doors. Main Street even had tree-lined pavements. For the first time in Mongolia I felt the genuine touch of urban life. Chulutt, Dariv, Hovd, Ölgii were simply gathering places for nomads, administrative centres with a random collection of derelict and largely irrelevant government offices. Should the towns vanish overnight – and most seemed on the verge of doing so – their inhabitants would simply have mounted their horses and ridden back to the family *ger*, the flocks of sheep and the wise migration of nomadic life. In Tsetserleg there were the usual suburbs of *gers*, and much of the traffic on the paved streets was horsemen from the countryside. But there were also people with a different history, permanent residents with a commitment to sedentary life.

I stayed in a hotel on the main street in whose bleak funereal interior the temperature mysteriously plummeted. The receptionist, an elusive woman whom we eventually discovered in the hairdresser's shop up the street, was able to offer two types of room: the standard at £1.20 a night, or a 'luxe' room at £1.80. I decided to live a little, and splashed out the extra sixty pence. The 'luxe' was a suite with a bedroom, a sitting room, a collection of precarious pieces of furniture, an ancient Russian television, and a pair of plastic slippers. Utilities were a trifle erratic. The electricity came on for four hours in the evenings, but the water only came once a week, on Sundays, when the hotelkeeper went through the rooms filling the bathtubs which served as our supply well for the other six days.

Opposite the hotel was the town hall through whose open windows drifted the clatter of typewriters. This impression of bureaucratic efficiency was undermined somewhat by the streams of typed forms which also drifted through the windows to wash back and forth in neglected waves across the small square in front of the building. In the market there was an exciting choice of root vegetables including some rare carrots. Along the back wall, at the butcher's stalls, the heads of sheep and cows, intact bar the fact that they were no longer connected to necks, nestled like trophies among the joints and chops of their own dismembered bodies. I assumed Mongolian shoppers, accustomed to an unusual degree of intimacy with their dinner, preferred to examine the face before purchasing a cut. But the heads themselves were prized cuts; cow's head in particular was in considerable demand for cow's head stew. Outside among the eclectic displays of the dry goods section was a large double bed, an object that seemed as exotic here as a dromedary in Covent Garden. It could hardly have attracted a bigger crowd if nude models had been draped across the mattress.

Every night the town resounded with the distressing sounds of canine sex and violence. In love and war the whining of the vanquished and the howling of the victorious were indistinguishable. The staff quarters of one of the rival armies was stationed in the yard at the rear of the hotel where a decrepit battalion of mongrels plotted their military adventures between brutal copulations. By first light the exhausted dogs had fallen silent, and I lay abed listening to the clip-clop of horses passing up and down Main Street.

All towns in Mongolia are the legacy of the great monasteries that dominated Mongolian life until the arrival of Communism in the 1920s. For centuries they were the only buildings and the only permanent settlement in the country. Urga, the old name for Ulan Batur, meant simply the Temple. Even the smallest and most abandoned of settlements, like the ghost town of Dariv, were originally the sites of temple monasteries. They were considerable institutions, many of them greater in wealth and influence than the monasteries of medieval Europe. Each stood at the centre of an ecclesiastical estate of pastures and flocks, and were the sole provider of the skills that pastoral society traditionally lacks – education, trade, and craftsmanship.

Though Buddhism had been present in Mongolia since before the days of Genghis Khan, it was, in its early centuries, the religion of the elite. It is said that the Chinese began to promulgate Tibetan Buddhism more widely in the sixteenth century in the hope that it might pacify their northern neighbours. After two thousand years the Chinese had finally come to accept that the Great Wall had failed them. Subsidies to the stonemasons were diverted to lamas who were sent north to the Mongol Hordes to accomplish what ramparts and watchtowers had failed to do: keep them in check.

Like Tibet under the Dalai Lama, the Mongolia of the pre-Communist era was an ecclesiastical state, founded by the first Living Buddha, the Jebtsundamba Khutuktu who, on his 'discovery' in 1650, claimed descent from Genghis Khan. In such a curious monocultural society an ecclesiastical career was the only route to power for men of ambition, and the lamaseries became centres of intrigue and corruption that would rival any Asian court. The priesthood burgeoned as it became customary for every Mongolian family to send at least one of their sons to a lamasery for the status and influence this would confer. By the beginning of the twentieth century Mongolia had well over 100,000 lamas, a third of the male population, who inhabited 700 large monasteries and over 1000 smaller ones. Their ruler was the Bogd Khan, a god-king who was the seventh reincarnation of the Jebtsundamba Khutuktu. Living in considerable splendour in a palace in Urga the Bogd Khan pursued a life of debauchery which would have made a Borgia pope seem like a model of moral reticence.

Mongolian lamaseries had a very poor reputation among the handful of foreign visitors who reached the country at the end of the nineteenth and beginning of the twentieth centuries. They routinely denounced them as feudal parasitical institutions that bore much of the responsibility for the backward state of the country. A heavy system of tithes, as well as the loss of productive manpower, were seen as a drain on the country's limited resources. Money-lending, at rates of interest up to 200 per cent, had become a profitable sideline for the monks. Bands of itinerant monks wandered the countryside selling indulgences, telling fortunes and generally preying on the credulous herdsmen. The epidemic of syphilis, which affected most of the Mongolian population by the beginning of the twentieth century, was blamed on the promiscuity of the lamas who kept harems of catamites and concubines. The great Mongolian historian, Charles Bawden, called the monasteries 'the curse of Mongolia'. When the Communists came to power they were determined to rid the country of them. But it was not just the feudal excesses that disturbed them. The clerics were the Party's only serious rival for power.

For the past seventy years Mongolian historians have tried to portray the arrival of Communism in Mongolia as the result of a popular uprising of oppressed herdsmen against feudal lords and their allies, a decadent church. But few countries were as devoid of revolutionary fervour as Mongolia in 1911, when the Chinese were obliged to depart after the fall of the Qing dynasty. Left to their own devices, the Mongolians would have slumbered on in a medieval state. The fact that the country became the world's second Communist state was due entirely to the turbulent events then convulsing its two giant neighbours: Russia and China.

When the Chinese departed, the Mongolian aristocracy declared the country independent under the theocratic rule of the Bogd Khan. The Chinese, who saw their absence from Mongolian affairs as a temporary hiatus, never fully accepted Mongolian independence, and in 1919 a Chinese warlord, General Hsu Shu-Tseng, attracted by the idea of all those back taxes, briefly reasserted Chinese control. Early in 1921 Hsu was turned out by a White Russian adventurer fleeing the civil war inside his own country, the mad Baron von Ungern-Sternberg.

That this remarkable and demented figure, at the head of a ragtag army of Tsarist officers, Cossacks, Polish renegades, and miscellaneous brigands, could take control of the country was a measure of how perilous was the notion of Mongolian nationhood in the early decades of the twentieth century. Having captured Urga, the mad Baron launched a Reign of Terror of psychopathic proportions. Styling himself the Khan of Mongolia and the God of War, he returned the Bogd Khan to his throne as titular head of state and embarked upon a brief but energetic period of office marked by barbarism and civic amenities. He started a bus service, organized electricity supplies, ordered the first street cleaning of Urga, built several bridges, published a newspaper and founded a veterinary laboratory.

On his own time he was flogging legions of prisoners to death and feeding them to his private pack of wolves. Meanwhile he was plotting with other Tsarist generals to cross back into Russia and restore the Grand Duke Michael to the Romanov throne.

The Baron provided the Red Army with the pretext it needed to enter Mongolia. By the middle of July 1921 ten thousand Bolshevik troops had arrived, ostensibly at the invitation of the Mongolian Revolutionary Party, a tiny organization barely a year old. Throughout the summer White and Red Russian forces, both aided by Mongolian irregulars, fought a number of bloody battles with the Bolsheviks gradually gaining the upper hand. Eventually abandoned by his own men, the Baron was captured by a Red Army patrol and taken to Novosibirsk where he was executed by firing squad in the middle of September.

Mongolia was the first of a long line of countries to discover how difficult it was to get the Red Army to go home. Communism was in the first flush of evangelical conviction, and the young political cadres attached to the Red Army set about recreating the Mongolian Revolutionary Party in their own image. Within a year fifteen of the leading members had been shot. Within two years they had dispensed with the charismatic nationalist leader, Sukhbatur, who is widely believed to have been poisoned by Russian agents. Had he lived Mongolia might have secured a more independent status.

The People's Republic of Mongolia, the first and the most slavish of the Soviet Union's client states, became the model for methods of control that the Kremlin would eventually practise throughout the world. Russian advisors and technicians flooded into the country to operate every modern facility from the railway to the security service which was set up by the NKVD, the forerunner to the KGB. Both Party and government were controlled by Russian political agents, and any sign of heresy was eliminated by selective assassination. From the years of early Leninism to the reforms of Gorbachev, Mongolian policy would mirror precisely the ideological shifts in the Soviet Politburo. In the circumstances it is surprising that Mongolia managed to retain its independence, however nominal. Stalin in particular was keen to absorb the country into the Soviet Union but a combination of realism in the Kremlin and latent nationalism in Mongolia thwarted his ambitions.

Throughout the dark years of his purges, Stalin had continually pressed Mongolian leaders to rid the country of the lamaseries which he considered the chief obstacle to complete Communist orthodoxy. A succession of leaders, who baulked at this assault on the nation's religious and cultural heritage, were deposed and murdered until finally Stalin had his own man, Choilbasan, in place as the General Secretary of the Party. A barely literate alcoholic, Choilbasan understood that his only chance of survival was complete co-operation. Ominously, he had spent part of his own unhappy childhood in a monastery where his destitute mother had abandoned him. Mistreated by the lamas, he had run away to become a street urchin in Urga.

In the early years of the revolution, the government had stripped the monasteries of their land and their privileges. Enormous taxes were levied on them, and many were forcibly relocated to unpopulated areas. In 1932, 700 monks were imprisoned or murdered in the wake of revolts against the confiscation of private property.

Back in Moscow, Stalin was demanding an even tougher line against the lamaseries. In the autumn of 1937, while the Party itself was being purged of its last discordant elements, the Final Solution began. In one of the darkest moments in Mongolian history, Choilbasan dispatched death squads across the country, chiefly composed of Russian secret police. In the space of a few months all of the country's monasteries were destroyed, well over fifteen hundred institutions, many of them hundreds of years old. Their inhabitants were purged. About 20,000 lamas were executed outright, most of them shot in the dark of night outside the burning ruins of their temples, and thrown into pits. The rest, up to 80,000 men, were sent to prison camps, many of them in Russian Siberia. Only a few ever returned. Almost overnight a quarter of the male population disappeared. With them went Buddhism in Mongolia, now officially a crime.

Buyandelgeruulekh Khiid in Tsetserleg was one of only a tiny handful of temple monasteries in the country that was allowed to survive as museums. In a previous incarnation the museum guide might have run the lamasery tavern. She was splendid landlady material, an overripe forthright woman who had reached an age when her wardrobe and her hips no longer agreed about her size. She wore a low-cut blouse and a string of fake pearls which roamed seductively across soft acres of cleavage. She had extravagant earrings, painted eyebrows and lipstick on her teeth. I found her in a side office, in an unbuttoned state, her feet up on a desk and her stockings rolled down to her knees.

The idea of the museum was that future generations, living in the rational sunlit uplands of a Communist society, would have the opportunity to guffaw at the primitive beliefs of their superstitious ancestors. Set against a hill overlooking the town, Buyandelgeruulekh Khiid was surrounded by the ruins of a much larger complex of temples whose fate had been rather more brutal. Most Mongolian temples drew their architectural inspiration from Tibet or China. Buyandelgeruulekh Khiid was of the latter persuasion, a group of single-storeyed buildings, one room deep, set round a courtyard between walls of lacquered and patterned screens, beneath soaring eaves.

Nyama's formidable bosom herded me along the stone paths between the buildings. She took little interest in the temples in her charge, loitering in the doorways, filing her impressive nails, while I looked round the cool interiors. She was a Russophile, an ironic guardian for these victims of Russian fanaticism.

She asked how I had come to Mongolia. She frowned when I mentioned Kazakhstan, but was delighted to hear I had been in Volgograd and had spent some time on the Black Sea. She had lived in St Petersburg for six years, she declared proudly. 'As a teenager,' she said, 'when I was young and beautiful.' She was an ardent admirer of Russian *kultura*. 'The Opera, the Ballet, the Literature,' she sighed, rescuing the pearls from the depths of her cleavage and twisting them round her fingers. 'Mother Russia. This is Civilization, no?'

I was easily seduced. I felt a bit starved of *kultura* myself. If I had a wish, a magic carpet to take me away from the steppes for a day out, St Petersburg would be high on my list of destinations: an afternoon in the Hermitage, tea on the Nevsky Prospekt, an evening at the Kirov followed by late dinner at the Astoria Hotel.

I asked Nyama if she had been to the Kirov.

'Tchaikovsky,' she murmured, dropping the name wantonly from her lips, an indecent sibilant sound. She swayed slightly as if remembering melodies. 'I saw *Swan Lake*.' She trailed a hand through the air. 'Such princes,' she sighed. 'Such swans.'

St Petersburg had left its stamp on her. With her heavy-lidded sensuality and her overpowering scent of powder she was the kind of character familiar to Pushkin's Onegin. I pictured her in a boudoir, on a chaise longue, entertaining a clique of young suitors.

Nyama was not the first echo from St Petersburg to reach Tsetserleg. It was the assassination of the Secretary of the Leningrad Party, Comrade Kirov, after whom the theatre was named, which triggered Stalin's purges of the 1930s. Like a stone dropped in a pond, the murder broke the surface of Soviet life and the fearful ripples would eventually wash across Asia to engulf every monastery and every lama in Mongolia.

With the introduction of religious freedom, Buddhism has returned to Mongolia, a shrunken presence struggling to regain ground in a secularized society. While Mongolians are eager to acknowledge the religion as part of their culture, it has not regained its former status.

One of the surviving buildings in Tsetserleg had been revived as a practising temple; a sign by the gateway announced the date it had recommenced its religious life: the 3 April 1990. Above a raised veranda of lacquered pillars the beams were decorated with garish skulls, meant to scare off evil spirits. Inside the tall temple doors, adorned with lion-head knockers, the monks were whispering Tibetan sutras into the incense-laden gloom. They were exactly as Friar William had described them over seven centuries ago. 'All their priests shave their heads completely,' William wrote, 'and dress in saffron colour . . . on the days when they go into the temple they put down two benches and sit opposite one another in two rows like choirs, holding their books.'

Buddhist rituals tend to go on a bit and the monks like to slot meals and snacks into the services. Tibetan scriptures were laid out on the low desks before them among the litter of breakfast – bowls of tea and plates of petrified cheese. Without interrupting the chanting a novice was making his way along the row replenishing the bowls from a great copper kettle like an attentive waiter. A tray of cakes arrived, produced by one of the petitioners who sat respectfully on a bench along the back wall.

The monks, a small assembly, were either very old or very young, survivors of the purges or novices who had taken up their vows since 1990. Among the latter was a plump fellow with a woolly cap who interrupted the chants at climactic moments with a blast on a long ecclesiastical trumpet as if he was announcing the end of the world. The old guard were represented by two ancient lamas at the end of the row. One accompanied the chants on a skin drum; his sense of rhythm might have been better sixty years ago. The other, a toothless chap, seemed to be having difficulty with the hard cheese. Their chanting was a little rusty but still mesmeric.

Buddhist monks are hoarders; they never seem to throw anything out. Regiments of tattered prayer banners hung from the ceiling, motheaten scarves were knotted round the pillars, old manuscripts that no one seemed to have looked at since the death of Genghis Khan were wrapped in dusty cloths and crammed into glass-fronted cabinets, rank upon indiscriminate rank of ornaments crowded every surface: statues of Buddha in every size and posture, framed-photographs of the Dalai Lama, endless paintings of fearsome guardians, creaking prayer wheels, butter lamps, crowds of miniature stupas like cheap holiday souvenirs. The clutter in the side aisles was so terrific that it was some moments before I noticed an ancient monk, like another dusty and forgotten artefact, who had nodded off in a corner with his stockinged feet nestling on the fender of a big Russian stove.

The surprise was that so much had survived. At the time of the purges, the Party had had a bit of a clear-out. Ancient manuscripts were burnt, prayers wheels were smashed, and gold and silver ornaments were melted down and shipped to Russia. The artefacts that crowd the revived temples are the things that people managed to rescue and to hide through the long decades of Communist suppression.

In a side office two women ran the Prayer Request Office. Here petitioners came to book prayers, sutras and blessings for particular concerns such as births, marriages, deaths, journeys, ill health, better pasturage, or good rainfall. A notice on the back wall listed the various options and the prices. The whole affair had an oddly bureaucratic air which I took for some legacy of Communism. There was a high counter, endless forms to be filled out in triplicate, a thick ledger where the requests were recorded, and receipts with official temple stamps. The women did their best to be slow and surly. There was even a queue.

I asked one of the women if it would be possible to visit any of the old monks who had been active before the purges. She mentioned the three elderly monks I had seen in the temple but advised me instead to go to see the oldest monk in the district who lived not far away, in Ikh Tamir. He had been attached to the Tsetserleg temples in the 1930s. He was ninety-seven, she said, but his mind was still clear.

I went to find a jeep immediately. With a man of ninety-seven, delay seemed inadvisable.

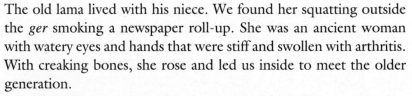

The old lama lived with his niece. We found her squatting outside the *ger* smoking a newspaper roll-up. She was an ancient woman with watery eyes and hands that were stiff and swollen with arthritis. With creaking bones, she rose and led us inside to meet the older generation.

At first the *ger* appeared to be empty. I had the sensation that I had come to visit a ghost, the spirit of a lama, perhaps evoked by the small Buddha in the glass-fronted box on a chest. An amber light seeped through the walls of the tent. A clock ticked in the silence.

'*Akhaa*,' the octogenarian niece croaked. 'Wake up. A foreigner has come to visit you.' She went across to one of the cots against the wall and prodded a blanket. A tiny head stirred on the pillow; beneath the blanket the body made hardly more impression than a rumpled sheet.

I helped her raise the old monk to a sitting position. He was as weightless as a moth. His slippered feet, swinging down from the bed in slow motion, landed so lightly on the earth he might have been afloat, there on the edge of the cot. His connection to the physical world seemed tenuous, irrelevant. His hands fluttered across the blanket, locating his amber prayer beads and his snuff bottle. I sat on a low stool at his knees. He was the size of a child.

The century had distilled him to some essence of life – a minute frame, an economy of movement, a delicacy of touch. He wore a red satin robe. Like the blanket, its folds seemed to contain almost nothing. His hands, protruding from frayed cuffs, lay in his lap, a collection of neatly folded bones, draped with translucent skin and decorated with blue veins. When he turned to look at me I could see that his old eyes, grown so pale they were blue, were almost blind. He had outlived gender. His thin shoulders, his small pursed lips and his delicate sagging skin, mottled with the stains of age, were sexless. Beneath a frosting of stubble, his skull looked as pale and delicate as porcelain.

'I was dreaming,' he said. On the threshold of sleep, his voice was a dry whisper.

His niece brought bowls of tea and I asked him about his life.

'I went to the monastery when I was eight,' he said. The words fell slowly like old leaves. 'I lived in the monastery in Tsetserleg. They were good times. The days were full of chanting. I was a monk for twenty-nine years.'

He could not remember how many lamas there had been in the old days. Perhaps a thousand, he said. It was one of the biggest monasteries in Mongolia, with many important lamas. When he was thirty-seven, the men had come from Ulan Batur, and the world of the monastery came to an end.

After sixty years he remembered that night as a series of confused images. The men came in trucks, the headlights shining into the courtyards. He remembered their shadows, stretching across the cobblestones and wavering across the walls of the temples. They had guns. One of the men read something, a proclamation. They said there was no God and no religion.

'Everything happened very suddenly,' the old man said. 'In the afternoon we had been monks in the temples. By the end of the night we were prisoners.'

First they took the older and more important lamas, men whom he had been taught to venerate.

'Like cattle,' the old man said. 'Herded together outside the gate in the light from the trucks. When I think of those lamas now, I can only remember their faces that night. Their eyes were white, and some of them were crying out. The men pushed them forward with their guns and loaded them into the back of their trucks and took them away. People said they were shot. I do not know what happened to them. But we never saw the old lamas again.'

Though he spoke slowly, the words seemed to slip from his mouth before they were fully formed. Dropping through toothless gums, the cluttered consonants stumbled over one another. Mandah translated my questions carefully but he never confused her role, turning with his replies to me, gazing sightlessly into my face, from time to time placing his hand on my arm to establish contact. His touch was so light, his bones might have been hollow.

'They made us burn the temples ourselves. First they took away all the sculptures, the precious things. Then they forced us to set fire to the buildings. But we were able to save some things. People had gathered at the rear of the temples, you see, on the slope above, local people, herdsmen. In the darkness we took things out to them when the men were busy below – texts and prayer banners and Buddhas – and the people took them away and hid them.'

With most of the ordinary monks he was sent to a prison camp that was built on the outskirts of Tsetserleg. He spent twelve years there, working in the camp as a camel herder carrying wood for the people in the town. Life was very hard, he said. They barely gave them enough food to survive, usually just plain rice. Some of the lamas died in the camp. When he was finally released he was sent to work in a herding collective in another district some distance away. He had lived there as a simple herdsman until the changes in 1990.

I asked if he had practised Buddhism in secret as some former lamas had done.

'No,' he said. 'It was not possible in those times. The Party members in the district were always warning me, not to give a prayer or a blessing, even to a member of my own family.'

'Didn't you chant, Uncle?' his niece asked. 'In secret?'

He turned towards her voice and an expression of mischief crossed his face. With his thumb and forefinger he lifted a pinch of snuff to his nose.

'Maybe.' There was the ghost of smile. 'A little. In secret.'

He turned back to me. 'All that was left of my temple was rubble. My sister managed to hide some of the precious things, manuscripts and a Buddha which had been in my *ger*. She went to collect them after I had been taken. She wrapped them in cloth and cow's dung and buried them near the river in Tsetserleg. When the reforms came and the temples opened again I directed one of my nephews to find them. They were safe after fifty years. I gave them to the new temple in Tsetserleg. Many people hid things in this way. You see we never lost *Buddagiin Shashin* – Buddha's faith. We suffered for fifty years but I am happy that I have lived to see the time when we can chant again.'

In recent years there have been government attempts to arrange compensation for monks. Officials from Ulan Batur had visited him and asked him to fill in a form listing the possessions that had been taken from him.

'They asked me about my livestock. My family's *ger*. They wanted to try to fix a price for these things. For compensation.' He smiled at me. 'What can I write for them?' he asked. 'I should try to count sheep for them after fifty years? How do I list the things I lost?'

He seemed relieved that nothing ever came of it.

'The men who came were like the first men who burnt the temples. They were the same. They asked a lot of dirty questions. About the names of the men who had arrested me, who had burnt the temples, who watched us in the prison camp. They wanted to make records, they said. But I told them nothing. It was a long time ago. Nothing can change what happened. Giving them names would not bring back the old temples.'

Mongolian monasteries may have had a poor reputation but this old monk's simple goodness was an inspiration. He was without bitterness.

'The past is irretrievable,' he said. 'You cannot live there.'

He wanted to go outside. A young man appeared and together we conveyed the old man to the door of the *ger*. His sharp elbow beneath my hand seemed the only point of substance. Outside we placed him gently on a chair in the late sun. He was apologetic about his infirmities.

'When I want to see there are no eyes, when I want to eat there are no teeth, when I want to walk there are no legs,' he said. It was very poetic in Mongolian.

The evening was scented with pine and the buttery smell of *gers*. On the far side of the river the pastures were raked with golden light. Coming home, the flocks trailed long shadows.

The old man sat with his head tilted like a bird, listening to the evening: the sound of sheep and the distant drawl of voices. How lightly, I thought, he perches on the world.

'I am waiting my turn,' he said. He lifted his face to the falling light. 'I seem to be the only one left.'

By the door of the *ger* an infant awoke and began to whimper. It was the old man's great great great great nephew. He turned his head towards the sound. 'He is like me, out of step with the world. He sleeps by day, and he is awake at night. We keep one another company while the others sleep.'

We took our leave.

'Do they give you good horses? he asked suddenly.

'Only when they trust me,' I said.

'You must insist. Tell them you have a lama's blessing. There is nothing so fine as a good horse. It makes up for anything.'

'*Sain yavaarai*,' he chanted. 'Good journey.' He waved his two hands briefly, like tiny wings flapping about his face. Then, exhausted by the effort, they fluttered to his lap and were still.

Chapter Thirteen

THE WEDDING BATTLE

Throughout the evening people came to warn me about themselves. They sat on the grass outside my tent, unburdening themselves with pre-emptive confessionals. The following day would be difficult, they said. Weddings were boisterous occasions. People became unpredictable. They counselled me about particular individuals then admitted that they themselves could be as bad as the next fellow. I would be wise to get away early before things got out of hand.

We had left Tsetserleg in the grip of a yellow apocalypse. A tempest of dust clouds and hot winds had engulfed the town. In the sulphur-coloured gloom a horseman had arrived at the hotel with four skittish horses. We wrapped our heads in scarves and rode away through the swirling streets.

By mid-morning the storm had abated. We crossed wind-scoured plains beneath high baroque clouds. The sky was washed and fresh. To the north, flocks of sheep were fanning out from the folds of plump hills. We rode with a river on our right heralded by a band of splendid trees showering yellow leaves. At midday we crossed at a ford where the water rose above our stirrups. I folded my legs over the pommel of the saddle and my horse stretched his neck forward in the charcoal-coloured water. He was a dark gelding with downy ears, a thoughtful face and an easy gait. I talked soothingly to him as he struggled for footing among the loose boulders of the stream bed, but he was calm and confident and lurched up onto the opposite bank without trouble.

The country on the far side was inhabited by poplars standing spaciously apart, and we rode through the latticework of their shadows where the winds had drifted the fallen leaves into curving currents. With their arboreal vaults, the trees had the air of memorial architecture. They were the only form in these landscapes to mark the long passage of time. In their rings one could find the record of decades. Perhaps this was why I was so pleased to see them. In the indifferent spaces of Mongolia, among the grasses and the endless wildflowers which seemed to last a summer or an eternity, they alone had a life like my own.

We climbed a rise and came down onto big open plains, treeless again, where two silent lakes had pooled among the grasses. Flocks of sheep lifted their heads as we passed. Hoopoes appeared around the edges of the lakes, dancing along the dust tracks that parted the grass. Towards the east the sky was streaked with mare's tail clouds.

Our horseman was the younger brother of the driver who had taken us to visit the old lama in Ikh Tamir. The temperamental difference between the settled town and the nomadic countryside cut through their family. The driver was a clean-cut sort with a house, a jeep, a watch, a pair of Levi's and a nose for commercial opportunity. The horseman was a nomad with a lively set of horses, a threadbare *del*, a poor sense of punctuality and a passion for marmot hunting. He was a gentle sentimental soul who saw us not as clients but as guests. Solicitous about our comfort and safety, he was keen that we should be happy in his home, in the embrace of these landscapes.

We rode on through the long afternoon, across vast yellow spaces into a blue distance where we came at last to an encampment of four *gers* afloat between flocks of sheep and cloud shadows as big as counties. It was the autumn camp of the horseman's in-laws.

On his advice we pitched the tents away from the *gers*. He too was worried about the fallout from the big wedding of the following day. Two women came across with a bucket of *airag* for us, followed in time by a stream of visitors to help us drink it. They sat on their haunches outside the tent with their horses snuffling at their backs and warned us apologetically about the coming festivities. Drink would be taken, they said. The festivities might attract the wrong sort. Things could get rowdy.

It sounded irresistible.

In the morning the groom and his supporters, a party of about seven or eight relations, set off to fetch the bride from her *ger* which lay some fifteen miles away. An old Russian truck, the equivalent of the wedding Rolls, had been specially hired for the occasion. When they arrived the groom would be obliged to search for his bride who by tradition must hide from him. It would not be too difficult. The tradition is that she hides under a bed in the neighbouring *ger*.

While we waited for their return we were given breakfast in the newlywed's *ger*. Over the past weeks it had been lovingly prepared by relations. It was like a show *ger* from Ideal Gers. Decorations included a poster of the inspirational figure of Batardene, the national wrestling champion, which had been hung in a prominent position above the marital bed. Biscuits, slabs of white cheese, and boiled sweets had been arrayed on every surface in dizzy tiers like wedding cakes. On a low stool stood a mountainous plate of sheep parts, arranged decoratively with the favoured cut, the great fatty tail, like a grey glacier on its summit. Younger sisters hustled in and out making last-minute preparations for the arrival of the groom, his bride and the guests. While we were at breakfast the first lookouts were posted to watch for the return of the truck bearing the wedding party from the bride's camp.

By mid-afternoon we were still waiting. Apparently a wedding breakfast would have been given to the groom and his accompanying party at the bride's camp, and complicated calculations were now performed concerning the number of miles to the bride's *ger*, divided by the speed of the truck, combined with the probable duration of the breakfast, and finally multiplied by the estimated consumption of *arkhi*. The unknown variable was the mechanical condition of the truck, an antique hybrid in which a Chinese engine had been grafted experimentally onto a Russian chassis by a camel herder from Uliastay.

At four o'clock a spiral of dust finally appeared beyond a distant ridge. When the truck drew up in front of the wedding *ger*, it was clear that the lavish hospitality of the bride's camp had been the cause of the delay. The back of the truck was crammed with wedding guests in such a state of dishevelled merriment that we had some difficulty persuading them to disembark. The bride's mother, apparently convinced that they were at the wrong *ger*, required four men to convey her to terra firma. The bride's elder sister, shrugging off all assistance, fell headfirst from the tailgate, bounced twice and came to rest, smiling, against a door post.

Once everyone was down from the truck, the bride and the groom stood respectfully to one side while the wedding party crowded into the new *ger* like football supporters at a local Derby. The groom was very tall and very thin with a long angular face. The bride, as round as he was linear, came up to his waist. Throughout the happy day they behaved like disappointed parties on a blind date, maintaining a glum countenance, and never once meeting each other's eyes. For the bride this was part of Mongolian tradition. She was meant to display a demure reluctance deemed to be commensurate with feminine modesty. Her new husband was part of a wider tradition: the nervous slightly shell-shocked bridegroom familiar in every culture. Their curious distance from the general jollity was exacerbated by the fact that they remained the only sober members of the wedding party.

Religion was represented by the kind of monk that Communists warned the populace about in the 1930s. A theatrical figure of porcine debauchery, the attendant lama would have made Falstaff seem both abstemious and thin. He was attired in a filthy *del*, a Manchu moustache, and a pirate's headband. Laying a fat hand on my head he mumbled a few words in *faux* Tibetan by way of a blessing, then offered me a bowl of *airag*. I liked him. He was jolly, lecherous, and very drunk.

Inside the newlyweds' *ger*, the two families took up positions on either side of the tent like opposing armies. Numbering fifty or sixty people, they were crowded together with the kind of intimacy usually reserved for the morning rush hour on the Tokyo subway.

The unexpected presence of a foreigner was seen as a sign of good fortune for the success of the union and I had been squeezed into the lap of one of the groom's brothers. At my back were the sharp knees of a long disapproving line of grannies and elderly aunts seated on cots.

Mongolian weddings suffer from an excess of hospitality. After the morning's blow-out at the bride's *ger*, it was now the turn of the groom's family to turn on the largesse, and they did not want to be outdone. Traditionally each guest had to drink three bowls of *airag*, and three of *arkhi*. Younger sisters were deployed as cup-bearers picking their way through the crush of limbs as they ferried the bowls back and forth.

With the arrival of the third bowl of *airag* each guest was obliged to offer a song. For even the shyest Mongolians this was a fairly painless turn as the whole assembly knew all the songs by heart and joined in *en masse* before the end of the first line. Sadly they were less familiar with the Irish air *She Moves Through the Fair*, and I was obliged to sing all four verses, unaccompanied, to a silent and bemused audience. It was only as I was coming to the end of the first verse that I remembered it was a song about a doomed wedding. Mongolians are very touchy about tempting fate and when they asked for a translation I suggested to Mandah that she should lie. She performed admirably producing a story about a boy looking for his favourite horse. The lama, a man familiar with duplicity, gave us a strange look. The novelty of Western music demanded an encore and I plumped for *The Skye Boat Song* on the grounds that the story – involving war, defeated chieftains, and domestic animals – would be a recognizable and fairly innocuous tale for a tentful of Mongolians.

No sooner had the third bowls of *airag* been polished off and the last songs died away than the bride's brothers carried in fresh supplies of drink from the truck, and the cupbearers started their rounds again. A rivalry was developing between the two families to outdo one another as bountiful providers. No quarter was to be given in an effort to ply the other side with liquor. Whispered instructions were quickly given to a couple of youths from the groom's side who hurried outside, took to their horses, and rode off across country to press-gang more supplies of *airag* from distant neighbours.

Under the pressure of drink, wedding guests on all sides were coming unstuck. Hats were askew, faces were turning green, and inanities were mumbled as wisdom. Even the sharp-kneed aunties were beginning to slobber. Meanwhile more and more guests arrived and the crush was beginning to make the assembly seem like a company of contortionists. People were stacked about me like interlocking crates.

The groom's brother, in his role as best man, was trying to bring some order to the proceedings, introducing members of the groom's family, welcoming the bride's family, directing the flow of *airag*. He wore the kind of peaked leather cap favoured by Lenin in the days when there was a revolution to lead. The resemblance was further underlined by a goatee and a tendency to stand and wave his arms about in declamatory fashion. He made several toasts. 'We will drink! We will feast! We will sing!' He made it sound like a Party directive.

One of the groom's brothers-in-law had taken a proprietorial interest in me. He wore a Homburg hat and a red *del* and had the smile and face of a friendly small-town bank manager. He lived nearby in a railway carriage. The great thing were the windows, he said. After a lifetime in *gers*, he loved the novelty of being able to see out. Also he found the fixtures quite useful. The emergency cord was ideal for drying sheepskins. The toilet compartment made a snug little byre for young lambs born when the nights were still frosty. But over the hubbub I was unable to discover the essential mystery of his carriage home: how it got here. The nearest railway was over 200 miles away.

The man in the Homburg let it be known that he was helping to pay for the wedding. He was a prosperous fellow with vast stocks of sheep. Drink had inflamed his generous instincts. I was to let him know if I needed anything. When it emerged that I was travelling by horse, he offered me his own horse, a Naadam winner, a priceless beast according to his own calculations. I demurred but he insisted. 'I'll kill a sheep tomorrow, you can take it with you,' he said. 'You are our guest. Whatever you need, food, horses, good luck, just let me know.' He held up his finger quizically. 'Have you a wife?' he asked. 'Don't worry. We'll sort something out in the morning.'

On the other side of the *ger*, among the bride's family, the most prominent figures were her two brothers. The first was a fine singer who was much called upon during the course of the afternoon for a song. The other brother could have played Wyatt Earp in a remake of *Gunfight at the OK Corral*. He had a broad-brimmed hat, a pencil moustache and handsome chiselled features. He had even mastered the cowboy trick of conveying an impression of intelligence and quiet dignity by never opening his mouth. When pressed for comment he invariably came up with the Mongolian equivalent of 'Yup.'

The drink and the crowded conditions had made for a terrific camaraderie. Sprawled in each other's laps, we were all becoming bosom chums. Even the overbearing Lenin was a pal. The bowls of *airag* came and went, and the company grew mawkish and lachrymose. Lenin was suffering an identity crisis. 'I have tried to do my duty, Stalin,' he appealed to me, his hands outstretched, tears welling in his eyes. 'I have done the best I could. I have tried to raise a good son. I have tried to be a good husband. I have tried to be good brother.'

A new fellow had squeezed in among us, an uncle of the groom with a dark whiskery face and a personal hygiene problem. He was rank as a camel. Lenin's tears had set him off, and he began to sob on Mandah's shoulder. He had a daughter her age, who had been adopted when she was a baby. His shoulders shook, and big tears descended his cheeks. By the time they reached his chin they were black. Only the man who lived in the railway carriage kept smiling. 'Do you travel with camels?' he asked. 'I can get you some very good camels.'

New reserves of *airag* were now arriving. An elder sister of the bride arose at this point with a rather sarcastic vote of thanks followed by the announcement that the family were now taking their leave. Apparently the feeling was that the groom's family were being rather too generous with the drink, and trying to belittle the bride's family by outdoing their hospitality of the morning. On cue Wyatt Earp and the singer rose to depart followed by the massed ranks of the bride's family. The groom's family, alarmed by this sudden turn of events, sprang to their feet. 'You must stay,' they cried. 'Food is coming. There is more *airag*. You must enjoy yourselves.' Beneath their protestations lay the idea that the bride's family were insulting them by not accepting their hospitality with good grace.

Much pulling now ensued. The groom's family pulled at the bride's family to keep them from departing while the bride's family pulled strenuously towards the door. In no time the pulling, common to the friendliest of Mongolian drinking circles, had degenerated into a brawl. Someone had pulled too hard and toppled forward, flattening a granny. Someone else accidentally upset a bowl of *airag*.

Suddenly the *ger* was in uproar, and blows were being exchanged. Wyatt Earp laid into a row of young men, felling three of them with a roundhouse right. The man who lived in the railway carriage, smiling more widely than ever, floored the singer, sending the stove and an elderly aunt flying. Lenin tried to rescue the situation with one of his speeches. 'We will drink! We will feast! We will sing!' he shouted above the mayhem. But no one was listening. He chopped two of the bride's sisters to the ground and tried to push his way towards the door to block their escape route. One of the sharp-kneed aunts at my back had taken up a horsewhip and was merrily flaying in the direction of her new in-laws. Eight bowls of *airag* had not done much for her aim and the blows were raining down on my own shoulders. The bridal couple, wisely taking no part in the fisticuffs, sat side by side, eyes politely downcast, as if the warfare that now raged about them was just another embarrassing speech. The only other non-participant was the lama, who viewed the fray with the beady eyes of a fight promoter while taking the opportunity of the general distraction to help himself to another bowl of *arkhi*.

The brawl came to an abrupt end with a strange good grace. It appeared fierce enough – there were at least a couple of bloody noses – but afterwards, with victory going to the groom's family for preventing what they saw as premature departure, everyone settled down to another round of drinking and songs. No one seemed to consider a wedding punch-up odd. With my own judgement slightly deranged by *airag* I was happy to fall in with this consensus, and decided that this mixture of camaraderie and violence, with a few songs thrown in, was a rather healthy business. It cleared the air nicely. A wedding reception where you got to give your new in-laws a good thumping was the kind of thing that people in the West could only dream about.

The bride's family of course were quite right to try to fight their way out when they did. A couple of hours later we were loading them into the back of the truck like sacks of potatoes. The bride stood to one side, on the threshold of her new life, watching the departure of her comatose family. Her last sight of them was the truck breasting a distant ridge. Silhouetted against the skyline was a single standing figure, the fat lama, one arm upraised, his robes flapping in the wind, the deranged captain of a devastated ship.

I was embarking on the final stage to Qaraqorum. The ancient capital lay four days' ride to the south-east.

The approaching winter had retreated temporarily, and the days basked in the warm sun of a brief Indian summer. We crossed a dry country where the wind blew the sandy soil raised by the horses' hooves through thin stands of grass. At a dying lake, four cows stood ankle-deep in marges of cracked mud. In the evenings the flocks of sheep gathered at wells where shepherds sluiced grey water into troughs. In a bleak place between two hills we passed a poor-looking *ger* where two naked children stood dumbly outside the door watching us, each clutching a talisman. The girl clung to a rag doll while the little boy held his penis.

On the morning of the second day we came down into the valley of the Orkhon river. Bounded to the east by distant blue hills, it seemed as wide as a country. We rode south with the river across grey flaking earth. Through the hot hours of midday, mirages fluttered across the flat expanses. Phantom trees came and went on the riverbanks to our left and far ahead herds of horses pranced in silver seas. Further south the country softened and men were gathering hay into oxcarts. The smell of the mown hay in the clear air was the smell of another country. Buildings had begun to appear among the *gers*, primitive constructions like Appalachian huts with empty doors and paper windows, the seasonal houses of people who were only dabbling with the idea of four walls. In the evenings the vast sunsets were the colour of fire. Splashing across the river channels, we camped on islands, on carpets of sweet grass fenced by willow scrub and water. The old moon sank behind screens of branches and we made huge fires of dead willow wood which cracked and sparked in the night air. Dogs howled from distant *gers* and the sky wore extravagant shawls of stars. In the mornings, we were awoken by great conclaves of ravens which gathered in the trees along the river, and the remains of our fires were cold moons of ash.

If this amorphous country has a heart, perhaps it is here, in the valley of the Orkhon. It has been a pivotal region in Mongolia since antiquity. Ogedei, Guyuk, and Mongke, the three successors to Genghis Khan, all spent months of each year in this valley where they held their *quriltais* or tribal gatherings. When the Mongol armies turned away from the planned sack of Vienna and rode home, it was here that they came. The valley is haunted by nomad tombs and there are remnants of pre-Mongolian settlement. The Uighurs, a Turkic people who now inhabit Xinjiang in north-west China, built a city here in the eighth century, known as Khan Balgasin Tuur. We rode in triumph through its empty shell.

In late afternoon we reached Qaraqorum. I had followed Friar William almost 5000 miles across much of the old empire, to this remote place. In his day it was briefly and unexpectedly the centre of the world, the focus of nations from the southern provinces of China to the Hungarian marches. Time has returned it to its natural state, a curiosity in remote grasslands. The long march of its white-washed walls rose from the steppe like another mirage. I spurred my mount up to the old city to lay my palm on the warm stone.

But the horse shied away, startled by the unfamiliar sight of walls and by the crows that flew suddenly through a gateway. To his nervous eyes the birds, flying out from the enclosed city, appeared to come from nowhere.

Unlike his brother Kubilai Khan, who would soon be building Beijing, Mongke Khan was too close to Mongol traditions to lock himself away in a city. When William arrived at the end of December in 1253 he found the Great Khan camped some distance from the city, preferring his *ger* to the luxuries of the capital. Mongke might rule the world but his chief concern was still good grazing for his sheep.

On 4 January 1254, William was summoned to an audience. After being frisked for weapons – concerns about the Assassins had resulted in tight security around the khan – they were taken inside the royal *ger* where they found Mongke seated on a low couch dressed in furs, examining some falcons. 'He is a snub-nosed man,' William wrote, 'of medium build, aged about forty-five'. Beside him sat a young wife and his grown-up daughter, Cirina, 'very ugly' according to the friar. Mongke asked them what they would like to drink and the friars settled for some rice wine. Their interpreter, who took his place next to the bar, was soon availing himself of refills. In no time he was drunk. William suspected Mongke himself of being a little tipsy.

Adopting a conciliatory tone in his address, William said he prayed for the khan 'to whom God has granted great dominion on earth' that he may have a good and long life. He explained their journey across Asia, from Sartaq to Batu, and then here to the court of the Great Khan. He concluded by asking leave to remain at court for at least two months to recuperate and await warmer weather. His colleague, Friar Bartholomew, was now so weak, William explained, that he could not ride further without risk to his life.

Mongke replied that the friar was quite right about his great power. 'Just as the sun spreads its rays in every direction,' he graciously conceded, 'so my power spreads to every quarter.' At this point his inebriated interpreter lost the plot and the rest of the royal address came in rambling and unconnected phrases. But in spite of the quality of the translation the audience passed off reasonably well and permission was granted for the friars to remain in the camp.

If the Mongols had hoped that the interview would cast some light on that most vexed of questions – the reason for William's visit – they were disappointed. While Mongke contented himself with diplomatic platitudes, various court officials interrogated William at length about his intentions and the letter he bore from the French King, Louis IX. They wanted to know if the French desired to make peace with them. William replied that as the two peoples were not at war, a peace mission was redundant. This made no sense to the Mongols. Their inflated view of their empire meant that they considered all peoples to be part of it. To them France was either submissive, recognizing the suzerainty of the Mongol khan, or opposed to it, and thus in a state of rebellion.

Part of the understandable confusion that dogged William's mission concerned Louis' letter. It had been written in the mistaken belief that Sartaq, the Mongol prince to whom William was originally sent, was a Christian. Though William did not know the contents of the sealed letter he understood it to be an appeal to the Mongols to unite in friendship with other Christians and to oppose those who were enemies of Christ. Unfortunately it had been translated by Armenians who seem to have made the French request rather more explicit by urging the Mongols to send troops to wage war against the Muslims. In light of the letter, William's insistence on the unofficial and religious nature of his journey must have seemed a trifle odd.

In all this confusion it is difficult to escape the impression that William was an unwitting pawn in a bigger game. Louis's previous contact with the Mongols had been the mission of Friar Andrew of Longjumeau, despatched explicitly to seek military alliances against the Muslims in the Holy Lands. Andrew got as far as the camp of Guyuk's widow in Central Asia where he was met with a frosty reception. The Mongols interpreted his presence as French submission, and sent him home with demands for tribute.

Unwilling to risk further rebuffs, Louis had supported William's mission because he was travelling as a missionary and not as an ambassador. Louis must have hoped that William would provide the Mongols with the opportunity to make overtures to Europe, if they were disposed to do so, without putting his own reputation on the line. He must also have hoped that the report he encouraged William to write would provide useful information about the disposition and size of the Mongol Empire, the character of its important princes and the nature of Mongol society, all mysterious issues to Europeans. William may have believed he was a humble missionary but his patron doubtless saw him, as the Mongols did, as an unwitting envoy and a potential spy.

The Mongols of course had their own agenda. To them France was merely a part of their universal empire that they hadn't yet had time to visit. They pestered William with questions about the country, particularly about the important matter of how many sheep, cattle and horses it contained, 'as if they were due to move in and take it all over forthwith'. William found their arrogance infuriating. 'I would preach war against them,' he rails in a rare outburst, 'to the best of my ability, throughout the world.' He seemed, momentarily, to have forgotten that he had come to save Mongol souls.

William was not the only foreigner at the Mongol court. As the unlikely capital of a vast empire Mongke's camp had become the diplomatic centre of the world. Ambassadors came and went like delivery men. During William's time Mongke received envoys from the Greek emperor, the Caliph, the King of Delhi, the Seljuk Sultan, the Emirs of Jezireh and Kurdistan, and various Russian princes. The King of Armenia was expected any day.

There were also numerous prisoners who had been captured in the European campaigns – Hungarians, Alans, Ruthenians, Georgians, Armenians, Germans, Frenchmen, even a mysterious Englishman named Basil. Most were retained because of their particular talents. They were treated tolerably well and lived like other inhabitants of the city. In Qaraqorum William became great friends with a French silversmith, William Buchier, whose brother had a shop on the Grand Pont in Paris. At Mongke's camp they met a woman from Metz in Lorraine, a trader who had the misfortune of being in Hungary at the time of the Mongol invasions. Transported across Asia as part of the Mongol booty, her life had been a misery until she met and married a Russian builder whose skills allowed the couple the protection of the court. William enthused about the wonderful meal she prepared for the two friars, the first European food they had eaten in months.

If William had expected to be the sole evangelist at Mongke's court he was bitterly disappointed. The tolerance that the Mongols traditionally showed to other religions meant that Mongke's camp was crawling with religious proselytizers of every persuasion who followed the court 'as flies do honey', according to William. There were Buddhist monks, Muslim clerics, Christian priests and native shamans, all vying for the ear and the souls of the Mongol power brokers. Each believed they were on intimate religious terms with the khan and daily awaited a conversion that would place them in a position of influence. The khan for his part saw no reason to choose between them. 'On such days that his soothsayers prescribe feasts . . . the first to arrive are the Christian clergy (who) pray for him and bless his cup. As they withdraw, the Saracen (Muslim) priests appear and do likewise; and after them come the idolater priests who do the same . . . He makes them all gifts, and all of them . . . forecast his good fortune.'

One of the more notorious clerics was an Armenian monk called Sergius. A 'swarthy and lank' fellow, Sergius had learnt Mongolian and seemed to have acquired a Rasputin-like influence at court, particularly among the khan's wives. He was an outrageous charlatan; William would later learn that he had never taken orders and was in fact an illiterate cloth-weaver. When lodgings were assigned to the two French friars, they found themselves sharing a *ger* with Sergius.

The Armenian proved to be the tent-mate from Hell. For a start there were the fingernails. Uncut and coloured with henna, they gave William the creeps. But the fingernails were only the beginning. Everything about Sergius irritated William. He was vain, presumptuous, deceitful, and self-serving. He wore a cap with peacock feathers and an iron girdle, and made for himself a chair 'such as bishops are wont to have'. Like the Nestorians, a heretical Eastern sect whose missionary zeal had taken them throughout Asia, he dabbled in shamanistic practices. He claimed to be fasting during Lent, William reported, when in fact he was feasting on almonds, grapes, dried plums and other fruits hidden in a box beneath his altar. He boasted that Mongke had agreed to be baptized by him though predictably nothing came of it. He was so aggressive with the Muslims that the Mongols were obliged to move his tent further away to avoid open hostilities. In continual conflict with the Nestorians, he eventually poisoned their archdeacon. A medicine man of some mean repute, Sergius almost killed the silversmith Buchier with his special patent laxative, a mixture of finely chopped rhubarb and holy water. For William the final straw was that he kept borrowing William's wine to entertain his guests and never replaced it. 'What a martyrdom,' the friar lamented.

One day in February William and Bartholomew agreed to join Sergius and a few other priests on a religious tour of the camp, dropping in on various members of the royal family to whom the Armenian had such an easy entrée. Under Sergius' guidance it developed into a clerical pub crawl.

Things got off to a bad start in Mongke's *ger* where Bartholomew was arrested for treading on the threshold, a capital offence in the Mongol criminal code. Still a bit shaky on his pins after crossing Asia, poor old Bartholomew found some difficulty in walking backward as they were leaving the royal presence and had tripped over the raised doorway. Pleading ignorance of Mongol customs, he managed to get off with a warning and an official ban from the khan's tents, but it was a touchy business that might have seen him in front of the archery squad.

At the *ger* of Mongke's eldest son, the clerics received an enthusiastic welcome when the young man leapt up from his couch, prostrated himself and struck his forehead on the ground in adoration of the cross. Then they settled down to a few rounds of *airag* overseen by the boy's tutor, a Nestorian priest called David, 'a great drunkard' according to William. Next they went to the *ger* of Kota, Mongke's second wife, 'who practised idolatry'. Despite finding her ill in bed, and 'so feeble she could scarcely stand on her feet', the overbearing Sergius forced her to get up and make a series of protestations to the Cross.

Lunch was taken in the *ger* of another young wife – mutton with 'a good deal of drink' – before they went on to the *ger* of Cirina, the ugly daughter. After a brief bout of prostration and head-banging in front of the cross, she poured the drinks and the priests downed a few more bowlfuls. Finally they pitched up at the *ger* of an older neglected wife of Mongke. She too was an idolater but was perfectly happy to worship the cross as a prelude to opening the drinks cabinet. All in all it had been a merry day. When finally the priests made their way home, it was, William reports, with 'a great howling as they chanted in their drunkenness – a state not viewed there with disapproval either in a man or a woman'.

The different nationalities at Qaraqorum allowed William the opportunity of some ethnographic research. A Tibetan monk told him about China which lay twenty day's journey to the south-east beyond the Gobi. He described their use of paper money and how they wrote with a brush, 'in a single character making several letters that comprise one word'. This was the first reference to Chinese writing in Western literature.

But William was very much the medieval man and he was most concerned to learn about the 'monsters and human freaks' depicted on the maps of his time and described by classical writers like Isidore and Solinus. Where were the dog-headed men and the monopods, the race with one leg? Sadly the Mongols informed him that they had never seen such people. The Tibetan however had some good tales. He told William of a mountain race called the Chinchin who were barely two feet high and covered in hair. Their knees did not bend and they moved with a jumping motion. Men hunted them by leaving intoxicating wines in the hollows of rocks. When the little people emerged from their caves, they drank the liquor, merrily crying 'Chinchin'. Once they had fallen into a deep sleep from the effects of the wine the hunters crept forward, opened a vein in their necks, and extracted drops of blood which was the base for the purple-reddish dye used for the monks' robes.

There were many such tall tales current at the Mongolian court. Beyond China there was said to be a country where men never aged. The King of Armenia was told of another country beyond China where women had the use of reason, like men. Naturally, he refused to believe it.

William spent three months at Mongke's camp before the court moved to the capital at Qaraqorum for the spring festivities. They arrived there on Palm Sunday in 1254. It was exactly a year since William had preached in Haghia Sophia. Along the Orkhon river, where we had camped, he gathered willow branches in lieu of palm leaves to carry into the city.

William was unimpressed with the Mongol capital. It was smaller, he commented, than the village of St Denis outside of Paris. As well as numerous palaces for court officials, there were two chief quarters, one of Muslim merchants and the other of Chinese artisans. Religion was represented by twelve idol temples of different persuasions, two mosques, and a Nestorian church. The city was walled and the gates acted as markets. At the eastern gate they sold millet and corn, at the western sheep and goats, at the southern oxen and carts, and at the northern horses. The khan's palace stood outside the walls on a raised mound.

The city of Qaraqorum lasted only a few decades. By 1260 new winter and summer capitals had been created at Beijing and at Shang-tu, Coleridge's Xanadu, and Qaraqorum fell into decline. In the sixteenth century the ruins were used to build one of the first Buddhist lamaseries in Mongolia, Erdene Zuu, enclosed by the long white walls, turreted with stupas, that survive today.

At a distance across the grassy plains the walls promise much. But when I passed through the southern gates, I found only a small cluster of temples in one corner. The rest of the city had been conquered by grass. Beyond the overgrown outlines of a few foundations nothing remained but birds and wind. The metropolitan centre of the nomads' empire has returned to pasture.

Before the purges of the 1930s Erdene Zuu was home to thousands of monks and contained up to a hundred temples. Only three survive, pressed against the western walls. The oldest halls were as weathered as barns. Spindly weeds sprouted between the roof tiles, the timbers were cracked, and the richly coloured beams had faded to a muted sepia. For almost thirty years they had been locked to the faithful until they opened as a museum in 1965.

The interiors were barnacled with Buddhist clutter – thangas, banners, drums, cymbals, gongs, long horns, glass cases of miniature stupas, tiered mandalas, Tsam masks decorated with skulls. The Gods seemed as numerous as the trinkets. Buddhism in Mongolia has a bewildering array of minor deities, a veritable crush of Bodhisattvas, tutelary demons, witches, local gods. Many were transplanted from Hinduism. Others came from Mongolian shamanism. When the Mongols took up Buddhism the lamas conveniently announced the simultaneous conversion of many of the old spirits who were given new employment in what is one of the largest pantheons in the world.

Presiding over this rabble are the Buddhas, prissy, demure, rather distant figures, with blue hair and red lipstick, adorned with amber and coral beads, silk scarves and elaborate crowns. Their superior air can be irritating, and I found myself gravitating towards the fierce guardian gods who flanked the doorways. Blood flowed in their veins. They rode horses, and smote enemies. One was depicted squatting on a naked malefactor. Another, with four arms, bared teeth, and an elaborate hat decorated with pheasant feathers and skulls, was drinking from a human skull. You felt these guys had all the best tunes.

The side halls, once reserved for meditation, were full of Tantric symbolism. Kalachakra Buddhism encourages the use of 'baser' human instincts, like lust or anger, for spiritual enlightenment. This is the excuse for the terrifying guardians as well as the recurrent representations of gods copulating in acrobatic positions. Among the visions of Paradise crowding the walls, rich with flocks of sheep, fine-looking *gers* and splendid horses, were intimate scenes of religious eroticism. A young woman, wearing little more than a string of beads, was straddling the Kalachakra deity and his divine member. At this splendid moment one envied him his innumerable arms. It was little wonder that the Mongolian monks, surrounded by such carnal visions, had a reputation for licentiousness.

As for the ancient capital of Qaraqorum, the only visible remains are two stone markers, part of a quartet that once delineated the perimeter of the city. For horsemen of the steppes, the markers took an unusual form: turtles.

Like the city itself the turtles are an imported idea. They are a Chinese symbol for longevity, no doubt brought by one of the many Chinese architects who worked at Qaraqorum. Standing in the open steppe beyond the sixteenth-century walls, the turtles, remarkably, are our only physical connection to the great Mongol Empire that so transformed the world of the thirteenth century. Perhaps this is as it should be. From a distance of seven centuries there is an unreal quality to the empire. The Mongols made a splendid entrance onto the world stage, stepping unannounced from the darkness of remote Asia into the spotlight of history in the course of a single season. Their exit was just as mysterious. For two centuries they were the pivotal players in world politics, yet when they departed, we never heard from them again. They trooped home to live exactly as they did before they ruled the world. They left nothing of their own behind. Travel the breadth of Asia and you will not find a single physical trace of the Mongol Empire. There is nothing to compare to the splendours of Tamerlane's Samarkand or the Raj monuments of British India or the Roman remains that litter Europe and North Africa. Of the Mongols we have only the stone turtles, lost in the long grass beyond the walls of Qaraqorum. Nothing captures so eloquently the surreal nature of the whole enterprise.

During Friar William's time at Qaraqorum Mongke ordered a great theological debate. 'Here you are,' the khan declared, 'Christians, Saracens [Muslims] and *tuins* [Buddhists], and each one of you claims that his religion is superior . . .' A conference was arranged for each to put their case. Three of Mongke's secretaries would act as umpires. A date was set: the eve of Pentecost. Mongke laid down the only ground rules: 'No man shall be so bold as to make provocative or insulting remarks to his opponent, and no one is to cause any commotion that might obstruct these proceedings, on pain of death.' William managed to ensure that he would be allowed to speak before the Nestorians, whose heretical views, he feared, might undermine the Christian case.

On the appointed day a huge crowd assembled. Representatives of the various religions had turned out in force, though the majority were Buddhists. One of their number, a monk from China, was the first to speak. He enquired what William would like to debate first: how the world was made, or what happened to souls after their death. William declared that all things begin with God, and therefore they should first debate the question of the Divine. God, William realized, was the weakest point of the Buddhist argument.

Unwisely allowing William to set the agenda, the Buddhists declared that only a fool would claim there is only one God. They attempted to create an analogy which they thought would appeal to Mongke. 'Are there not great rulers in your country, and is not Mongke the chief lord here? It is the same with Gods, inasmuch as there are different gods in different regions.'

When William defended the notion of a single omnipotent God, the Buddhists were quick to identify the most difficult aspect of this belief. 'If your God is as you say, why has He made half of things evil?'

'It is not God who created evil. Everything that exists is good.'

To the Buddhists this looked like an own goal.

'Where then does evil come from?' they asked, sensing they had the friar on the ropes.

William realized he was venturing onto difficult ground, and tried to shift the direction of the argument again. 'Go back to the first question,' he insisted, 'whether you believe that any God is all-powerful.'

When the Buddhists replied that no God was all-powerful, the Muslims burst out laughing. William seemed to have the Buddhists where he wanted them, and pressed home his advantage. 'So, then,' he said, 'not one of your Gods is capable of rescuing you in danger . . . He does not have the power. Further,' he went on, in a point likely to appeal to Mongke, 'no man can serve two masters, so how it is you can serve so many Gods?'

According to William this point left the Buddhists speechless, and the debate moved on. The Nestorians took to the floor to explain the Trinity, always a tricky subject, and one on which they were notoriously unsound. The debate soon degenerated into theo-logical detail, and William took little further part in the proceedings.

When it was all over the Nestorians and the Muslims, believing they had won the day, 'sang in loud voices while the *tuins* remained silent'. William was less sanguine. The debate had only served to remind him how unsuccessful had been his mission to the Mongols. 'No one said, "I believe,"' he noted sadly. 'No one said, "I want to become a Christian."'

Afterwards the assembled clerics pitched into the *airag* and in no time everyone was roaring drunk.

The successor to the great capital of the Mongols was the village of Kharkorin, a collection of old Russian buildings standing among yellow-leafed birch trees around what passed for a municipal square. Our hotel bore a faded red star on its forehead like a tattoo that wouldn't come off. Dead leaves drifted through the open doors into the hallway where a wide staircase led up to the rooms on the first floor. The boys of the town stole into the hall after school to slide down the banister until the hotelkeeper, a formidable woman with a tall dark face, chased them out. A caretaker carried pails of water from the river twice a day and stood them in the large tiled bathroom. I persuaded the hotelkeeper to heat one for me so I could wash in the tin bath. There was no lock on the bathroom door and a stream of curious passers-by came to view the naked foreigner, lathered in soap and sluicing himself with cupfuls of water. The hotelkeeper was so bemused by what she saw that she fetched her friend from the shop next door to come and have a look.

Our horseman did not linger. He was nervous about the town. His anxieties centred on the fact that there was a flour mill in Kharkorin. The people were not herdsmen, they were workers, who earned wages and lived in houses. From his perspective, a more dangerous and more dissolute people, it was hard to imagine. It was the age-old antipathy, the nomad's distrust of towns with their narrow streets, their confining walls, and their calculating inhabitants.

I had decided to go to Ulan Batur by jeep. Time was now short. We were well into September, and the Mongolian winter was close. I wanted to ride into the Khentii mountains in the north-east, to the Holy Mountain of Burkhan Khaldun, where the tomb of Genghis Khan is rumoured to lie.

Chapter Fourteen

ANOTHER COUNTRY

After a thousand miles of sheep and pasture the grey dreariness of Ulan Batur can seem exotic. From the window of my hotel room – reminiscent of a council flat I once knew in south London – I gazed in wonder at the ordinary facts of urban life. A man on his way to work, carrying a briefcase, waited on the pavement below for the lights to change. A woman stopped at a street kiosk to buy a morning paper. A trolley bus disgorged passengers on the pavement opposite, then rattled away down an avenue as bleak and wide as a parade ground. Regiments of high-rise apartments crowded the horizon between distant smokestacks belching brown clouds. Dark cars glided between government buildings with curtained windows. When a horseman trotted round the corner of a tenement, past parked cars, some temporal wind might have blown him in from another age. A metropolitan miracle conjured out of grasslands, Ulan Batur was so unlike anywhere else in Mongolia it was less a capital city than another country. Only its failure – the tented suburbs where a quarter of a million people still live in *gers* beyond the reach of paved streets and municipal facilities – offered any connection to the Mongolia I knew.

Youth is part of its strangeness. Ulan Batur would make Kansas seem antique; my father was older than most of the buildings. Constructed under Russian supervision during the 1930s and 40s, the city was a showcase for the sterile delights of Soviet architecture.

It shares the depressed anonymity of provincial cities from Poland to Siberia, taking nothing from local initiative and everything from government directive. Ulan Batur was a city that bureaucracy built, full of arbitrary avenues and monolithic public buildings. Without the moderating influence of an older and more gracious age, the result is brutality.

The shallow character of the modern city prompts curiosity about its predecessor, the native Mongolian settlement before the Russian building crews set to work. On old maps it appears as Urga, astride the caravan route from Lake Baikal to China. In the beginning, sometime early in the seventeenth century, it was a migratory encampment of tents which moved as the seasons and the pastures dictated. It settled at its present site, on the banks of the River Tuul, late in the eighteenth century, when it began to achieve pre-eminence among other Mongolian settlements because of the presence of numerous important temples including the great Gandan monastery. In those days in Mongolia religious devotion was the only reason to erect four walls. Other than the monasteries Urga did not contain a single building until the Russians built a consulate in the late nineteenth century. The secular population numbered six thousand; the lamas may have numbered sixty thousand.

The Urga of the nineteenth century resembled the strange ecclesiastical city of Lhasa before the Chinese colonized it, a shambolic filthy place where gilded temples rose from a chaos of tents and mean stockades. Processions of burgundy-robed lamas rubbed shoulders with wild-looking horsemen, Mongol princes, Russian exiles, Chinese merchants, and the ragged hordes of the criminal and the poor drawn here for the opportunities that temples and crowds presented. Caravans of camels covered with the dust of the Gobi pushed through the throng, past the Mongol carts and the tethered sheep, to makeshift bazaars where traders, butchers, fortune-tellers and beggars gathered beneath the overlapping awnings. The great Russian explorer Przhevalsky was struck by the terrible stench.

All the filth is thrown into the street and the habits of the people are loathsome ... crowds of starving beggars assemble in the marketplace; some of them, mostly old women, make it their last resting place ... No sooner is a fresh corpse thrown into the street than packs of wild dogs tear it to pieces.

Alioshin, a White Russian who had come here in the wake of the mad Baron, reported that the dogs were eager to extend their attentions to the living. No one risked going out without a stout stick.

Ruling over this weird place, rarely venturing beyond the walls of his palace, was the Living Buddha, a syphilitic god-king, Champion of the Divine and Supporter of Civilization. In the hierarchy of Tibetan Buddhism the Bogd Khan was third only to the Dalai and Panchen Lamas. In Mongolia he was the spiritual ruler who took the reins of temporal power into his enfeebled hands when the Chinese departed. As a monk he was meant to be celibate. As a ruler he managed to provide a consort, a ten-year-old heir and the scandal of pubescent mistresses.

His Holiness was surrounded by a praetorian guard of five thousand lamas, from simple servants to fortune tellers, from medical practitioners to the Councillors of God who formed the government. A separate and mysterious class of lamas lived apart in their own *gers*. All had had their vocal chords severed, rendering them mute. They were the Living Buddha's secret weapon, the poisoners who eliminated disobedient abbots, Chinese spies, political agents, and common criminals alike.

The Bogd Khan was rarely seen by his followers; even the excitements of Mongolian wrestling could not draw him out of his palace. At the Naadam festival, attended by the intrepid Mrs Bulstrode who toured Mongolia in 1913, his throne remained empty throughout the festivities. He appeared only fleetingly when it came time to receive the taxes and 'presents' gathered from his subjects. Mrs Bulstrode described him as 'decrepit, bloated, dissipated and uninspiring'. Dr Frederick Ossendowski, a Polish geologist fleeing the Bolsheviks, who passed through Urga en route to China, spent several afternoons with the great man. He records him as 'a stout old man with a heavy shaven face resembling those of the Cardinals of Rome'. Drink or venereal disease had robbed him of his sight. 'He Who Could Do No Wrong' was generally plastered by mid-afternoon. His cabinet meetings invariably degenerated into drunken brawls.

His subjects believed him to be the richest and most powerful monarch in the world, not an odd assumption given the level of religious taxes. Like all monks he was a hoarder. He was rumoured to own a thousand white camels and two thousand white horses. Ossendowski was given a tour of the royal treasury where he found presents from rulers and lamas in every corner of the Buddhist world. There were gold nuggets from Bei Kem, boxes of musk and ginseng root sent by the Orochons, a ten-pound lump of amber from the coast of the 'frozen sea', precious stones and bags of pearls from Indian rajahs, walrus tusks, tortoiseshell boxes and carved ivory from China. Chests contained a conservationist's nightmare: every kind of rare fur from white beaver to blue sables to black panther. The library was full of Tibetan, Indian and Chinese manuscripts as well as a collection of cuneiform tablets from Babylonia which may well have been part of the Mongol campaign loot from their conquest of Mesopotamia in the thirteenth century. His zoo was famous and included giraffes, elephants, a sloth, a boa constrictor and several seals, presumably a trifle morose at being so far from the sea. He owned the country's first gramophone and motorcar, acquired on a shopping trip in Shanghai.

The car's battery proved to be one of his chief amusements. The Bogd Khan ordered wires to be attached to its terminals and thrown over the walls of his palace. When the faithful kneeled to kiss the wires they believed the shock to be a divine blessing. Listening to their squeals at an upper window the Living God fell about in paroxysms of laughter.

When he died prematurely in 1924, Soviet agents ensured that no reincarnation was recognized, and that old Urga should die with him. With the revolution the city was renamed Ulan Batur, Red Hero. The monasteries were destroyed, wide public avenues were cut through the dense warren of alleys, the old temple square at the heart of the city was remade as Sukhbatur Square, named after the revolutionary hero who 'invited' the Russians in. Where Tsam religious dances were once performed by monks dressed in spectacular masks, diffident herdsmen from the countryside now pose for photographs in an empty steppe of paving stones against the

familiar backdrop of Sukhbatur's equestrian statue and tomb, modelled on Lenin's. It is a souvenir snapshot that features in many
gers in Mongolia, like a talisman, proof that Mongolians too are
part of the modern world of nations, with a city to call their own.

If Ulan Batur is Mongolia's anchor in the modern world, most of
its inhabitants are still moored to the countryside and the nomadic
ideal. Over half a million Mongolians now live in Ulan Batur, a
quarter of the country's population. But the drift to the metropolis
has not brought the usual disdain for the less sophisticated life
they have left behind. All Mongolians hanker for the steppes. The
landscapes, the horses, the livestock and the round womb of the
ger provide their identity however divorced they have become from
them in the capital. Everyone understood that Ulan Batur was not
Mongolia, and they could not truly be Mongolians in this place.

The arrival of relatives from the country with sheep carcasses,
jugs of *airag* and news of the pastures were glorious occasions in
their cramped flats. During the summer months parents were in
the habit of sending their children to their grandparents in the
countryside to fatten them like sheep. They felt the city made them
weak and prone to illness, and that it undermined their confidence
and their identity. Only the connection to the countryside could
keep them healthy.

I had lunch one day in a modern restaurant with a friend and
her six-year-old daughter who had just returned from a month in
Arhangay with her granny. The countryside, according to her
mother, had done the child a world of good. She had returned
flushed and energetic and alert.

'Just like a Mongolian,' she said to me.

Energetic and alert was certainly not a description of the city
during the seven decades of Communist rule. In Ulan Batur stories
are told of the old days of central planning by people bewildered
that they had once been part of it. In offices and workplaces comrades were required to keep a diary of what they planned to achieve
each year. Supervisors would check the diaries religiously to insure
that they were in line with the Party's Five Year Plans. After a time,

the planning diaries became quarterly. Managers liked them because they were something tangible that could be managed without leaving their desks. Workers liked them because they could crib from each other's plans, and they were a happy substitute for work. The plans were becoming addictive. Soon detailed written plans had to be submitted every month. Then weekly plans were added to the regime and finally, with workplaces now in the full grip of planning mania, the plans became part of the daily routine. From receptionists to supervisors, workers spent a couple of hours a day on the planning diaries, ensuring that they had the right revivalist tone and that they were in keeping with the resolutions of the latest Party Congress. As well as work plans there were ideological plans with workers planning which books to study and which Party reports to read, and general plans like New Year's Resolutions in which comrades planned to work harder and achieve more.

The plans became everything. They flowed back and forth on tides of paper. An entire level of management was devoted to reading and checking the plans, advising amendments and suggesting future goals. It was an Orwellian world in which plans had become the chief industry. Implementation was considered a dangerous and intractable business, with its threat of failure and culpability. It also took time away from planning. Everyone in the system, from office juniors to under-secretaries, recognized they had a vested interest in the plans and that the thing could be easily upset by a rogue zealot who wanted to take action. Such people were quickly squeezed out.

Nothing so illustrates the enfeeblement of the country as this demented planning. In trying to adopt to the ways of a modern bureaucratic society Mongolians had made a fetish of one element. In Ulan Batur a race of hardy nomads, a swashbuckling people who swept across the face of Eurasia conquering all the great civilizations of its age, had been reduced to a city of compulsive penpushers and timid functionaries.

The plans are gone but the dead hand of seventy years of Communist rule still lingers. The lack of initiative, the sloth, the unwillingness to take any action however innocuous in case it exposes you to criticism, will remain part of the mentality of urban Mongolia for years to come.

But perhaps it is too much simply to blame Communism. A Mongolian friend, only half joking, blames the empire for the country's lethargy. When Genghis Khan set off to conquer the world, he said, the best Mongols followed in his wake, riding to China, to Persia, to the Volga, to take charge of the new imperial provinces. Mongolia, he said, had been left to the dullards who preferred to stay at home and look after sheep.

The removal of the best and the brightest however is far more recent than the thirteenth century. It is only sixty years since Mongolia's small population lost its most promising citizens. By 1928 the Russians had got rid of the independent leadership of the infant Mongolian People's Party and installed their own stooge, the Stalinist Choilbasan, in power. Following the Russian lead, the purges began. Opponents and unorthodox comrades were eliminated with equal enthusiasm.

In Ulan Batur a new Museum of Political Repression records this nightmare. It occupies one of the few older buildings in the city, a Russian building, just south of the square. The ground floor is devoted to the names of the victims, like a war memorial recording some colossal carnage. It is said that 100,000 people perished in the purges of the thirties. Their names fill the four walls in small dense script.

Upstairs the names come to life in old photographs, letters, and personal effects – an author's spectacles, an antique gramophone, a pipe, a snuff bottle, the ordinary possessions of comrades too independent or too Mongolian for Moscow's agents. It was the record of a nation's shame that until very recently had also been its secret. The guide, a grey exhausted woman, pointed out her own father. The blurred black and white photograph was dated 1924. Posing in a photographer's studio in the uniform of the Mongolian Red Army, a young man gazed out at us, excited to be caught up in momentous events, innocently unaware that the shutter's click was capturing an image to record his own persecution, here on the walls of this room. Six years later he was sentenced to eight years in prison in Irkutsk. He was accused of being a rightist or a leftist, a revisionist or a Trotskyist, she wasn't sure. It hardly mattered. He never came home. He must have died there, she said. Conditions were very primitive. Or perhaps they executed him. No one knew. She was only a baby when he vanished. She did not remember him, she said, turning her empty hands upward.

The rooms were as hushed as a funeral parlour. Families, remembering lost ancestors, passed through in a huddle of whispers and soft footfalls. At the windows even the outside world seemed muted, a murmur of traffic and birdsong. Filtered through decorative lace, the autumn sun cast patterned flowers across a glass case that contained a love letter in vertical Mongolian script, a string of prayer beads, a photograph of a woman, and the thin shirt of a prisoner.

They were all here, a lost generation, an assembly of ghosts, brought together as if they were once a united company, to convey some meaning to us, gazing at us from the walls, silently pleading to be remembered – Mongolian princes, Chinese shopkeepers, intellectuals, artists, lamas, Party members trapped on the wrong side of a discussion. The executioners were here too – the avuncular Stalin, the stiff Choilbasan, and a long rogue's gallery of interrogators with dull merciless eyes. The contrast with the victims was startling. The photographs of the disappeared showed intelligent open faces; they had been part of one of Mongolia's rarer resources: its tiny intelligentsia. At the behest of an imported ideology, almost every educated man and woman in Mongolia perished. By 1940 when Tsedenbal succeeded Choilbasan as Party General Secretary, there were only five people left in the entire country with a secondary school education.

Friar William's endeavours to woo the Mongols away from the horrors of Buddhism have been unexpectedly revived in recent years. Since 1990 and the arrival of democracy, there has been an influx of latter-day Williams to Mongolia. His successors are American evangelicals. William might find them as dodgy as the Nestorians on matters theological but he would admire their robust fundamentalism with its stubbornly medieval logic.

One Sunday morning I went with Mandah to her 'church', a small community hall where a congregation of about thirty people was struggling with *O God Our Help in Ages Past*, encouraged by a theatrical individual playing an electric organ. I settled in the back row, feeling like a spy in the House of the Lord.

When the congregation had settled into their seats again a young woman came forward to read the St John's Gospel in Mongolian. American missionaries have paid for the translation, publication and distribution of the Bible throughout Mongolia. Compared to the arcane Tibetan sutras of Buddhism read exclusively by monks, they are aware of the appeal of a free book, in your own language, in your own hands, packed with good tales and clear instructions.

The week's preacher was an elderly white-haired American who introduced himself as Reverend Steve, or rather as 'shrevershand shtivsh'. He had lost his false teeth – there was an incomprehensible explanation about denture powder and a chamber maid – and he hoped the congregation would bear with him. Fortunately there was a translator rendering his words into Mongolian but anyone who had come along to improve their English comprehension would have struggled. Without his teeth Reverend Steve's English sounded like something spoken by an inebriated Finn.

He began by announcing how delighted he was to find the Lord Jesus at work here in Mongolia. As a scriptural reference for his sermon he took the story of Cain and Abel, exploring the idea that we are our brother's keeper. It was a fairly plodding discourse though, to be fair, laborious translation and loose consonants whistling through the gaps in his teeth rather precluded any hope of oratorical flourish.

Afterwards he asked members of the congregation to stand and tell the others how they would like to be included in their prayers over the coming week. One by one they got to their feet, hesitantly at first, then with more confidence after the example of others. The congregation was mainly young and female; many were teenage girls. We were asked to pray for ill relations, for a university place for a young woman with a long pony-tail, for a good school for the son of another, for a job, for a happy marriage, for a hoped-for flat, for the safe return of a sister on a long journey.

In that moment the hall seemed indistinguishable from the shaman's tent. If Christianity was superior to shamanism as an ethical force, there was little evidence of it in their requests. Each of the petitioners sought divine intercession, some advantageous alteration of their own fate. The god might have been different but the people who came to kneel arrived with the same desires. They wanted to improve their chances, to cleanse their lives of baleful influence and bad karma. They sought the aid of spiritual forces in a difficult and unpredictable physical world. There didn't seem any particular reason to come to the Christian God rather than to Dayanderkh other than the expectation that his magic was stronger. That it was stronger was self-evident to anyone with a television where America bestrode the world as the new land of milk and honey. Dayanderkh could hardly compete with the Reverend Steve's god who had bequeathed on Americans, his chosen people, such lavish success. In the minds of these aspirants, encouraged by the evangelical fervour of the new missionaries, the message of Christ, the idea of salvation and the American Dream had become inextricably entwined.

One afternoon I went to call on Choijampts, the abbot of the Gandan Monastery which is to Mongolia what Westminster Abbey is to England. It was one of the few monasteries to escape the purges, being granted exceptional leave to continue as a living museum of the Buddhist faith with a ghostly coterie of practising monks under the strict control of the government. In the worst years it acted as a perverse showcase of the Party's tolerance for gullible visitors. It was not without its casualties of course; aside from most of its monks it lost the monumental statue known as Magjid Janraisig, built by the Bogd Khan in 1911 in the hope of restoring his failing sight. At the time of the purges the statue was shipped off to Leningrad where it was melted down for ammunition.

With the new religious freedoms, Gandan is active again with 350 lamas in residence. One of their first endeavours has been to recreate the Magjid Janraisig with funds from public subscription and international donations. Eighty foot high and weighing twenty tonnes, encrusted with gold and precious stones, the new copper figure of Avalokitesvara was unveiled in 1997. As a symbol of the renaissance of Buddhism in Mongolia and of the country's independence from its Russian overlords, Magjid Janraisig has no equal.

Misunderstanding eased me through the layers of clerical officials that surround the august person of Choijampts. Apparently they thought I was someone else. The speed with which I was handed up the chain of command made me wonder if they had mistaken me for an emissary from the Dalai Lama. The gatekeeper dispatched me to the doorman, who sent me on to the keeper of the appointment diary who led me through a long series of empty rooms to the office of Choijampts' secretary. After a brief consultation on an old Bakelite telephone the secretary ushered me through to the office of his personal assistant. A moment later I was in the inner sanctum of the office of the great man himself.

Choijampts rose from behind his desk to shake my hand. He was a plump robed Buddha with narrowed eyes and huge ears with fat elongated lobes. His office was a pleasant study with the latest technology – a television and video player, a fax machine, a mobile telephone – prominent among the bookcases and the Buddhist shrine that sat in the far corner. On the long coffee table in front of my chair were plates piled with shortbread biscuits. The room bore the odours of sanctity and pleasure, of candle wax and fresh baking.

If he had been expecting someone else, he was far too polite to show it, and his welcome was effusive and warm. We conversed in fractured English. He was a chain snuff taker, helping himself to continual pinches of snuff from an old film canister on his desk. It was almost one o'clock and throughout our conversation I could hear the great man's stomach rumbling like a train.

Among its ecclesiastical hierarchy Tibetan Buddhism seems to promote hilarity. Like the Dalai Lama, Choijampts was addicted to jokes and fits of giggles. In this mood he was difficult to divert into serious discussion; laughter kept breaking through.

I brought him greetings from Smith & Sons Tobacconists in the Charing Cross Road. Before leaving London I had bought some tins of snuff as gifts for people in Mongolia. The sales assistant had mentioned that Choijampts, whom he described as the Head Monk in Outer Mongolia, was a regular customer, dropping in for his supplies every time he was in London. Remarkably he had been in the shop only the week before, buying in bulk.

'Charing Cross Road,' Choijampts threw his hands up and let out a great belly laugh. 'Smith's Snuffs. Very good.' He rummaged in a drawer and drew out a small tin bearing the shop's imprint: Snuff Blenders and Cigar Importers Since 1869. 'George IV blend. Please, try some.'

'Tell me,' he went on. 'The Mouse-Catcher. It is still catching the audience?'

'The Mouse Trap. Absolutely. Still there.'

His shoulders shook with merriment.

Keen to get the conversation away from the anachronisms of London's West End, I asked about the Christian missionaries, the rivals of the Mongolian lamas struggling to reintroduce Buddhism in their own land.

'Many are not traditional Christians,' he said, suddenly serious. He was watching me carefully, not wishing to cause offence. 'Americans,' he shrugged. 'Not exactly archbishop of ghanterbury fellows.' A mischievous smile was playing at the corners of his mouth. 'But they are very good basketball players.' He exploded into laughter again. 'Yes, yes, very good. Dunk shots every time.'

Many of the more recent American missions had taken to sending tall athletic fellows to preach the gospels. They set up basketball games, a big draw for young urban Mongolians in thrall to American culture, and talked about Jesus, the divine coach, at half time.

'We poor Buddhists,' he giggled. 'Too short.'

I asked about the distinctive qualities of Buddhism in Mongolia.

'Oooh,' he giggled. 'We are different. We are Mongolians.' He leaned across the desk towards me, waggling his head. 'I am having six childrens. Big difference.' He gestured towards his lap and, presumably, towards his penis. 'All part of God's plan. For the man.' A great belly laugh was welling up again. 'We are showing our bottom to the moon,' he roared. What I assumed was a euphemism for lovemaking was accompanied by an elaborate pantomime – taking down his trousers, patting his bottom, then pointing upwards to the moon. He slapped his desk and threw his head back. Convulsed with laughter, he repeated the pantomime several times. 'Ooooh, we like this,' he cried, gasping for air between rollicking peals of laughter. 'Showing our bottoms to the moon.'

Then the laughter ended abruptly, as if a switch had been thrown. Suddenly serious, he said, 'That is a difference.'

A call to lunch, delivered by his assistant, cut our interview short.

'We must meet again in London,' he chuckled, seeing me to the door. 'We will go to the Mouse-Catcher. Very good. The English like the whodidit stories too much. Murder and mayhem.' He paused at the door. 'There is another one. Very good my friends tell me. What is it.' His brow darkened. 'Oh yes,' he brightened. 'No Sex Please, We are English.' And another great gale of laughter filled the room.

Chapter Fifteen

IN SEARCH OF GENGHIS KHAN

In the Khentii mountains autumn blazed through the forests. Conflagrations of fiery leaves consumed the slopes while forks of sunlight raked the yellow grass. Along the tracks the willows were scarlet and blue. Winter was so close now that it made nightly forays into the country, like a hunter under cover of darkness. In the mornings we found the milk frozen in its tin and at the river I had to break thin plates of ice to wash. Once, I woke in the middle of the night and crept outside. In cold moonlight the colours had leaked away, leaving a ghostly monochrome world. In pastures of frost the horses stood like statues, their breath uncurling from their nostrils in tall plumes.

We were riding in uninhabited country. For six days we saw no one. Stags trumpeted in the woods, deer fled like ghosts through the trees, and every morning we found the fresh tracks of wolves where sandy soil cleaved the grasses. On the second day, from a low pass where a rickety *ovoo* was adorned with blue scarves and elk antlers, we caught our first sight of the great mountain, Burkhan Khaldun, its head turbaned with snow.

We dismounted and circled the *ovoo*. Then standing with our backs to the wind, we gazed over the crimson forests towards the mountain.

'Oh my high mountain, Burkhan Khaldun,' our horseman, Zevgee, recited. 'Every day I shall honour you with offerings. Every day I shall worship you. My children's children should always remember this.' They were the words of Genghis Khan, as reported in *The Secret History of the Mongols*.

The home of powerful shaman spirits, Burkhan Khaldun is the Mongol Garden of Eden, a landscape of innocent origins. *The Secret History* tells of a blue wolf and a fallow deer who came to these regions from across the seas. Their offspring was a human child, Batacaciqan, the first Mongol, born at the head of the Onon river.

We mounted again and descended the far side of the pass, turning our horses up a long autumnal valley where the larch trees were tongues of fire. The mountain loomed over the surrounding country, its white summit entangled in a heaven of clouds and columned sunlight

The discovery of *The Secret History of the Mongols* by a Russian scholar working in archives in Beijing in 1886 rocked an academic world accustomed to the idea that nomads were as averse to literature as they were to fresh vegetables. Written in the Year of the Rat, either 1228 or 1240, the book records the rise of the Mongol people, the long genealogy of the family of Genghis Khan, the great man's difficult early career, and his eventual triumph as leader of the empire. The 'secret' of the title probably refers to the fact that the book was only to be read by members of the imperial line. While the earliest sections are clearly mythical, the value of the later parts as an historical source is a matter of debate. Arthur Waley, its English translator, calls it 'a pseudo-historical novel'. Most scholars accept the bare bones of its biography of Genghis as reasonably accurate while discounting the heroic embellishments as the stuff of legend.

For a man who once controlled most of the known world, remarkably little is known about Genghis Khan. No contemporary likeness was ever produced, though there is a portrait, painted by a Chinese court painter a generation after his death, that shows the Mongol chieftain in the idealized style of a Chinese emperor with silk robes and a wispy beard. It hung for centuries in the Forbidden City in Beijing until Chiang Kai-Shek and his retreating Nationalist forces took it to Taiwan. A thirteenth-century Persian historian described Genghis as tall, vigorous, and robust, with cat's eyes and a white beard. 'Some of the devils were his friends,' he adds, rather undermining the veracity of his account.

According to *The Secret History*, Genghis was born near Dadal at the junction of the Onon and the Balj rivers, sometime in the 1150s or 60s. His name was Temuchin; Genghis Khan was a later title meaning universal ruler. His father, a clan chief, had been poisoned when Temuchin was nine years of age. Rejected by the rest of the clan and hunted by enemies, the family lived as fugitives in the region of Burkhan Khaldun. With time a charismatic mystique developed around the young exiled chieftain whose followers grew as he began to defeat rival clans in a series of daring raids. A decade or more of internecine tribal conflict ensued, culminating with Temuchin drawing the divided Mongol clans to his own banner. For the first time in generations the Mongols were united under a single dominant leader who was now proclaimed, at the age of thirty-nine, as Genghis Khan. To the authors of *The Secret History*, this was his great achievement. After the conquest of Mongolia, the conquest of the world paled into insignificance.

Beyond the borders of Mongolia, Genghis' stock tends to plummet. His demonization in Western historical tradition is unparalleled until the twentieth century gave us Hitler. When Bram Stoker searched for a suitable ancestry for Dracula, Genghis was the natural choice. But for Mongolians, he is a figure not just of veneration but of worship. For one brief shining moment under his leadership the Mongols had ruled the world. For an enfeebled country often dependent upon the patronage of outsiders, Genghis Khan became the sole historical argument for national virility and pride.

Like the lamas and the intellectuals, Genghis Khan fell foul of Marxist orthodoxies. Stalin commissioned a damning biography of the great Mongol leader and the official line was that he was a feudal reactionary figure. During the seventy years of Communist rule in Mongolia, the great national hero was a non-person.

In 1962, in an unexpected outbreak of nationalism, there was a short-lived attempt to rehabilitate Genghis on what was taken as the 800th anniversary of his birth. Commemorative stamps were to be issued and a stone monument was erected at his birthplace of Dadal. The unveiling was attended by Tomor-ochir, a leading member of the Politburo and President of the Mongolian-Soviet Friendship Society. Unfortunately the Mongolians had misread the liberalizing trends in the Kremlin. With memories of the Hungarian uprising still fresh in his mind, Khrushchev decided to stamp out this revisionism before it went too far. The stamps were hastily withdrawn. Tomor-ochir was attacked in *Pravda*, dismissed from the Politburo and expelled from the Party while lesser officials connected with the celebrations of the anniversary were arrested. The revival of the cult of Genghis Khan was aborted.

It was only with the collapse of the old system that Genghis finally came out of the closet. In modern Mongolia Genghis is now omnipresent, a cross between royalty and the latest pop star. He is a cult figure and his image, or at least the Chinese version of it, is everywhere from banknotes to stamps, from T-shirts to the label of the most popular brand of vodka. It is strangely fitting that a medieval figure should be the national icon of this most medieval of societies.

After 1990 a Genghis Khan Society was set up in Ulan Batur with the aim of erecting monuments, palaces and museums in his honour as well as sponsoring expeditions to search for his tomb, near the mountain of Burkhan Khaldun. Contributions were sought from abroad; the Mongolians naively believed that the rest of the world held Genghis in the same high esteem as they did themselves. Begging letters were sent to world leaders, including the Queen. A large contribution would ensure them a seat inscribed with gold letters at the Society's Great Council. Sadly no money was forthcoming, and the world missed the opportunity of seeing Elizabeth II installed as an Honorary Advisor to Genghis Khan.

For Genghis Khan, Burkhan Khaldun was a sanctuary in death as it had been in life. It became his only permanent abode in 1227 when his body was returned to Khentii to be buried somewhere in the vicinity of the great mountain. The few sources that we have for his funeral hint at elaborate rites conducted in total secrecy. Forty maidens decked in jewels and a company of fine horses were placed in the tomb to accompany him to the next world. Sadly the expeditions to find his tomb (most organized by the Japanese) have so far come up with nothing. It remains one of the great archaeological mysteries.

We camped at the foot of the mountain in a grove of yellow trees. I was looking forward to tempting a few lenok from the stream that ran beneath the camp with the Woolly Bugger of Pall Mall when Zevgee, the horseman, announced we must start for the summit. It was mid-afternoon. I had presumed we would wait until morning, to allow us a full day to tackle the mountain, but Zevgee assured me that we had sufficient time for the climb. Leaving Mandah to look after the camp, we mounted the horses and set off.

On the rising slopes the pines closed ranks until the shafts of sunlight were extinguished between their mossy trunks. In the gloom we came to a spectacular *ovoo* constructed not of stones but of branches, woven together, in a tall pyramid. Tattered rags adorned the dead boughs. In the narrow spaces between the trees, the *ovoo* seemed disproportionately large, as if belief had prompted a freakish and unruly growth here in the wild wood. On a boulder altar were the usual bric-a-brac offerings: cartridges, coins, the bones of horses. A few feet away a great iron cauldron was full of dry horse dung.

Zevgee and I plucked hairs from the tails of our horses, tied them to the *ovoo*, then mounted again and rode on. On the steep ground the horses lurched their way upwards, scrambling for footing. Dislodged stones clattered back down through the trees like pebbles dropping into a deep well. We followed a vague trail which switchbacked precipitously between dark trunks, fallen trees and dense thickets of undergrowth, stopping frequently for the horses to catch their breath. Flecks of spittle dribbled from their lips, and their leg muscles trembled. I would long since have proceeded on foot but Zevgee, like all Mongolians, was loath to dismount. Mongolian horses are accustomed to difficult terrain; their surefootedness would make a mountain goat look clumsy.

But eventually the incline was too steep. We dismounted and clambered upwards, in places on our hands and knees, levering our way through the trees while our mounts floundered after us among the sharp branches. I called up to Zevgee to suggest that we tether the horses here and continue alone, but he waved dismissively at me, and climbed on, pulling his horse behind him through the narrowing aisles of undergrowth.

Eventually we emerged above the tree line on the shoulders of the mountain where snow had drifted into deep banks. After half an hour of floundering through the drifts we gained a ridge on the mountain's edge where the winds had swept the rock bare. I peered down over the edge. A thousand feet below, a mountain lake shone with the reflections of yellow trees. Silhouetted against the sky above me, Zevgee was a medieval figure leading his horse, climbing upwards with a stick he had cut from the forest.

At the top we were met by a new wind. To the north, an assembly of mountains shouldered pearl-blue provinces of sky. At our backs the sun was tipping into a crowd of lesser hills. Across the summit, a flat expanse hardly larger than a village square, scores of small stone *ovoos* littered the bare rock. In the dying light, with their elongated shadows, they looked like gravestones.

On the far edge stood an *ovoo* that was considerably larger than the others: a rough pyramid of stones over ten feet high. It was known as the Seat of Genghis Khan where, according to legend, he had come as a young man to honour the great mountain and to survey his lands. I realized why we had not left the horses behind. For a Mongolian to turn up at such a sacred site without a horse, like a vagrant, would have been undignified. With the horses, Zevgee and I solemnly circled the shrine three times. Among the offerings – a brick of Chinese tea, the leaf springs from a jeep, someone's boot, a stirrup – were the long hollow-eyed skulls of horses, mounted like spirit masks among the piled stones.

Having performed our circuits we settled down in the lee of the *ovoo* to drink a ritual bottle of vodka. Zevgee, rubbing his hands merrily, was delighted with my respect for Mongolian tradition, though a trifle disappointed that I had opted for such a small bottle. I poured the drink into a bowl and handed it to him. He threw a pinch of liquor to the sky, another to the *ovoo* and then downed the rest himself, before handing it back for me to do the same with the next bowlful.

'It is late,' I said to Zevgee. He looked at me with his rheumy eyes. Zevgee was a rarity among my guides: I did not like him. He had a squashed face, like a bat whose radar had malfunctioned. He was evasive and duplicitous and had a good line in theatrical complaint.

'It is late,' I repeated in my rudimentary Mongolian. 'The climb is long. The sun is setting. It will be dark when we go down.'

But Zevgee only gazed at me blankly and threw back another bowlful of the Genghis Khan.

The man was an idiot, and I cursed myself for being such a fool as to allow him to have led me onto this mountain so late in the day. I briefly considered pushing him over the edge to his death, but in such a sacred site, I decided foul play was probably ill-advised. I took another slug of the Genghis Khan instead.

Enthroned on flat rocks, we sat with our backs to the *ovoo*. Mongolia lay at our feet. Mountains careered between the horizons, their anvil heads cleaved by canyons of russet-coloured shadow. Beyond the mountains lay Siberia. In the long reaches of these landscapes no lights broke the gathering dusk. The only sound was the wind keening softly among the multitude of tiny cairns of stone gathered about us on the summit. They were personal *ovoos*, raised by pilgrims in this remote place to record and promote their hearts' desire. Bathed in an eerie rose-grey light, they were crowded together in unseemly chaos, a lost tribe of memorials marking the graves of spent hope.

We finished the Genghis Khan and stood up. I went across to the western edge of the summit and raised my own little pile of stones, facing the setting sun. Then we started our descent.

In the twilight we picked our way back down across the steep snowfields. By the time we reached the trees it was dark and the vodka was kicking in. The next three hours were a nightmare. In the darkness the forest had the logic of a labyrinth. We blundered into trees and impassable thickets of brush. Peering into the gloom, we found the ground suddenly disappearing beneath us in a precipitous drop, and had to backtrack and search for another path. In places the undergrowth was too dense to turn the horses, and we had to persuade them to reverse between snagging branches. Time and again we stumbled over unseen obstacles, slipping downward through scree and shrubs, with the horses crashing behind us, until some other unseen obstacle broke our fall. We had long since lost direction, other than downward, and had no way of knowing if we were heading for the camp or drifting across the face of the mountain into other valleys.

In this dark world full of invisible threat, most horses would have panicked and become uncontrollable. But throughout our disorderly descent, our horses remained calm and steady. I have never admired Mongolian horses more. Nothing seemed to intimidate them.

The same could not be said of Zevgee. The dark forest had robbed him of his last defence against despair. He moaned, he whimpered, he sat down among boulders and wailed. At one point he found a box of matches in the depths of his *del* and began to wander this way and that, lighting his way among the trees, as if he was searching for the chair lift. Being Chinese matches, they didn't last long, and we were soon alone again with the dark.

Eventually I spotted a campfire through the trees, a long way to the right and far below us. It disappeared from sight almost immediately as we dropped into a gully but I took an orientation from the stars and directed our farcical descent towards it. An hour later, cut, bruised, and exhausted, we staggered out of the trees into the clearing where Mandah was making tea on the fire.

'What's taken you so long?' she asked.

For the next three days we trudged east through gloomy forests. The wonderful winds that had swept us into Khentii had died away and now in the boggy interminable valleys we seemed to be marking time. The days dragged into one another. The forests were unrelenting. The horses, wearied by the soft ground, were sluggish. Under leaden skies the crimson leaves had turned to rust, and our camps were damp and sunless. In the claustrophobic grip of this wilderness, among the endless trees, I longed for the clarity of the open steppe.

On the third day we began to emerge at last into a more spacious world. The valleys widened and the abrupt wooded slopes unravelled as we came down to one of the tributaries of the Onon river. The gloomy pines were replaced by spacious stands of birches, their white trunks shedding pages of bark, their leaves shimmering in the newly arrived sun. Meadows and wind-blown reaches of sky opened between the trees. The horses caught the mood of the changing landscape and quickened their pace.

On the morning of the fourth day, in a valley of auburn grasses we saw a herd of horses, and an hour later, a *ger* pitched among roving flocks of sheep, the first habitation we had seen in almost a week. We spurred our horses to a gallop. Sunlight scudded ahead of us. A high whistling wind blew across the meadows, and the trees along the river showered clouds of yellow leaves. We crossed a wide saddle of hills and galloped down the far side, hollering like outlaws, into an vast plain of grass and wildflowers and wind. The world seemed young again, as it had on that first morning in Namar-jin, over three months ago.

In this mood we galloped into Batshireet. It was a Gary Cooper Moment, somewhat spoiled by the attitude of the sheriff. Within half an hour I had been arrested.

Perhaps incarceration was to be expected in a town that had such a Siberian feel to it. The people were Buryat Mongols, the majority of whom lived across the border in Russia. The women tended to headscarves and the men to pot bellies and leather jackets. Russian influence and plentiful trees meant that the idea of houses had made something of an impact here. The town was composed of one-roomed cabins of the sort that had ceased to be the thing on the American plains around 1905. Batshireet might have been Caspar, Wyoming after the arrival of the first wave of wagon-trains, a town of pine planks, hitching posts, and big men partial to snuff. The wood cottages found charm in their dilapidation and the glori-ous trees made them picturesque. The hotel was a low building with carved Russian windows, sagging doors and potbellied stoves. I was chopping kindling for the stove when there was a knock on the door.

The policeman was a lugubrious sad-eyed character in an uncon-vincing disguise: a herdsmen's *del* and a floppy golf hat. In a con-spiratorial whisper he invited me to attend the governor in the town hall next door. Unaware of his official position, I replied, perhaps a trifle testily, that I would come when I had sorted out the stove, paid the departing horseman, had a wash and a cup of tea. The secret policeman stood awkwardly in the doorway chewing on his lip.

'But you must understand,' he whispered. 'You are under arrest.'

It was not the first time that I had had occasion to remark on the vast improvement in Mongolian manners over the centuries. Seven hundred and fifty years ago they were pillaging and raping in a manner that could only be described as uncouth. These days even a criminal arrest is delivered with a polite manner and a shy voice.

Zevgee watched me go with the look of a man who had just been informed his salary cheque had bounced. Mercifully the policeman didn't bother with handcuffs or a blanket over my head as he led me next door to the town hall to help with enquiries. Upstairs in the governor's office we were seated in front of a dour tribunal. Batshireet enjoyed a relatively low crime rate, and in the absence of a backlog of remand prisoners, it seemed we were going to proceed straight from arrest to trial.

In the best traditions of Asian judicial systems, judge and chief prosecutor were the same fellow: the governor, a stern young man with a calculating face, clearly an SDP hard-liner. A Nuremberg judge would have looked less forbidding. On either side of him sat my arresting officer, looking morose, and a third man who was clearly soft cop. He said little, but forgot himself sufficiently to smile occasionally.

The tribunal did not want to spoil the fun by revealing the nature of my crime at the outset. Instead they cross-examined me about our journey, how many days we had been travelling, what route we had taken, what districts we had passed through. But I knew where their enquiries were leading. Burkhan Khaldun was a restricted area and permits were required to travel there. In practice few people bothered with these permits; the process for acquiring one was arcane and time-consuming. They ignored the regulations knowing that they were unlikely to meet an official in ten thousand square miles of uninhabited wilderness, and if they did, he would not want to spoil a welcome encounter with questions about permits. But I was different. I had come to Batshireet, and I was a foreigner who could afford a juicy fine which could go straight into the governor's savings account.

I decided to forestall him before we got onto my criminal activities. Sidestepping his enquiries about our route I enthused about the natural wonders of the area. I was a writer, I explained, and I would be returning to London to prepare a book on Mongolia in which Batshireet was to feature prominently. When people in Europe read the book, Batshireet was sure to form part of their future holiday plans.

The governor's line of questioning faltered, then ground to a halt. He made a few doodling notes on the paper in front of him then spoke *sotto voce* to the secret policeman. Finally he cleared his throat.

He was delighted, he said, that I should have chosen to visit Batshireet. He had asked me here today, he announced, to welcome me officially. He hoped I would enjoy my stay. He would send a dead sheep round to the hotel in the morning with his compliments. I was to let him know if there was anything he could do to be of assistance. The promise of tourists, all lacking the proper permits, had completely gone to his head.

In no time the whole of Batshireet was in thrall to the coming tourists. The tiny museum, which had been shuttered for years, was opened and swept out for my inspection. The governor conducted my tour personally. We examined the mug shots of the first doctor, the first teacher, the first postmistress. We looked over the stuffed animals, and consulted a chart showing the rising livestock numbers during the Communist era. The chart ended rather abruptly in 1990. The governor was keen to explain that the rising numbers had continued during the years of SDP stewardship. It was just that they found it difficult to secure the felt-tip pens to keep the chart up to date.

The hotelkeeper was in a state of parlous excitement about the tourist hordes, though she worried that Batshireet's future as a holiday destination might be threatened by the state of the hotel toilets. They consisted of a pair of rickety outhouses perched precariously over deep pits. The timbers supporting them, she confessed, had been weakened by age and the corrosive effect of urine. She reckoned they were safe for Mongolians for a couple of years yet. But tourists, she knew, were large people. She had seen a group of tourists once in Ulan Batur, when she had been visiting her sister, and their size was their most distinctive feature. Some of them, she reckoned, must weigh as much as two Mongolians. Her fear was that one of the outsize tourists might send the outhouse plunging into the feculent abyss.

I took a degree of mischievous pleasure in leading the governor astray, but the hotelkeeper was good woman and her excitement and anxieties made me feel like a heel. I advised her privately not to spend any money on underpinning until the first tour group had actually made a booking.

I sought refuge in the library, a plain room of pine planks and old books. There was an iron stove, and a high counter for reading three-month-old newspapers. Passing boys peered through the windows with cupped hands. In the back shelves there were volumes of Turgenev, Tolstoy and Chekov. Mandah found a copy of *Eugene Onegin* and was lost to the world for the next three days. English Literature was rather less well represented. The librarian fetched the single example from a top shelf and asked if I thought it would appeal to the tourists. I told him that they would probably be too busy exploring the surrounding countryside to have time for *Stress Factors in Reinforced Concrete Structures*.

The librarian spent his afternoons outside on a bench in the pale sunshine, reading Turgenev as the old leaves gathered about his feet. A willowy young man with a soft voice and a delicate manner, he was impossible to fit him into the life of the steppes. I could not imagine him squatting in a *ger* over sheep bones, or picture him on a horse. He had studied at university in Ulan Batur where he had learned to speak a good if rather literary English. Health problems had cut short his studies and he had come home to Batshireet where the librarian's post had offered some sanctuary. Among the birch trees, he was an ethereal figure. When he looked up from his book, he seemed to struggle slightly to take hold of the world again.

The librarian was bemused by my journey. He did not understand why I should want to visit Mongolia. What was there to see, he said, except landscape?

'Landscape is a great pleasure,' I said. 'Particularly in Mongolia.'

'You do not have to travel a thousand miles to understand that the sky is blue everywhere.' He was quoting Goethe. It occurred to me I would need to travel a thousand miles to find anyone else who had heard of Goethe.

'I wanted to see nomadic life,' I said simply.

'What is interesting about nomads?' he asked. His questions were polite but pointed.

'Their world is so different from my own. Nomads do not feel the need to settle and to put down roots,' I said. 'Their only commitment is to movement. The security that settled people find in building – a wall, a field, a storage barn – nomads seek in migration.'

'But the movement is only physical,' the librarian said. He had folded his book into his lap, the long fingers entwined in the pages, marking his place. He looked across towards the river where the trees were releasing delicate squalls of leaves onto the grey water. 'Nothing changes here.'

He was right, of course. It is the irony of nomads, people whose lives were wedded to movement, that their world was so static. It was a society without diversity and without ferment, as if a life of migration had exhausted their quota of restlessness. Nomads adhered to a way of life that most of the world had abandoned millennia ago. Even their *gers* were still built and arranged exactly as Friar William had described them over seven hundred years ago. Time and again I had heard people say, about some facet of their lives, from saddling a horse to butchering a sheep, 'this is the Mongol way', a statement that was meant as an argument and a defence against innovation. The passage of time went unmarked by alteration. An alien, descending from the heavens, would find it impossible to tell if the world of the herdsmen, like the landscape itself, was ancient or brand-new, the product of an eternity or of an afternoon.

Perhaps this was a kind of freedom, or a remarkable kind of confidence. It is difficult not to admire the insouciant indifference of a people who do not feel the need to mark their place or their

passage. But the result was sterility. The restless notions of aspir-
ation, so central to the creative energies of cities, were curiously
absent here. The steppes created nothing. The glamorous romance
of a fluid Arcadia located among migrating herdsmen, of a free-
wheeling nomadic consciousness, unfettered by walls and the
unyielding demands of the soil, was as substantial as the wind.

The governor had arranged a lift for us with the Butcher, a man
in possession of a jeep. He took us to Binder a short distance to
the east. The Butcher was a mountain of a man with no neck and
a wheeze that at first I thought came from the car's heating system.
The journey was something of a crush. The Butcher himself took
up half the car. The other half was shared between two cows (dead),
five dismembered sheep, eight people and a mysterious sack that
dripped blood onto my boots.

Mercifully the journey was short. Above the Onon river we
arrived at two log cabins surrounded by a collection of wooden
corrals where boys were cutting horses from a herd in a tempest
of dust and clattering hooves. In these regions, where cabins had
become as common as *gers*, I was reminded again of the American
west circa 1900: the big unfenced landscapes, the log corrals, the
buckboard wagons, the tethered horses, the wooden wheels leaning
against the rough walls of cabins, the rain barrels abandoned in the
long grass. Two young boys took turns riding a turn-of-the-century
bicycle across a pasture, like some newfangled contraption that had
turned up from back east.

The Butcher introduced us to Oyunna, a tough middle-aged
woman who inhabited one of the cabins with a brood of innumerable children. In answer to my enquiries she explained that the
cabin was only a seasonal structure. They would leave soon for the
winter pastures. They would shut the door, and ride away to valleys
near Öndörkhan where they would spend the winter in their *ger*,
a more suitable structure for the Mongolian cold than a draughty
cabin. Over a dinner of boiled marmot, she agreed to guide us to
Dadal, my last destination. Her mother lived there, and it would
be an opportunity to visit her.

In the morning we sorted horses. Most of the herd was in from the hills so there was an excess of horseflesh to choose from. Under the guidance of one of Oyunna's teenage sons I settled on a paint gelding with big hair. While the other horses were charging point-lessly round the corral he stood in a corner watching them with an air of condescension.

'He is a good horse,' the boy reassured me. 'Quite fast'. This proved to be Mongolian understatement.

When we led him out of the corral, he had the irritated look of a chief executive who had been inconvenienced by the doorman. He was a sturdy horse with muscular shoulders and a broad back, one of the few Mongolian horses who wasn't dwarfed by my Western saddle. His untrimmed mane was so thick that the reins got lost among the dark roots. Over his forehead the mane rose into a gravity-defying quiff. His hairstyle and his air of intelligent disdain reminded me of one of my more dissolute friends, so I called him Fred. Too late, I realized he was the shaman's warning, the horse with the man's name.

We departed in a great party of riders, composed chiefly of young men in battered trilbys on their way home from some gathering on the other side of the valley. Fred immediately took charge, shouldering past the other horses to get to the front of the group. As leader of the pack, he cut a glamorous figure, wilful, aloof and charismatic. I tried to hold him so that I might ride beside the others, but Fred hated the idea of being in step. I learned later from Oyunna that he had run in the Naadam races when he was younger, an honour reserved for the best horses. He had only come third, an experience that had clearly marked him psychologically, like a bright child who had unexpectedly failed his eleven plus. The result was that Fred had a massive chip on his shoulder. He had devoted his life to proving he was a contender. In any group of horses he insisted on being at the front. With time I learnt to control him but only after developing cramp in my hand trying to rein him in. When I allowed him to run he went like the wind. He was tireless, and astonishingly quick. He was the best horse I had in Mongolia, and I loved him.

Fred led the group of riders up a tawny slope towards a wind-swept ridge of grass and larch trees. On the far side we descended through trees where the young men stopped to pick wild geraniums for one another which they laced into their saddles. At the bottom of the wood we emerged on the banks of the Onon river where a ragged ferryman operated a raft on a hand-pulled cable. The horses walked aboard without any trouble. The river was dark and swollen. A pair of whooper swans rose from a side bay when we were in midstream, their wings beating in slow motion as they lifted over the pine trees.

On the far bank we rode away to the north-east through empty valleys. One by one the young men peeled away from the group towards distant *gers* until we were alone with our guide. Oyunna was accompanied by her six-year-old daughter, excited at the prospect of a visit to Granny's. The little girl rode a pretty black colt. It was the foal of Oyunna's mare. Together, the little girl and the little colt, never strayed far from their mothers' side.

We rode in a landscape of winds. Blond grasses rippled through the valleys, birch trees bucked their heads along the river, and gusts of leaves fluttered over the cold water. Across the tall skies squalls of clouds streamed eastwards while skylarks tumbled away over the meadows like paper. The winds pushed at our backs, flapping our coats and tearing the words from our lips. In these hills, smooth and fluid as dunes, the whole country might have been sculpted by the prevailing westerlies. Fred, when I let him go, flew across the plains as if the wind was another horse he was trying to outrun.

At this season, all Mongolia was on the move. *Gers* had been dismantled and packed, and families were migrating to their winter pastures. Trains of loaded camels rose over the low passes led by horsemen bent against the wind. Flocks of sheep were blown across the slopes and straggling lines of yaks, their long coats beating like banners, breasted the skyline. A herd of horses, some thirty strong, came thundering through a narrow vale, drawing up suddenly at the sight of our small caravan. When the gusting winds delivered our scent, they tossed their heads and swung away to the south, their tails unfurled. Even the birds were departing. In the water meadows raucous flocks of herons had gathered. Hopping about in quarrelsome groups, they hoisted their wings like sails, waiting for the signal to go. Nothing seemed secure.

In these restless landscapes, the winds were hurrying me towards the one destination I did not desire: journey's end.

Dadal, where the Onon and the Balj rivers meet, was the birth-place of Genghis Khan. There are two memorials to the great man in the area. The most recent, apparently erected since 1990, was an enormous white rock on which a line drawing of Genghis had been etched. Its domineering scale would have appealed to Stalin.

About a mile away was Deluun Boldog, the memorial which had so upset Khrushchev in 1962. It was a simple innocuous slab of stone inscribed in old Mongolian script with the date of Genghis' birth. On the hill above was a stone *ovoo* adorned with blue scarves, a Mongolian symbol of respect. The site had a quiet dignity. From the hill one looked down over an oxbow of the Balj river. Cattle were adrift in the meadows beyond and groups of tall birch trees threw trailing shadows down the slopes.

It seemed an idyllic place for a childhood. Genghis' exile to the forests of Burkhan Khaldun must have been bitter indeed, just the kind of trauma that drives men to great deeds. *The Secret History* charts the connections between his departure from this sylvan place and his life of conquest.

In many ways the empire of Genghis Khan would appear to be without legacy. The Mongols founded no great cities, built no roads, brought no culture to the nations they conquered. Beyond the dramatic upheavals of his own time, it could be argued that the man from Dadal had made no enduring impact on the course of history.

But the Mongol Empire did have one remarkable legacy. The initial tempest of conquest was followed by a long period of peace in which the barriers to medieval travel and trade had been dismantled across a vast portion of the world. The *Pax Mongolica* lasted for over a hundred years during which distant nations, many for the first time, were suddenly in contact with one another. The pioneering journeys of John of Plano Carpini and of William of Rubruck were soon followed by numerous others, most notably that of Marco Polo. The East lay open to enquiring Europeans. Pegolotti, who wrote a fourteenth-century handbook for European merchants travelling in Asia, was able to claim that 'the road you travel from Tana (at the mouth of the Don) to Cathay is perfectly safe'.

The conditions and pressures that led to the European Age of Discovery are many and complex involving economic growth, technological advances and political developments. But one of the first catalysts for this great push across the world's oceans to other continents, the voyages that would change for ever how we viewed the world, lay with the empire of the Mongols. When, later in the fourteenth century, Islam eventually closed the Asian trade routes and China withdrew again behind its walls, Europe did not forget what it had seen during the Mongol era. The East was no longer a myth; it was now a memory. Marco Polo's widely published account of his years in China became the inspirational text for European explorers from Christopher Columbus onwards, all searching for sea routes to the riches of Cathay, all seeking to re-establish the glamorous trade they had enjoyed briefly under the Mongol Empire.

This was the legacy of the Mongols, and of the boy who had grown up here among the pastures of Dadal. By pushing beyond their own ill-defined frontiers, the nomads of the steppe had set the whole world in motion. It was their historic role, to provoke change among the settled peoples whose societies they disrupted. When eventually the Mongols returned home, they went back to their old life, as if nothing had happened. For the rest of the world, nothing would be the same again.

Fred and I arrived in Dadal like a storm breaking. We had left the others behind valleys ago. We crossed autumn plains as if we were in flight, chased by the wind through a landscape of exhilarating simplicities. Pulling against the reins, Fred sought ever greater excesses of speed, as if there was no limit to him. From time to time I forced him to rest, stopping him on the ridges where we paced among the trees like fugitives. Then I swung into the saddle again, and spurred him down the slopes into heart-pounding reaches of grassland. He was full of running, and I could not resist him. We were both intoxicated with this headlong flight.

On the final pass, where the wind keened among the trees, I held Fred long enough to survey the town below. Like Batshireet, Dadal was a village of log cabins, its air scented with pines and wood shavings. Chimney smoke bent in the wind, and a single horseman was plodding between two cabins. We fled down the long slope to the town, and swept through it before the inhabitants had time to gape. On the far side we cantered up a long hill to Gurvan Nuur, an old holiday camp about a mile beyond the town, where we would stay.

We took the low picket fence in a single bound, thundered past an open-sided dance hall and a gymnasium colonized by sparrows, and charged between the prim cabins and the grassy walkways at full gallop. On the lakeshore we drew up in a cloud of dust, snorting and lathered with sweat. It was a final deranged Gary Cooper Moment. Typically there was no one about to witness it. Gurvan Nuur seemed deserted.

In the sudden stillness I swung down from the saddle. The journey had come to an abrupt end, in a run-down out-of-season holiday camp. Fred and I walked around, catching our breath. Full of the turmoil of movement, I had suddenly run out of destinations. I mounted Fred again and we cantered about the camp, past the cabins, through the woods, and back down to the lake shore, as if I was looking for something. But it was no use. There was nowhere further to go. I had run into the brick wall of arrival.

The sky lowered and a fine rain washed across the lake, deepening the silence of the place. After a time I saw the others, coming up the slope through the rain from the direction of the town. I dismounted again, and hobbled Fred. Then I unstrapped my saddlebags, undid the girths and lifted my saddle down for the last time. The horse with the man's name had brought me to this unwelcome end.

In the old days Gurvan Nuur was a resort for Party officials and prizewinning herdsmen. The idea had come from Russia, that cadres and worthy comrades should be provided with some reward for the hard grind of building a bright future, a week in the country where film shows, communal meals and pit toilets were meant to foster the collective spirit and the Party Line. When the idea was imported into the wilds of Mongolia the rustic character of the holiday camp was rather lost. Oyunna, my guide, had spent two weeks at Gurvan Nuur twenty years ago, as a reward for high milk-yields. For her the camp was a symbol of modernity. She had been impressed by the glass windows in the cabins, the sprung beds, the Russian stoves, and the open-air cinema where they had watched socialist romances shot in Minsk.

Now it was the usual story of abandonment, the spectral remnant of another era. Dotted about the grounds were the dilapidated instruments of healthy activity – a weed-strewn sand-pit for horse-shoes, a running track consumed by grass, parallel bars no longer parallel. The old sanatorium building, rumoured to have once provided hot baths and saunas, was boarded up, and on the edge of the lake a rowing boat had sunk in weedy shallows. The ghosts of camp counsellors seemed to flit between the cabins trailing images of nature treks, botanical quizzes, and hearty singsongs. There was a boy-scout atmosphere, an out-of-doors wholesomeness that seemed, in this remote place, curiously suburban. It was an absurd place to end my journey.

With its scent of pine needles and its rows of identical cabins Gurvan Nuur reminded me forlornly of a summer camp I had gone to as a child. For two weeks, an eternity at the age of ten, I had been miserable. The camp was run with the kind of regimented efficiency that would have delighted Baden-Powell. Nothing happened of one's own initiative; the days were parcelled into pre-ordained segments, marked by bells, and devoted to scheduled activities. Canoeing, hiking, hill climbing – all were robbed of their excitement by pedantic counsellors and the community of other boys. It was a place where adventures were domesticated.

The camp had been an unwelcome intrusion into the months I had come to love. Summer was a whole world of adventures with the dreaded return to school far off over a distant horizon. In the back gardens of my own neighbourhood, a fine and boundless country riddled with dark secrets and dangerous territories and splendid hiding places, there seemed no limit to time or to possibilities. It was a country of the imagination. Among the dahlias and the rose beds, pirates were slain, jungles explored, and kingdoms toppled. Once, I had pitched a tent and spent the night alone by the big maple tree. It felt as remote and as fabulous as any expedition to Outer Mongolia, a sensation not in the least compromised by my mother's arrival with hot chocolate and biscuits.

But the summer camp was not like that. When we marched through the woods, they were not explorations of Amazonian jungle but nature hikes to identify trees. When we canoed on lakes they were not high seas, but just lakes. Some notion of exile still adheres to my memories of that place. It was a kind of settling down, a confinement to a sedentary world. That camp too had marked the end of something.

Oyunna and her daughter departed the next morning. Their journey had been in vain; Granny had left for Ulan Batur to visit relations the previous day. I held Oyunna's mare while she fastened the other horses in a train with their lead ropes. Fred was cross at the indignity of being tethered like a stock pony. I stroked his flanks. His muscles quivered beneath my hand. He gazed at me briefly with an accusing eye, then tossed his mane and looked away.

From the ridge above the camp I watched them ride down through Dadal, disappearing from view between the wooden huts, then emerging again beyond the town. They swung away from the river across the plain, heading west, two riders and three riderless horses. A thin sullen rain filled the growing distance between us. This was the moment I had dreaded, the final departure of the horses. I watched them diminish across the far slope to the pine ridge. For a moment between the trees they stood against the sky. Then they vanished, dropping out of sight into all that landscape, the way we had come.

INDEX

INDEX

INDEX

INDEX